D1241185

RETURNING TO FREUD

CONTRIBUTORS

Jean Clavreul

Marcel Czermak

Jacques Lacan

Serge Leclaire

Eugénie Lemoine-Luccioni

Charles Melman

Jacques-Alain Miller

Michèle Montrelay

Moustapha Safouan

Jean-Claude Schaetzel

René Tostain

Returning to Freud:
Clinical Psychoanalysis in the
School of Lacan

Edited and Translated by
STUART SCHNEIDERMAN

New Haven and London
Yale University Press

Designed by Sally Harris
and set in VIP Electra type.
Printed in the United States of America by
Vail-Ballou Press, Binghamton, N.Y.

Library of Congress Cataloging in Publication Data

Main entry under title:

Returning to Freud.

   Includes index.
   1. Psychoanalysis—Addresses, essays, lectures.
2. Psychology, Pathological—Addresses, essays,
lectures.   3. Lacan, Jacques, 1901–   —
Addresses, essays, lectures.   I. Schneiderman, Stuart,
1943–   [DNLM: 1. Psychoanalysis. WM460 R439]
RC506.R45   616.89'17   80–11927
ISBN 0–300–02476–2

10   9   8   7   6   5   4   3   2   1

Contents

Translator's Preface

I have described below the reasoning that dictated some of my choice of terms in translating these articles. In most cases I have discussed my decisions with Jacques Lacan and Jacques-Alain Miller.

First, I have chosen to translate the French *sens* and *signification* as, respectively, "sense" and "meaning." The reasons for this choice may seem obvious, but Alain Sheridan has chosen in his translations of Lacan to use "meaning" and "signification," respectively. Certainly in some contexts *sens* is a bit closer to what we call meaning, but the word translates perfectly well as "sense," and the two share approximately the same equivocation. This of course liberates the word "meaning" to translate the French *signification*. In my judgment the English word "signification" is too archaic to be useful and does not have the familiarity that *signification* would have to a French reader.

Second, the concept of *sujet supposé savoir* has been wrongly translated by Sheridan as the "subject who is supposed to know." This is erroneous because Lacan means by his concept that the subject is supposed and not the knowing. Thus I have opted for the expression "supposed subject of knowing."

Third, the French *aggressivité* has been rendered by Sheridan as "aggressivity." Unfortunately, this word does not appear in any dictionary that I have been able to find, and thus I have chosen the word "aggressiveness," which is commonly used in the English language. The reader will have no difficulty in distinguishing "aggressiveness" from "aggression," since the former refers only to intended aggression or an aggressive attitude.

Fourth, Lacan's concept of *manque-à-être* has been translated as "want-to-be," and to me, at least, this expression is unsatisfactory. One of the scenes of the word "want" is "lack," but this is not rendered in the idea of "want-to-be." Thus I have adopted, with Lacan's approval, the expression "want-of-being" where the genitive can be either subjective or objective.

Fifth, I have not succeeded in finding an English equivalent for *jouissance*, which refers to the experience of sexual satisfaction. I have, at Lacan's suggestion, left it and the concept of *plus-de-jouir* in French. This latter refers to a surplus, something that is left over after the experience of jouissance. Generally I conceive of it as something left to be desired.

Sixth, I have not in all cases followed the English translation of Freud's terms in the *Standard Edition*. It seems to be fairly well accepted now that the German *Trieb* should be translated as "drive" and not as "instinct" (see the *Standard Edition*), and I have followed this. Another difficulty I encountered in the *Standard Edition* was the translation of the word *Besetzung*. The editors of that work chose to invent a word, "cathexis." In German the word means "occupation," in the sense that an army occupies a village or that a pay toilet in use bears a sign reading "Occupied." In French the word has always been translated *investissement*, which is perhaps a bit closer to the German *Einsetzung* than it is to *Besetzung*. Thus I have opted, taking my risks, for the word "investment" rather than "cathexis." Neither translation is perfect, but in such a case I prefer to use a word that belongs to the English language.

The principal danger in translating articles by Lacan or by those who are members of his school is to become so enamored with the "text" that one renders it in what I would call anglicized French. Many of the translations of Lacan that have already appeared in English have done so, and therefore readers have found these works even more impenetrable than they are normally. I have thus decided in this translation to be scrupulously faithful to the syntax and semantics of the English language. To be truthful, had I wanted to do otherwise, the group of editors of Yale University Press would never have permitted me this peculiar self-indulgence. The reader who finds these articles lucid and intelligible should know that not only the present translator was responsible, but also Jane Isay, Matthew Gurewitsch, and one anonymous outside expert. I will even be so immodest as to single out Jane Isay, without whose vision, imagination, and persistence this book would still be an unfulfilled wish.

I have retained and expanded footnotes to the French text that seemed valuable for English readers. Notes that are bracketed are my additions.

Stuart Schneiderman
New York City
November 1979

RETURNING TO FREUD

Lacan's Early Contributions to Psychoanalysis

Anglo-American readers of Lacan's writings have found themselves face-to-face with an alien terminology. Too often they have reacted to this encounter with Otherness by turning away, unwilling to question themselves or their masters. However much Lacan bases his theories on those of Freud, he has introduced a number of new terms into psychoanalytic theory, and since this is a part of the problem, a brief discussion of them here is in order.

I have avoided producing yet another list of definitions. Such lists are by now rather common, and their uselessness is all that people seem able to agree upon when discussing them. In any case, the reader who craves definitions can find most of Lacan's terms defined, for better or worse, in a book entitled *The Language of Psychoanalysis*, written by J. Laplanche and J. B. Pontalis (New York: Norton, 1974).

The problem of definition is compounded by the following consideration. Except in a few instances, Lacan has not stuck to a single definition for a single term. Changes in meanings of course reflect part of the experience of any teacher who is obliged to backtrack and redefine his terms in different contexts— that is, if he wants to be understood.

It also happens that Lacan is not a systematic author. He does not follow an argument or a topic until he has exhausted it but prefers to move around, seemingly at random, asking a question today and proposing an answer six months or six years later. Or else it may happen that he will simply reformulate the original question. It takes considerable time and effort before the reader sees or recognizes a conceptual unit.

Many American analysts have openly stated their annoyance and even outrage at the apparent randomness of this procedure. It would probably be vain to justify it by saying that this is the way an analysis unfolds or even that this is how one learns language. The fact that a reader can perfectly well appreciate the justification for Lacan's presentation of theoretical material will not make him like it any better. It may well be that Lacan's idiosyncrasies and aristocratic tone will finally be unacceptable to people whose tradition is democratic, but after all, this remains to be seen. It is best to avoid prophecies that might, I would say, self-fulfill.

1

At present two books by Lacan are available in English. They are a selection of the *Ecrits* and one seminar, *The Four Fundamental Concepts of Psycho-analysis*. This sampling is perhaps representative, but it does not in any way permit the reader to follow the development of Lacan's thought over the years. One day, when more of Lacan's work is available, an informed judgment will be possible.

An overview of Lacan's early contributions to psychoanalysis properly be-gins with his first work as a psychoanalyst, which is marked by his discovery of the "mirror stage." A first version of this concept was presented at a congress of psychoanalysts in 1936. This time must have corresponded with the end of Lacan's analysis with Rudolph Loewenstein. The 1936 paper was later rewritten and was published in 1949.

Between 1936 and 1949 Lacan worked on the problems of narcissism and aggressiveness, being careful to distinguish the latter term from aggression. In his paper "Aggressiveness in Psychoanalysis," he established the fundamental inter-relation between narcissism and aggressiveness. Later, in the early 1950s, he introduced the categories or registers of the imaginary, the real, and the sym-bolic. As an organizing principle this triptych has remained the fundamental reference for psychoanalytic treatment performed by analysts in his school. Another statement, made in 1953 and spurred by dissensions within the French analytic group, was the now renowned "Function and Field of Speech and Language," in which Lacan declared that the instrument of analysis is speech and the field of its work is language. Lacan's borrowings from linguistics and anthropology, influenced by the publication of Claude Lévi-Strauss's *The Elementary Structures of Kinship*, appeared at this moment, although only to the extent that these disciplines made relevant contributions to clinical work.

Ferdinand de Saussure's concept of the signifier was introduced by Lacan to grasp what Freud had variously called the functions of switch-words, key-words, and nodal points. Contrary to Saussure's definition of the sign as the unit formed by signifier and signified, Lacan declared that the signifier could only function in combination with another signifier and that it represents not a signified but a subject. In short, signifiers always come in pairs.

During this time Lacan came to define the ego as the image the child encounters in the mirror. Certainly there is an identity between the child and his image, but this is a mistaken identity. The child is not in fact identical to this alien image; he simply acts as though he were. This occurs through what Lacan calls a "misapprehension" (*méconnaissance*) that is normative, though not in any way normal.

Lacan saw the inadequacies of the theory of ego psychology and thus introduced the concept of a subject distinct from the ego. Early in his career he defined the subject as whoever is speaking. The subject is determined retroactively by the act of speech. To the extent that what is spoken rarely coincides with what the ego intends to communicate, there is a splitting between ego and subject. Ultimately the subject is the subject of the unconscious, and it speaks most truthfully, as Freud stated, in slips of the tongue and other errors showing that the ego's censorship is suspended.

In "Function and Field" Lacan defined the act of speech by saying that there is no speech without a reply, even if that reply is an enigmatic silence. Speech is addressed to an Other, and it is only by taking into account the response of the Other that the subject can know the sense of his own speech. Lacan defined the Other as a place rather than a subject. The Other is neither complete nor whole—it is not simply another name for a Self. We would perhaps be more accurate if we followed Lacan's suggestion and translated the term as "Otherness."

The Other is deceptive, a trickster, and if the subject knows anything, he knows that in having a fault or a lack, the Other is desiring. In English we can say that the Other is wanting. The question that establishes the subject's relationship with the Other is, "What does the Other want from me?" This Other, this quality of Otherness, is also distinguished rigorously from the "other," my counterpart, who resembles me and is my equal.

Lacan's Otherness is the Other scene that Freud, after Fechner, said was the place of dreams. The Other has a discourse that predates the subject's entry into the world of speaking beings, and Freud called this discourse the family romance or myth, whose structure is written as the Oedipus complex. Otherness is always and irreducibly outside the subject; it is fundamentally alien to him. Insofar as the discourse of the Other agitates a singular subject, it forms the Freudian unconscious. Otherness is structured, and the principle of its structuring is the Law of the prohibition of incest. Freud identified this Law as being that of the murdered father.

Another of Lacan's major contributions is the clarification of the place of desire as organizing human existence. Where the *Standard Edition* translated Freud's *Wunscherfüllung* as "wish fulfillment," French analysts have called it the "realization of desire." Desire is realized in the dream, and Lacan added that this is always the Other's desire. That desire must find expression in dreams suggests that it is a desire that the subject cannot accept as his own or cannot act upon.

The neurotic is someone who does not know what he wants. His transference will be structured around the idea that his analyst knows and can tell what he knows. As Lacan put it, in the transference the analyst will be thought of as the supposed subject of knowing. This states not that the analyst does not know anything but that he is not the subject of his knowing. It is thus impossible for him to speak what he knows.

This leads to still another of Lacan's major contributions, the object *a*. For the psychoanalyst the important object is the lost object, the object always desired and never attained, the object that causes the subject to desire in cases where he can never gain the satisfaction of possessing the object. Any object the subject desires will never be anything other than a substitute for the object *a*.

With this overview in mind, let us examine the mirror stage more closely. It is inaugurated for the child at the age of approximately six months, in the instant of a look. Trapped in a motor incoordination, or what Lacan called a "fragmented body," the child finds in the unified field of the mirror image a sense of wholeness or togetherness, and he takes it upon himself. He puts the image on, or as Lacan would say, he assumes it as his own.

This experience is not sufficient to make the child a subject; it anticipates the subjectivity that he will gain when he acquires speech. This will occur according to the same dialectic as that by which he assumed his mirror image. The child assumes the words of the Other as though they were his own.

The child does not merely see his image in the mirror. He sees that image surrounded by a world of objects. This world is certainly integrated with the ego; the ego as image is its center. This integration is effected only at the cost of a misapprehension: the ego may be thought of as a subjective center of the world; in fact it is the first object of the child's look.

We must add that when the child first recognizes his image in a mirror, he greets the discovery with jubilation. He is transfixed by the image; he is fixated, even captured, by its immobility as well as by its wholeness. In a sense the child will invest his image narcissistically because it responds or appears to respond unfailingly to his cues. This is again a misapprehension of the fact that he himself has been captured within the field of the mirror.

The responsiveness of the world of objects is taken by the child as a sign of love. When the child demands objects, he is in fact demanding a sign of love from those whose task is to provide those objects. This love maintains and solidifies the child's identification with his mirror and is thus a barrier against the dread of fragmentation.

The end of the mirror stage comes at the age of approximately eighteen months, when the child can recognize that his parents are not entirely responsive to inarticulate demands. Otherness is first denied, and the child will acquire language through mechanisms that appear to be rooted in the mirror stage.

First, imitation of sounds plays an important role, and second, the child will attempt to repair the Other's defect by naming what he wants. If parents do not read the child's mind and do not give what he demands, then language comes to hold the promise of letting them know unambiguously. A problem then arises, concerning the fact that the speaking of the demand alters it, and the child who receives the demanded object will discover that he no longer wants it. Love, we might say, is no longer sufficient, and the child has entered into the world of desire.

Essentially there are two ways in which the child enters this world. First, when he perceives that a parent desires an object that is other than he, he will want to be that object, to be the desired object. Second, when he perceives a parent desiring an object, he himself will then consider that object desirable. Here he will identify with the Other's desire. Obviously, in this second case there will be a competition for the desired object.

The imaginary order derives from the mirror phase. The world is visible; it is present to consciousness through the agency of perception. At the same time it is captivating. In the imaginary the child has the illusion of being in control of a world that has enslaved him. This is one reason why Lacan has never been very enthusiastic about the idea of ego control. Another reason is dialectical: if we want to posit the ego as a master, then we must ask who or what its slave is. There are no masters without slaves.

In general terms we might say that the way in which the child relates to his mirror is determined by the way in which he is held by a parent before the mirror. In introducing this Other as determinant, Lacan says that the dual relationship between the child and his image is defined by the intervention of a third party. We may then ask what there is about this first Other, generally a mother, that determines the way she negotiates this crucial moment in the child's development. To answer this question we would want to know something about the history of this person, her relationship with her family and her husband, and the place the child has come to occupy for her within her own history.

The importance of these elements cannot be denied, but they are unknown to the child. At the time that the mirror stage is occurring, he is unaware of the forces that determine whether the phase occurs satisfactorily or unsatisfactorily. These factors form the material of the symbolic. For Lacan the structure of the imaginary is determined by the symbolic. The symbolic is a structure of differential athematic elements, whether they are the phonemes of language or what Lévi-Strauss calls the mythemes of myths. What counts here is that these elements exist within a structure, and this supersedes their content or meaning or form. Being structured, the elements of the child's prehistory hold together in much the same way that the child perceives his image in the mirror as being together. In fact, the symbolic should come to replace the imaginary as structuring.

In psychoanalytic work the symbolic manifests itself in the form of the family romance or the mythic structure of the Oedipus complex. This discourse is the conjuncture into which the subject was born, and it determines the success or failure of his maturation and development. When there is a failure of psychosexual or psychosocial maturation, relating it to a moment in a developmental process is secondary to analyzing the specific signifiers that the patient uses to talk about it. These signifiers are related to the constellation of signifiers that constitute the discourse of his family history. Since the symbolic order has the quality of Otherness, there is no subject in the symbolic.

Excluded from the symbolic, the subject is reconstituted in the real. The real is the scene of the trauma; the subject is constituted in an encounter with a traumatic situation. At one time Freud called this trauma the "primal scene." The fact that this scene is impossible to remember excludes the idea that something in the scene itself is traumatic. What it does mean is that the child bears witness to the conjunction of two beings from whose act he was conceived. The subject never truly escapes this trauma; in fact, he becomes it. The trauma always returns him to the same place, and we can say that this is where he lives, more truly than in the reality that philosophers and psychologists have arrived at by abstracting.

The patient ought to reach a point where he articulates the signifiers that inscribe him in the real and determine his destiny. His avoidance of the real is patent in his will to live out his fantasies. If Freud mistook the fantasies of his first hysterical patients for real seductions, it was at least an instructive error. In his fantasy the subject participates in, but does not bear witness to, the primal scene.

Trauma is not merely an encounter with sexuality; it is an encounter with sexuality signifying death. If what the subject seeks to encounter is the answer to the question of his existence, the trauma represents a failed encounter, one from which the subject retreats, knowing that death is the only answer to his question.

What stands between the subject and his desire for death is narcissism. The relationship between narcissism and aggressiveness makes for the fact that narcissism, the ecstatic affirmation of one's being alive, is always enacted at someone's expense. The affirmation of one's life entails the exploitation of someone else's life.

In the mirror stage the fragmented body arrives at a false sense of wholeness, of Self, through identification with an image. As several analysts have noted, there is no such thing as an inborn true sense of Self. While this sense evolves in the imaginary, a parallel process will take place in the symbolic, in which the important point is not the subject but rather the name. In bearing a name, man gains, not a sense of wholeness, but rather a sense of an otherness that is neither whole nor complete. Lacan's most recent representation of this otherness is as a hole.

The neurotic subject seeks to avoid the distressing encounter with the real. In place of the real, he promotes the symptom, the psychic symptom, with which he lives in an uneasy coexistence. In his earliest work on hysteria, Freud defined the symptom as the moment when a part of the body enters a conversation at the place where a word should have been spoken. What is in play is not an attempt to shore up the impending ruin of the body image but the maintenance by the hysteric of the supposed integrity of the communication that is supposed to be taking place. One major characteristic of hysterical structures is the belief that words are too weak or feeble to express true feelings.

In the hysterical symptom a part of the body is sacrificed to fill in a gap in the Other, to make him understand or respond. The symptom is signifying. It speaks a reply that the hysteric cannot pronounce—this because she must await it from an Other body. When the symptom manifests itself, the hysteric is alienated from a body whose speech is actually addressed to her but in a language that she does not understand. The hysteric habitually identifies with the object a in her willingness to sacrifice her own happiness to cause the desire of a man, originally her father.

In Lacan's later work the crucial concept will be the object a. Lacan himself considers this to be one of his major contributions, and I will discuss it in some detail, using its definition, provided above, as an object that causes someone to desire.

In addition, the object a is circumscribed an disengaged by the drive, assuming that an analyst permits his patient to get beyond narcissism. The role of the object a in the drive is played by one of the four objects Lacan has named as objects of drives, namely, the breast, the voice, the look, and excrement.

We can distinguish the object a from the imaginary phallus attributed to the mother. The object a is not the representation of a denial of a lack; it indicates the place of the lack and its irreducibility. The object a is a trace, a leftover, a remainder. We can summarize its concept by saying that it leaves something to be desired. There is no such thing as the perfect crime—we have all heard this phrase—and we can add that there is no such thing as the perfect sexual act, the act that is totally satisfying.

The clue, the trace of the criminal's passage, causes the desire of the detective. In erotic relations it can be the beloved's look, the tone of his or her voice, the curve of a body, that causes a lover to desire. It is always a fragment that causes desire, never the imaginary wholeness of the partner's being.

In fetishism the object that causes desire, this little bit of nothing that is detached from the body, becomes itself the object of desire. For an alcoholic it is the one more drink, or else it may be the bottle or the glass. In a phobia the object causes desire and revulsion at the same time. Anxiety, Lacan has said, is not the fear of nothing, the flight or fright before a void, but rather the encounter with the object *a* that marks the spot where there is a lack.

One might have the impression that in the case of obsessional neurosis, the object *a* is excrement. It also happens that obsessionals are intensely interested in the visual. Even in the case of the Rat Man, in the midst of a tale that aims at nothing if not anal erotism, we cannot fail to notice that the event unleashing the episode that led the patient to Freud was the loss of his glasses—exemplary manifestation of the object *a* as look. The object *a* here is not the patient's look, but his father's—and this is manifest in the scene where, examining his sex in the mirror, the Rat Man opens the door of the hallway just enough to attract the look of his dead father.

The object *a* represents the step beyond the Oedipus complex. The death of the father, as the Rat Man demonstrates, is not the end of the father but rather the beginning of his Law. Where we would say that the *a* is a fragment of a name, we note that in Freud's myth of the primal horde, it is the body of the murdered father that becomes fragmented. The importance of the name tells us not that man relates to his body through the image that he found in the mirror but rather that his relationship to the image is simply a precursor for his relationship with his name, which will determine his sense of his body.

In Freud's myth the band of brothers devour the body of the murdered father in order to make his influence disappear, to free themselves from the Law prohibiting incest. And here we encounter a radical impossibility; such a total devouring is impossible. There will always be a remainder, a trace of the father's passage among the living. Freud said in the last paragraph of *The Interpretation of Dreams* that desire is indestructible. We may thus conclude by saying that there is always something left to cause desire. If the analyst during an analysis will come to be this object, he will also at the end of analysis not be it. He will submit himself to the fate greeting any object that stands in for *a*, and that is to be discarded.

The Other Lacan

This book is a collection of clinical studies by psychoanalysts who base their practice on the teachings of Jacques Lacan. My intention in editing and translating these articles was to bring to the attention of the English speaking world the most important aspect of Lacan's work.

I have made every effort to choose articles that can be read by people who are not thoroughly steeped in Lacanian theory. Thus the reader will find that when theoretical points are introduced, they are related to clinical material. I would go so far as to say that any approach to Lacan that does not see his theory in its relationship to analytic practice is doomed to an irreducible obscurity and confusion.

Lacan has often said that his teaching has only one purpose: to train psychoanalysts. The procedures for training analysts have always been subject to intense debate. Instead of arguing the questions raised by Lacan's training methods, I have chosen to present evidence of the results. The informed reader will judge the effectiveness of Lacan's teaching by evaluating the work of his students. We can pose the relevant question as follows: has Lacan developed a theory that is transmissible to others, or are the positive effects of his own therapeutic work merely the result of the force of his personality?

It goes almost without saying that an American reader picking up a copy of the English translation of Lacan's *Ecrits* will not see the practical application of what appear to be rather abstract theoretical considerations. This reader may well be willing to see Lacan as a thinker, a master of hermeneutics, or even a self-indulgent metaphysician.

In Paris, of course, Lacan's presence as a practicing analyst has made it difficult for readers to think of him merely as a philosopher, a moment in intellectual history. Since most Americans have not had the advantage of seeing Lacan in practice, I requested that he contribute to this volume the transcript of a patient interview. Since Lacan responded favorably to this request, the reader is provided with a unique opportunity to study in depth the technique that has developed from Lacan's clinical and theoretical experience. I say "unique" because no transcript of an interview by Lacan has ever been published before anywhere.

This book, then, is devoted to Lacan as a practicing analyst and a teacher of analytic candidates. Since this is not the Lacan whom most Americans have encountered in articles previously published in English, I take the liberty of saying that this is the Other Lacan.

To begin with a question, let us ask what makes a therapeutic procedure specifically psychoanalytic. The question of the specificity of psychoanalysis implies a distinction between analysis, on the one hand, and medicine and psychology, on the other. The problem is to define psychoanalysis without falling back on analogies with medicine and behavioral science. A second and related question is the following: how can we declare that Lacan's teaching is eminently clinical, given that he never writes case studies?

There is a fairly widely held assumption that the most effective way of talking about analytic work is to write up entire cases. This idea seems to be based on an analogy with medicine, and not merely in following the form of diagnosis, prognosis, treatment, cure. It is also analogous in prescribing what I will call a standard analytic procedure for similar symptoms. In medical cases the anonymity of the patient is no obstacle to the transmission of correct procedure. No one, I think, would make this assertion for psychoanalysis.

A second aspect of the medical case study is that it is the illness that counts and not the words that the patient uses to describe the illness. The medical patient talks about his symptoms, and the words are in a sense transparent; their function is to attract the physician's look to the affected part of the body. To the extent that testing is necessary to diagnose physical illness, the patient's words become of even less significance.

In contrast to medicine, psychoanalysis is concerned most directly with words. Whatever general interpretation we may have for a psychic symptom, whatever developmental phase we connect it with, psychoanalysis will not resolve the symptom without taking into account the words the patient uses to describe it. Not only is the interest in words specific to psychoanalytic treatment, but a particular choice of words is specific to a particular patient. An analyst who concerns himself with discovering a universal meaning for psychic symptoms will miss the specificity of the patient's language.

Psychoanalysts are thus especially attuned to nuances in verbal expression, and when they formulate an interpretation, they must address it to the specific analysand who will hear it. Effective interpretations are received by analytic patients as referring specifically to them, not as universal truths or as applications of general knowledge. If this is true, then a psychoanalytic interpretation cannot

be preprogrammed, it cannot come straight from a handbook as the one definitive answer to a patient's problems. To a certain extent the effect of analytic
interpretation is unpredictable; the analyst cannot be assured of the correctness of
his interpretation until he receives confirming material from the patient.

We may also note that medical treatment (to the extent that medical knowledge has advanced) provides an answer to the patient's suffering. When the
physician knows the cause of an illness, he aims at that cause with his treatment.
Here we can appreciate Freud's discovery that the hysterical patient knows the
cause of her suffering and that it is sufficient to let her talk for that cause to be
discovered. According to Lacan, the analyst does not retain the answer to his
patient's question. What the analyst offers when he interprets is a decoy answer,
one that will arouse the patient's opposition and will lead him to offer a new
response to his own question. This is properly a dialectical procedure and is at
the heart of any analytic activity. (A supplementary question is whether the
analyst knows, when he offers his answer, that it is in fact a decoy.) We see here
some of the reasons that led Lacan to place so much emphasis on speaking and
language in psychoanalysis.

Another aspect of speech has a direct bearing on the question of writing
psychoanalytic case studies. Whereas a medical practitioner who wishes to demonstrate a treatment procedure will describe that procedure, when Lacan wants
to describe analytic practice, he is very likely to write about something other than
analytic practice. In passing we should mention one reason for this, namely the
problem of confidentiality. An analyst who is as well known as Lacan can fully
expect that any cases he writes up will be the object of intense study by analytic
candidates and even by people completely outside the psychoanalytic milieu. As
we know from Freud's cases, this kind of intense interest will eventually lead to
the revelation of the identity of the person being written about. In this context we
should say that Lacan's decision not to write up cases is simply a mark of
professional responsibility toward his clients. The subject of a psychoanalytic
case study can never enjoy the total anonymity that the subject of a medical case
study has. Thus Lacan has spoken about analytic cases by referring to poems,
plays, and even philosophical texts as paradigms. Such a shifting of reference is
obviously inadmissible in medical cases or in behavioral science.

The following example will bring into relief the problem of shifting reference. It happens from time to time that people come to see analysts to talk about
sexuality. It also happens that there are several ways of talking about sexual
experience. Some analysands feel the need to offer a graphic description of their
experiences, as though the only way the analyst could understand them would be

to visualize, so that the analyst becomes an observer, a mute witness. Another patient may avoid descriptions to speak allegorically about sex, at times not knowing that his allegory makes sense only in that context.

If we may say that this latter patient thinks that he is talking about one thing and is really talking about another, why may we not say the same thing for the first patient? When he is talking about sexuality, perhaps the first patient is talking of something that is not fundamentally a sexual relationship—the trans- ference, for instance. Such considerations suggest that the analyst does not take the discourse of his analysand at face value. He must always hold open the possibility of a reference to something else, something that is only alluded to or suggested in the discourse he hears.

Just as the "what" being talked about is indefinite in analysis, so is the "who" talking. Everyone knows that the analysand's unconscious reveals itself more clearly in a slip of the tongue, a word that slips out while he is not paying attention, than in a correctly thought-out, well-formulated utterance. If we think we know who is speaking a well-formulated utterance, if we think that the ego maintains control over such a statement, then who is responsible for the slip? Lacan has answered that this other speaker, this other subject, is the subject of the unconscious, precisely the subject whose being we are never conscious of.

Many analysts believe that the slip of the tongue, this pure manifestation of the unconscious, ought to be integrated into conscious discourse. The question is, what happens to our normal discourse, our well-formulated utterances, when we let the unconscious speak in their midst? We assume that they are not going to remain untouched; rather, they will in some way become poeticized (I use this word to preclude the assumption that people who have completed psychoanalysis speak pure poetry), this because for Lacan, metaphor and metonymy are essen- tial aspects of the structure of the unconscious, not defense mechanisms.

These concerns form an essential aspect of Lacan's approach and one that should be borne in mind, for many of the case studies in this volume have a poetic quality not often found in analytic writing and never found in medical textbooks. I will leave it for the reader to decide whether Lacan is successful when he proposes to talk about the analytic cure by referring to Edgar Allan Poe's "The Purloined Letter" or when he offers Plato's *Symposium* as an exemplary text on transference. I do want to establish that in analysis one may talk about one thing while in fact referring to something else and that the metaphoric quality of the discourse is not gratuitous.

For Lacan the index of an analytic cure is the way things are said. This index is eminently social and excludes the indices of thinking, insight, con- sciousness, and so forth. The same index holds true for the analyst, and not only because he has been psychoanalyzed himself. The analyst is not an objective observer. He is rather a subjective participant in the experience of the transference. We might say that he is necessarily touched by what he hears. An essential element in the dialogue, the analyst through his activity or lack of activity often determines what is spoken and what is not. As Lacan has said, speech is dialogue. The analyst's role is to let his analysand speak what had heretofore been unspeakable.

I distinguish, then, the analyst's bearing witness to his practice from his witnessing of the analysis. If the analyst were merely a witness, then psychoanalysis could be conceived according to an experimental model such as we find in laboratory science. The notion that analysis takes place in a setting like a laboratory leads to the assertion that some standard or correct procedure will give a specific predetermined result. This assumes that there is an ideal procedure to follow and that there are analysts who know what this procedure is. Without going into the theory behind the question of the ideal analyst, we can certainly recognize that such assumptions constitute a prejudice endemic to candidates and that the practice of supervision is designed precisely to counteract it.

Candidates in analytic institutes are often more concerned about whether their supervisor will approve or disapprove of their work than they are about being responsive to their analysand's discourse. When the candidate is in session, he is often wondering what his supervisor will say about his actions, and he will thus address his interpretations to his supervisor rather than to his analysand. His remarks will not be specific to his analysand and will be taken by him as addressed to someone outside the session.

One of the difficulties inherent in such an idealization is that it may precipitate an acting out on the part of the analysand. We know that in an acting out, the analysand enacts an unconscious fantasy outside the analytic session. The acting out, which has the quality of being staged so that it can be told to the analyst, is an element of the transference whose articulation within the session has been blocked precisely by the analyst's not wanting to hear about it. It is not the acting out that sidetracks analysis, but rather the analyst's failure to bring it into the enactment of the transference. The acting out should be considered an element of the analytic dialectic, an occasion for the analyst, as Lacan says, to offer a better response. A responsive intervention is not one that provides the answer or the interpretation of the acting out.

Analysis is a dialectical process in which the analysand analyzes. He analyzes not the Self but rather the Other, insofar as the analyst in the transference is supposed to occupy its place. Because of the nature of the transference, the analysand will form an idea of what the analyst wants to hear and will speak accordingly. If the analyst decides that he wants to hear a specific answer or that he wants to hear an affirmation of the correctness of his interpretations, he will enter into a complicity with the patient's ego that will have the effect of blocking the patient's verbalizations.

Not only does the analyst not have the answer to the analysand's question, he knows that there is only a series of tentative answers that the analysand has used to formulate his neurosis. The analyst's desire is indefinite; he does not want to hear the one answer proving that he is right; rather, he awaits another articulation of the question. His role is to bring the analysand to recognize that this Other that had been supposed to have the answer is defined as lacking something, as defective at precisely the place where the answer should have been forthcoming.

At this point the reader may wonder how one conducts a Lacanian analysis. Although there is no simple formula, some markers can be used by the analyst to situate himself better in relation to the analysand's discourse. The first marker has to do with the importance of verbalization. The analyst should direct his interventions to what has been said or to the way in which it has been said. The analyst should not interpret nonverbal expressions; nothing is to be gained by telling the patient why he hesitates before lying down on the couch. Does this mean that we overlook the well-known preverbal element in human behavior? Not at all. Instead we say that if anything is to be analyzed from nonverbal expressions, they must be assumed to have a sense. Unfortunately, this sense is totally opaque if we do not know what words the patient chooses to describe it. And if the preverbal child, for example, is performing acts that make sense, then this is because the world in which he lives has been organized by beings who are thoroughly verbal. The fact that a child cannot speak does not mean that he exists outside the net of language; on the contrary, to the extent that he cannot speak, I would assert that he is more thoroughly captured in that net.

If an analyst decides to interpret a gesture without knowing the exact verbal expression that the analysand chooses to describe it, his interpretation can only be received as addressed to a generalized individual. It is thus alienating, or more precisely, it reinforces an already existing alienation. Finally, the analyst may also find that an analysand will feel persecuted by such interpretations, and in my judgment, rightly so. Obviously enough, if the patient perceives that he can communicate nonverbally, through symptomatic behavior, then he will have little incentive to translate that behavior into speech.

A psychic symptom is not cured by the analysand's understanding of the universal symbolic meaning of the symptom. Often enough, analysands know these meanings as well as analysts do. The resolution of a symptom is based on the analysand's recognition of the signifying function of the terms he uses to describe his symptom. That an analysand chooses some terms and not others to talk about his symptoms is of the greatest importance, and these terms will eventually be seen to resonate with signifiers that are attached to key events in his history or prehistory. By prehistory I mean the history of his family before his birth, history that is inscribed in certain key signifiers and should not be confused with the supposed preverbal period.

The discussion above suggests a second marker: the analyst ought to be especially attentive to elements of the patient's history that are not part of his lived experience. Events in the history of his family, the events that brought his parents together, are often of great significance, even though the analysand knows about them only because he has heard of them.

This reasoning leads to a crucial question for analysis: precisely what is enacted in the transference? Clearly an experience that can be remembered does not need to be enacted in the transference. We will declare, then, that an event enacted in the transference was not simply forgotten but is outside the remembered, this because it does not count among the analysand's subjective experiences. Experience enacted in the transference may have been lived by a parent with his parents, before the analysand was born. It is thus irreducibly Other for him. The cases in this volume demonstrate clearly how elements of prehistory are determinant for a subject's neurosis.

A third marker is that the analyst should direct the treatment but not the patient. This suggests that the analyst ought to intervene in relation to the transference as it has been articulated and not in terms of some ideal pattern of behavior that he may wish to engender. Nor should the analyst respond to transitory improvements in his patient's condition, even if they concern the disappearance of symptoms. Every analyst knows that symptoms may vanish overnight if a patient feels that this disappearance will satisfy the analyst and will help the analysand to escape encountering a difficult question.

These considerations lead to a fourth marker, which I define as the analyst's obligation to recognize his analysand's desire. Obviously this recognition complicates matters, for to recognize excludes granting approval or permission.

The neurotic patient presents himself for an analysis because he does not know what he wants. During the course of his analysis, the analysand will continue his everyday existence and will discover some things that he desires. Not all of the analysand's actions outside the analysis constitute an acting out, a manifestation of transference. Differentiation can be a problem. By what index may we determine whether the analysand involves himself in a relationship because he desires to do so or whether the relationship simply manifests a resistance?

Unfortunately there is no very clear-cut guideline that we can follow here. There is no way to relieve each analyst of the responsibility for formulating a judgment in relation to each of his patients. If we accept with Lacan the view that the analysand's desire is not determined by his ability to adapt to a standard of normality, we do not contend that his desire is simply for the abnormal. In the absence of a firm guideline, we may look to Lacan for a direction that will help us determine where the analysand has accepted his desire or where he has evaded it.

An analyst should base his decision to recognize his analysand's desire on the way in which that desire is articulated. Certainly, a wish that is stated as a demand for approval or permission is not a desire but rather an aspect of transference love. Nor is desire presented to the analyst as a fait accompli, a fact that he is supposed to be obliged to recognize. But when the patient's desire does become known to him, when the analysand has discovered some part of it, he ought to act on that desire—and I would hasten to add that in psychoanalysis thinking about an act is not identical with performing it.

These are merely some of the issues that should be raised when we question desire. And the only correct response here is to leave the question open. Such is, after all, the way Lacan has taught.

PART ONE. THE PSYCHOANALYTIC INTERVIEW

1   A Lacanian Psychosis: Interview by Jacques Lacan

TRANSLATOR'S NOTE

The text that follows is a translation of the unedited transcript of an interview conducted by Jacques Lacan with a hospitalized psychiatric patient before a group of psychiatrists and analysts. The names have, of course, been altered, but in changing them Jacques-Alain Miller was careful to maintain the resonances that the original names had for the patient.

Translating such a text poses special problems. The transcript retains the particularities of a spoken discourse. I have rendered these in equivalent English forms. Also, the patient has a rather special way of using the French language, especially as concerns verb tenses and neologisms. In almost all cases I have retained the verb tense used by the patient, even where, for example, his use of the pluperfect or imperfect seems awkward in English. For the neologisms, wherever possible I have used an English neologism and have included the French term in parentheses. In short, I have translated good French into good English and broken and erroneous French into less than perfect English. At present, the original French transcript is unpublished.

THE PRESENTATION OF MR. GÉRARD PRIMEAU

DR. LACAN: Sit down, my good man. You have found a great deal of interest here. I mean that people are really interested in your case. You spoke with your psychiatrists. Many things have been somewhat clarified. Tell me about yourself. (Mr. Primeau is silent) I don't know why I would not let you speak. You know very well what is happening to you.

MR. PRIMEAU: I can't manage to get hold of myself.

DR. LACAN: You can't manage to get hold of yourself? Explain to me what is happening.

MR. PRIMEAU: I am a little disjointed in regard to language, disjunction between the dream and reality. There is an equivalence between the . . . two worlds in my imagination, and not a prevalence. Between the world and reality—what is

Jacques Lacan is the director and founder of the Ecole Freudienne de Paris. He practices psychoanalysis in Paris.

called reality—there is a disjunction. I am constantly making the imaginative flow.

DR. LACAN: Speak to me about your name. Because Gérard Primeau, is not . . .

MR. PRIMEAU: Yes, I had decomposed, before knowing Raymond Roussel. . . . When I was twenty, I was studying *maths supérieures*. . . .[1] Since then I was interested in physical facts, and there is a lot of talk about intellectual strata and substrata. Language could present strata and substrata. For example, I had decomposed my name into *Geai*, a bird, *Rare*, rareness.

DR. LACAN: *Geai Rare* . . .[2]

MR. PRIMEAU: *Prime Au*. I had decomposed, in a somewhat ludic way, I had fragmented my name to create. What I have to tell you is . . . (silence)

DR. LACAN: And then—what then? What do you call—this is what I have been told—*imposed* speech?

MR. PRIMEAU: Imposed speech is an emergence which imposes itself on my intellect and which has no meaning in the ordinary sense. These are sentences which emerge, which are not reflexive, which are not already thought, but which are an emergence, expressing the unconscious. . . .

DR. LACAN: Go ahead. . . .

MR. PRIMEAU: . . . emerge as though I was perhaps manipulated . . . I am not manipulated, but I cannot explain myself. I have a lot of trouble explaining. I have trouble getting hold of the problem, trouble getting hold of this emergence. I do not know how it comes, imposes itself on my brain. It comes all at once: *You killed the bluebird. It's an anarchic system.* . . .[3] Sentences which have no rational meaning in banal language and which are imposed on my brain, on my intellect. There is also a kind of counterbalancing. With the physician who is named Dr. D—— I have an imposed sentence which says *Mr. D—— is nice*, and then I have a sentence which counterbalances, which is my reflection; there is a disjunction between the imposed sentence and my sentence, a reflexive thought. I say, *But I am insane.* I say *Mr. D—— is nice*, imposed sentence, *But I am insane*, reflexive sentence.

DR. LACAN: Give me other examples.

MR. PRIMEAU: I have a lot of complexes, at times I'm very aggressive. I often have a tendency . . . .

DR. LACAN: You are "aggressive." What does that mean?

---

1. [This term refers to the first of two years of study preparatory to entrance into one of France's best private universities. A student in this course of study has graduated from the equivalent of high school with an outstanding record.]
2. [Pronounced exactly like *Gérard*.]
3. ["Anarchic system" is in English in the original text.]

MR. PRIMEAU: I've explained.

DR. LACAN: You don't appear to be aggressive.

MR. PRIMEAU: When I have an emotional contact, I am aggressive inside.... I can't say any more....

DR. LACAN: You are going to succeed in telling me how that happens.

MR. PIMEAU: I tend to compensate. I am aggressive, not physically but inside. I tend to compensate with imposed sentences. I am expressing myself badly, it is clearer now.... I tend to recover with the imposed sentences. I tend to find everyone nice or beautiful, ... then at other times I have aggressive, imposed sentences....

DR. LACAN: Take your time, take plenty of time to find out where you are.

MR. PRIMEAU: There are several kinds of voices.

DR. LACAN: Why do you call them "voices"?

MR. PRIMEAU: Because I hear them, I hear them inside.

DR. LACAN: Yes.

MR. PRIMEAU: Thus I am aggressive, and inside I hear people by telepathy. From time to time I have emerging sentences, which are meaningless, as I just explained.

DR. LACAN: Give a sample.

MR. PRIMEAU: *He is going to kill me the bluebird. It's an anarchic system. It's a political assassination, ... political assastination* [assastinat], which is the contraction of words between "assassination" [*assassinat*] and "assistant" [*assistanat*], which evokes the notion of assassination.[4]

DR. LACAN: Which evokes... Tell me, no one is assassinating you?

MR. PRIMEAU: No, they are not assassinating me. I am going to continue with a kind of unconscious recovery. Sometimes I have emerging sentences, aggressive and insignificant, or rather, nonsignifying, nonsignifying in everyday language, and sometimes I recover from this aggressiveness, and I tend to find everyone nice, beautiful, and so on. This beatifies, canonizes, certain persons who I call saints. I have a friend who is named Barbara, and that gives "Saint Barbara." "Saint Barbara" is an emerging sentence, but me, I am in an aggressive phase. I always have this disjunction between the two, which complete each other, according to the influence of time, and which are not of the same order: one is emerging, and the other is reflexive.

DR. LACAN: Yes. Then let us talk more specifically, if you want to, of the

---

4. [In a French psychiatric hospital, an *assistant* is a physician who has completed his residency and is thus a staff member bearing primary responsibility for patient care. A psychiatrist who seeks this position in France is obliged to take a competitive examination called the *assistanat*.]

emerging sentences. Since when have they been emerging? This is not an idiotic question. . . .

MR. PRIMEAU: No, no. Since I did . . . I was diagnosed as having paranoid delusions in March 1974.

DR. LACAN: Who said that, "paranoid delusions"?

MR. PRIMEAU: A physician, at the time. And these emerging sentences . . .

DR. LACAN: Why do you turn toward that man?

MR. PRIMEAU: I felt that he was mocking me.

DR. LACAN: You felt a mocking presence? He is not in your field of vision. . . .

MR. PRIMEAU: I was hearing a sound, and I felt . . .

DR. LACAN: He is surely not making fun of you. I know him well, and he is surely not making fun of you. On the contrary he is very interested. That is why he made a noise.

MR. PRIMEAU: The impression of his intellectual understanding . . .

DR. LACAN: Yes, I think so, that is more like him. I tell you that I know him. Besides, I know all the people who are here. They would not be here if I did not have full confidence in them. Good, continue.

MR. PRIMEAU: On the other hand, I think that speech can be a world force, beyond words.

DR. LACAN: Exactly, let's try to see. You have just presented your doctrine. And in fact, it's one hell of a mess, this story of . . .

MR. PRIMEAU: There is a very simple language that I use in everyday life, and there is on the other hand a language which has an imaginative influence, where I disconnect the people around me from the real. That is the most important. My imagination creates an other world, a world which would have a sense which is equivalent to the sense of the world that is called real, but which would be completely disjoined. The two worlds would be completely disjoined. On the other hand, these imposed sentences, to the extent that they emerge sometimes to go and aggress a person, are bridges between the imaginative world and the world that is called real.

DR. LACAN: Yes, but finally the fact remains that you maintain a clear distinction.

MR. PRIMEAU: Yes, I maintain a clear distinction, but the language, the fluency of imagination, is not of the same intellectual or spiritual order as what I say. It's a dream, a kind of waking dream, a permanent dream.

DR. LACAN: Yes.

MR. PRIMEAU: I don't think I'm inventing. It is disjointed, but that has no . . . I cannot . . . in answering you I am afraid of making a mistake.

DR. LACAN: You think that you have made a mistake in answering?

MR. PRIMEAU: I have not made a mistake. All speech has the force of law, all speech is signifying, but apparently at first they do not have a purely rational sense.

DR. LACAN: Where did you find this expression "all speech is signifying"?

MR. PRIMEAU: It's a personal reflection.

DR. LACAN: Right.

MR. PRIMEAU: I am conscious of this disjointed world, I am not sure of being conscious of this disjointed world.

DR. LACAN: You are not sure of . . .

MR. PRIMEAU: I am not sure of being conscious of this disjointed world. I do not know if the . . .

DR. LACAN: If the . . . ?

MR. PRIMEAU: . . . the dream, the world constructed by imagination, where I find my center of myself, has nothing to do with the real world, because in my imaginative world, in the world that I create for myself with speech, I am at the center. I tend to create a kind of minitheater, where I would be at the same time the creator and the director, while in the real world, my only function is . . .

DR. LACAN: Yes, there you are only a *geai rare*, if indeed . . .

MR. PRIMEAU: No, the *geai rare* is in the imaginative world. The Gérard Primeau is the world commonly called real, while in the imaginative world, I am *Geai rare prime au*. It is perhaps from my word *Prime*, which is the first, the one which codifies, which has force. I used a term in one of my poems. . . .

DR. LACAN: In one of your poems?

MR. PRIMEAU: I was the solitary center of a solitary circle. I do not know if that was said before. I found it when I was rather young. I think it is by Novalis.

DR. LACAN: Precisely.

MR. PRIMEAU: I am the solitary center, a kind of god, the demiurge of a solitary circle, because this world is walled in, and I cannot make it pass into everyday reality. Everything which masturbates . . . well, which is created at the level of the interior dream—I was going to say "which masturbates". . . . (silence)

DR. LACAN: But finally, what do you think of this? According to what you say, it would appear that you feel that there is a dream which functions as such, that you are the prey of a certain dream?

MR. PRIMEAU: Yes, it's a little like that. A tendency, in life, also, to . . . (silence)

DR. LACAN: Tell me.

MR. PRIMEAU: I am tired. I do not feel very well this morning; I am not in the mood to talk.

DR. LACAN: Why the devil not?

MR. PRIMEAU: Because I was a little anxious.

DR. LACAN: You were anxious. Which side is that on?

MR. PRIMEAU: I don't know. I am anxious. Anxiety is also emerging. It is some-times related to the fact of meeting a person. On the other hand, the fact of meet-ing you, and . . .

DR. LACAN: It makes you anxious to speak with me? Do you have the feeling that I understanding nothing of your problems?

MR. PRIMEAU: I am not sure that the interview can release certain things. Once I had an emerging anxiety which was purely physical, without any relation to social fact.

DR. LACAN: Yes, my way of introducing myself into this world . . .

MR. PRIMEAU: No, I was afraid of you because I have a lot of complexes. You are a rather well-known personality. I was afraid of meeting you. It was a very simple anxiety.

DR. LACAN: Yes. And what is your feeling about the persons who are here, who are listening with a great deal of interest?

MR. PRIMEAU: It is oppressing. That's why it's difficult to speak. I am anxious and tired and that blocks my tendency to . . .

DR. LACAN: Who did you see in 1974?

MR. PRIMEAU: Dr. G——.

DR. LACAN: G——, he wasn't the first psychiatrist you saw?

MR. PRIMEAU: Yes, he was the first. I saw Dr. H—— when I was fifteen.

DR. LACAN: Who took you to him?

MR. PRIMEAU: My parents. I was opposing my parents.

DR. LACAN: You are their only child?

MR. PRIMEAU: I am the only son, yes.

DR. LACAN: What does he do, your father?

MR. PRIMEAU: Medical salesman.

DR. LACAN: Meaning that he does what?

MR. PRIMEAU: He works for a pharmaceutical laboratory. His work consists in going to see physicians to present their products; he is a kind of representative.

DR. LACAN: He works for . . . ?

MR. PRIMEAU: D—— Laboratories.

DR. LACAN: You, did you have career counseling? You told me that you studied maths supérieures.

MR. PRIMEAU: That's right, yes. At the *lycée P——*.

DR. LACAN: Tell me a little about your studies.

MR. PRIMEAU: At what level? I was always a rather lazy student. I was naturally gifted. . . . I always tended to count on my intelligence rather than on work. In maths supérieures, I dropped out because I have . . .

DR. LACAN: I have . . . ?[5]

MR. PRIMEAU: There was a problem with a girl.

DR. LACAN: You had a problem with a girl?

MR. PRIMEAU: I was worried about a problem with a girl. I began maths supérieures in November, and then I cracked after two months because of a problem with a girl. Afterward I abandoned maths supérieures because I had a nervous breakdown.

DR. LACAN: You had a nervous breakdown linked to. . . . ?

MR. PRIMEAU: To this disappointment with the girl.

DR. LACAN: This disappointment concerned whom?

MR. PRIMEAU: A young woman I knew at summer camp. I was a counselor and so was she.

DR. LACAN: Yes. I do not see why you would not say what her name was.

MR. PRIMEAU: Hélène Pigeon.

DR. LACAN: Yes. That was in 1967, then. Where were you in your "school-work"? We must call it that.

MR. PRIMEAU: I had had problems because I was lazy. Laziness is an illness. I had already had a lot of problems since I was fifteen, and I was having affective palpitations because of my stormy relations with my parents. It happened that I had memory losses.

DR. LACAN: You speak of your parents. You have already situated your father a little. And your mother?

MR. PRIMEAU: I was brought up by my mother because my father, a medical salesman, was working in the provinces. My mother was a very anxious, very silent woman, and since I myself was very retroactive, very, very reserved, the evening meal was very silent; there was no true affective contact from my mother. She was anxious, her mental state was contagious. . . . It is not a virus but concerns the environment. Thus I was brought up by this mother, very anxious, hypersensitive, exposed to family fights with my father when he came home for the weekend. The atmosphere was tense and anxiety-provoking. I think that by osmosis I myself was very anxious.

DR. LACAN: When you speak of osmosis, what is your idea of the osmosis in question, you know so well how to distinguish the real . . .

MR. PRIMEAU: . . . from the imaginary?

DR. LACAN: Yes, that's it. Between what and what is there osmosis?

MR. PRIMEAU: I believe that there is first a becoming conscious between what is called the real . . . There is a psychological tension created, anxiety in relation to

5. [The French *j'ai* ("I have") is a homophone of *Geai* and *Gé*.]

the real, but carnal, that is to say, in relation to the body, and which then passes by osmosis to the mind. . . . Because I have a problem: it is that I cannot . . . I feel a little . . . Once I wrote a letter to my psychiatrist. . . .

DR. LACAN: To which psychiatrist?

MR. PRIMEAU: To Dr. G——. For a long time I was talking about the hiatus between the body and the mind, and there was a . . . I was obsessed by . . . I am speaking of then, and this is no longer valid. . . . I led a kind of . . . (Mr. Primeau seems very moved) . . . a notion of electrical bodies apparently linked and which apparently disjoined themselves. I could not manage to get hold of myself in relation to this body-mind situation.

DR. LACAN: "Then"—when was "then"?

MR. PRIMEAU: I was seventeen or eighteen. I was saying, what is the moment when the body enters into the mind, or the mind into the body? I do not know. I am obsessed—how?—by the body composed of cells, of all kinds of nerve cells. How does a biological fact become a spiritual fact? How is there a sharing between the body and the mind? In sum, how does thought have an interaction on the level of neurons? How is thought formulated? How, beginning with the interaction of neurons in the brain—how does thought come to emerge from these neuronic interactions, from these hormonal developments, from these neurovegetative developments or whatever. I had been led to think . . .

DR. LACAN: But you know that we don't know any more about it than you do.

MR. PRIMEAU: I had been led to think that, seeing that biology takes its waves as being in the brain, I had been led to think that thought, or intelligence, was a kind of projecting wave, a wave directed toward the outside. I do not know how these waves were projected toward the outside, but language . . . This is related to the fact that I am a poet, because . . .

DR. LACAN: Yes, you are incontestably a poet.

MR. PRIMEAU: I tried, at the beginning, to. . . .

DR. LACAN: You have some things written by you?

MR. PRIMEAU: Yes, I have some here.

DR. LACAN: You have some where?

MR. PRIMEAU: In the hospital. Dr. Z—— had asked me to bring them. But I would like to continue. I tried, by poetic action, to find a balancing rhythm, a music. I was led to think that speech is the projection of an intelligence which arises toward the outside.

DR. LACAN: Intelligence, speech. What you call intelligence is the usage of speech.

MR. PRIMEAU: I was thinking that intelligence was an undulating projection toward the outside, as if . . . I do not agree with you when you say that intelligence is speech. There is intuitive intelligence, which is not translatable by speech, and I am very intuitive, and I have a great deal of difficulty in logifying [à logifier]. . . . I don't know if that is a French word, it is a word I invented. What I see . . . Sometimes it happened that I said, when discussing with someone, "I see," but I cannot translate rationally what I was seeing. These are images that pass, and I cannot . . .

DR. LACAN: Tell me a little about these images which pass.

MR. PRIMEAU: It is like a cinema, what is called a "cinema" in medicine. It takes off very quickly, and I would not know how to formulate these images because I do not succeed in qualifying them.

DR. LACAN: Let's try to be more specific. For example, what is the relationship between these images and a thing which I know—because I was told—is very important for you? The idea of beauty. Do you center your idea of beauty on these images?

MR. PRIMEAU: At the level of the solitary circle?

DR. LACAN: Of the solitary circle, yes.

MR. PRIMEAU: That's it. But the idea of beauty as concerns the dream, it is essentially a physical vision.

DR. LACAN: What is beautiful, aside from you? Because you do think that you are beautiful?

MR. PRIMEAU: Yes, I think that I am beautiful.

DR. LACAN: The persons to whom you attach yourself, are they beautiful?

MR. PRIMEAU: What I look for in a face is its luminosity, always this projection, a luminous gift; I seek a beauty which radiates. It is not foreign to the fact that I say that intelligence is a projection of waves. I seek people who have a sensitive intelligence, this irradiation of the face which puts one in relation with this sensitive intelligence.

DR. LACAN: Let's talk about the person who preoccupied you in 1967, . . . whose name was Hélène. Did she radiate?

MR. PRIMEAU: Yes, she radiated. Finally, I met others. . . .

DR. LACAN: Other radiant persons?

MR. PRIMEAU: Other radiant persons, men as well as women. Sexually, I am as much in love with a woman as with a man. I was speaking of physical relations with men. I was attracted solely because of this radiance, at once intellectual and sensitive.

DR. LACAN: I see very well what you mean. I am not obliged to participate, but I see what you mean. But really, you did not have to wait until you were seventeen to be touched like that, by beauty. Who brought you to . . . ?

MR. PRIMEAU: About a question . . .

DR. LACAN: Tell me.

MR. PRIMEAU: . . . of opposition with my parents. My mother was very silent, but my father, when he came home for the weekend . . . about questions of education, about questions about everyday life, with the advice that he used to give me, I was rather refractory, in revolt, already very independent, and I was irritated by the advice my father wanted to give me, as though I already had the possibility of going beyond them by myself, without receiving advice from my father. It was then. . . .

DR. LACAN: What did he say to H——?

MR. PRIMEAU: I don't remember anymore.

DR. LACAN: He said that you opposed him.

MR. PRIMEAU: I don't remember anymore what he said. He made me speak, then he made me go out of the room, and he spoke with my father. He did not give the diagnosis when I was there. He made me take tests, undressed. I had a lot of complexes, sexually.

DR. LACAN: This word "complex," for you, signifies . . . It is especially centered on, let us say, sexuality. Is that what you mean? You have already used this word "complex" five or six times.

MR. PRIMEAU: It is not only about sexuality. It is also about relationships. I have a great deal of difficulty in expressing myself, and I have the impression of being, not rejected, but . . .

DR. LACAN: "But . . ." Why do you say "not rejected"? You feel that you are rejected?

MR. PRIMEAU: Yes, I have complexes about speech, complexes about social life. It is through fear, it is a certain anxiety, a fear of speaking, of. . . . I have an after-wit [un esprit de l'escalier], I have no sense of replies, I have a tendency to retreat into myself because of that. I have a lot of difficulty. . . . I stop myself sometimes, I cannot . . . The fact that I was afraid to see you, before, was an inferiority complex.

DR. LACAN: You feel yourself in a state of inferiority in my presence?

MR. PRIMEAU: I said "before." I have complexes about relationships. Since you are a very well-known personality, that made me anxious.

DR. LACAN: How do you know that I am a well-known personality?

MR. PRIMEAU: I tried to read your books.

DR. LACAN: Ah yes. You tried? (Mr. Primeau smiles) You read. It's within reach of everyone.

MR. PRIMEAU: I don't remember anymore. I read that when I was very young, when I was eighteen.

DR. LACAN: When you were eighteen you read some things that I had produced.

MR. PRIMEAU: Yes.

DR. LACAN: What year does that put us in?

MR. PRIMEAU: In 1966.

DR. LACAN: That had just come out.

MR. PRIMEAU: I do not remember. . . .

DR. LACAN: At that time you were . . .

MR. PRIMEAU: At the C—— Clinic for students. I saw it in the library. I must have been twenty.

DR. LACAN: What pushed you to open this damned book?

MR. PRIMEAU: It was under the influence of a friend who had spoken to me. . . . I leafed through it. There were a lot of terms which were very . . .

DR. LACAN: Very what?

MR. PRIMEAU: Very complex, and I could not follow the book.

DR. LACAN: Yes, that comes from the fact that the book has been making the rounds lately. Does that impress you?

MR. PRIMEAU: It pleased me. I did not read all of it, I simply skimmed through it.

DR. LACAN: Good. Let's go, try to come back. *Dirty political assassination*. Why these assassinations?

MR. PRIMEAU: No, there is "political assistants" and there is "assastination."

DR. LACAN: Is there a difference between "assistant" and "assassin," or is all that equivocal?

MR. PRIMEAU: Equivocal.

DR. LACAN: It's equivocal?

MR. PRIMEAU: I cannot . . .

DR. LACAN: . . . distinguish the "assistant" from the "assassin." When did this start, this mix-up which I will call "sonorous"? When did the words—we leave to the side the story of your name, *Prime-Au—Geai Rare*, that has some weight, the rare jay—but—"assistant" and "assassin," the words slide together. We cannot say that there the words take on weight, because the "dirty assassination" . . .

MR. PRIMEAU: Their weight, to the extent that it is not reflexive.

DR. LACAN: Which is to say that you do not add your reflection to them?

MR. PRIMEAU: No, it emerges, it comes spontaneously, in bursts, sometimes spontaneously.

DR. LACAN: In bursts?

MR. PRIMEAU: In bursts. Exactly; I thought that there was perhaps a rational relationship, even if this is not emerging, between *dirty assassination*, *dirty assistants*, and *dirty assastination*. But finally these contractions of words between "assassin" and "assistant" . . . I was also interested in the contraction of words. For example, I had known Béatrice Sarmeau, who is a singer. In going to see her at the V—— theater, I had known her. The feast of Saint Béatrice is February 13. I found that in looking through my dictionary—not my dictionary, my calendar—and since she had asked me to come back and see her again, because I had said some very lovely things about her concert, I had written a wish: "From the place where I read you, didn't Béatrice festive" [*De l'espace où je vous lis, ne s'est pas Béatrice en fête*]. I had written *dixt*, ten days: at the same time the fact I was wishing for ten days, the distance between thirteen and twenty-three, ten, and the formulation, I had not said [*dit*] it, because the ten [days] did not pass without there being a feast.

DR. LACAN: What is this "festive" [*en fête*]? Was that the feast?

MR. PRIMEAU: It was the feast. In the wish there was this word which was contracted. There is another word like *écraseté*, which is at the same time "crushed" [*écrasé*] and "exploded" [*éclaté*]. I had written a poem that I called "Vénure," which is a contraction of *Vénus* and *Mercure*. It was a kind of elegy. But I do not have it here, because... There was also a word "to fall" [*choir*] which I used to write *choixre*, to express the notion of falling and the notion of choice [*choix*].

DR. LACAN: And who else outside of Hélène, to call her by her name, and the *Vénure*—who "venurated" you? Tell me that.

MR. PRIMEAU: Then there was Claude Tours; I knew her at C——.

DR. LACAN: Tell me a little about her.

MR. PRIMEAU: She was also a poet. She worked alone on the piano, and she worked on four-handed piano playing, she danced, she drew.

DR. LACAN: She also was illuminating?

MR. PRIMEAU: When I knew her, she had a kind of beauty. She was very much marked by the medication she was taking. Her face was puffed up. Later I continued to see her, after she left the clinic; she had lost weight, she had a luminous beauty. I am always attracted by these beauties. I am looking for a personality in the room. Perhaps this lady with blue eyes who is wearing a red foulard. It's a shame that she is wearing makeup.

DR. LACAN: She resembled this lady?

MR. PRIMEAU: Yes, she resembled her a little. But Claude did not wear makeup. This lady has put on makeup.

DR. LACAN: Do you ever put on makeup yourself?

MR. PRIMEAU: Yes, it happens that I put on makeup. It has happened to me, yes. (He smiles) It happened to me when I was nineteen, because I had the impression... I had a lot of sexual complexes... because nature endowed me with a very small phallus.

DR. LACAN: Tell me a little bit about that.

MR. PRIMEAU: I had the impression that my sex was shrinking, and I had the impression that I was going to become a woman.

DR. LACAN: Yes.

MR. PRIMEAU: I had the impression that I was going to become a transsexual.

DR. LACAN: A transsexual?

MR. PRIMEAU: That is to say, a sexual mutant.

DR. LACAN: That is what you mean? You had the feeling that you were going to become a woman.

MR. PRIMEAU: Yes, I had certain habits, I used to put on makeup, I had this impression of the shrinking of the sex and at the same time the will to know what a woman was, to try to enter into the world of a woman, into the psychology of a woman, and into the psychological and intellectual formulation of a woman.

DR. LACAN: You hoped. . . . It is nonetheless a kind of hope.

MR. PRIMEAU: It was a hope and an experience.

DR. LACAN: Your experience is . . . that nonetheless you still have a masculine organ, yes or no?

MR. PRIMEAU: Yes.

DR. LACAN: Good, then how is it an experience? It was rather like a hope. In what way is it an experience?

MR. PRIMEAU: In hoping that it was experimental.[6]

DR. LACAN: Which is to say that you "were hoping to experience," if we can once again play on words. It remained at the state of a hope. . . . Finally, you never felt yourself to be a woman?

MR. PRIMEAU: No.

DR. LACAN: Yes or no?

MR. PRIMEAU: No. Can you repeat the question?

DR. LACAN: I asked you if you felt yourself to be a woman.

MR. PRIMEAU: The fact of feeling it psychologically, yes. With this kind of intuition of . . .

DR. LACAN: Yes, pardon me, of intuition. Since intuitions are images that pass through you. Did you ever *see* yourself as a woman?

MR. PRIMEAU: No, I saw myself as a woman in a dream, but I am going to try . . .

DR. LACAN: You saw yourself as a woman in a dream. What do you call "a dream"?

MR. PRIMEAU: A dream? I dream at night.

DR. LACAN: You ought nonetheless to perceive that they are not the same, a dream at night . . .

6. [The French word *expérimental* can also be translated "experiential."]

MR. PRIMEAU: And a waking dream.

DR. LACAN: And the dream that you yourself have called "waking" and to which, if I have understood, you have fastened imposed speech. What happens at night, these images that one sees when one is asleep—is that of the same character as the imposed speech? This is a very approximate way of saying it, but perhaps you have your own ideas.

MR. PRIMEAU: No, there is no relationship.

DR. LACAN: Then why do you call your imposed speech dreams?

MR. PRIMEAU: Imposed speech is not a dream; you have not understood me.

DR. LACAN: Please excuse me. I heard you very well when you used the word "dream" in that context. Even in adding "waking," it was you who used the word "dream." You remember having used this word "dream"?

MR. PRIMEAU: Yes, I used this word "dream," but the imposed sentences are between the solitary circle and what I aggress in reality. I don't know which is a part of. . .

DR. LACAN: Good. Then, what is this bridge which aggresses?

MR. PRIMEAU: Yes, it is the bridge which aggresses.

DR. LACAN: Then these words or speeches. . .

MR. PRIMEAU: No, they are sentences.

DR. LACAN: These speeches which pass through you express your assassination. This is very close to what you said yourself, for example, *They want to monarchize me.* This is something that you say, but it is an imposed speech.

MR. PRIMEAU: It is an imposed speech.

DR. LACAN: Good. The "they" in question are people that you harm and to whom you impute the will to "monarchize" your intellect. Do you agree?

MR. PRIMEAU: Yes, but I do not know if it is. . .

DR. LACAN: Thus either the speeches emerge as such, they invade you. . .

MR. PRIMEAU: Yes, they invade me.

DR. LACAN: Yes.

MR. PRIMEAU: They invade me, they emerge, they are not reflexive.

DR. LACAN: Yes. Then there is a second person who reflects on them, who adds what you add in recognizing that you play this part. You agree?

MR. PRIMEAU: Yes.

DR. LACAN: What do you add, for example? *They want to monarchize my intellect?*

MR. PRIMEAU: It has never happened that I add a sentence to this sentence: *They want to monarchize my intellect.* But *Royalty is not defeated* or *is defeated.* I do not know if. . .

DR. LACAN: It is you who make the distinction between the imposed speech and the reflection that you add on, and in general—this is not the only example—you add a "but." You just said, *But Royalty is defeated.*

MR. PRIMEAU: *They want to monarchize my intellect,* emergence. *But Royalty is defeated* is a reflection.

DR. LACAN: Which is to say, it's yours, you made it up?

MR. PRIMEAU: Yes, while the emergence has been imposed on me. It comes to me like that, they are like intellectual drives that come to me, which are born brutally, and which impose themselves on my intellect.

DR. LACAN: During our discussion . . . ?

MR. PRIMEAU: I have had a lot of them.

DR. LACAN: Perhaps you can reconstruct them.

MR. PRIMEAU: *They want to kill me the bluebirds.*

DR. LACAN: *They want to kill me the birds. . . .*

MR. PRIMEAU: *The bluebirds. They want to get hold of me, they want to kill me.*

DR. LACAN: Who are the bluebirds? Are the bluebirds here?

MR. PRIMEAU: The bluebirds.

DR. LACAN: What is that, the bluebirds?

MR. PRIMEAU: At the beginning, it was a poetic image, related to the poem by Mallarmé, "L'Azur," then the bluebird was the sky, the infinite azur. The bluebird was the infinite azur.

DR. LACAN: Yes, go ahead.

MR. PRIMEAU: It is an expression of infinite liberty.

DR. LACAN: Then, what is it? Let us translate "bluebird" by "infinite liberty." It is the "infinite liberties" that want to kill you? We must find out whether the "infinite liberties" want to kill you. Go ahead.

MR. PRIMEAU: I live without boundaries. Not having boundaries . . .

DR. LACAN: We must find out if you live without boundaries or if you are in a solitary circle, because the word "circle" implies the idea of a boundary.

MR. PRIMEAU: Yes, and of a tradition in relation to . . .

DR. LACAN: The image of the solitary circle . . .

MR. PRIMEAU: In relation to the dream—the nonimaginative [things] created by my intellect?

DR. LACAN: No, but we must nonetheless get to the bottom of this.

MR. PRIMEAU: It is very difficult, because . . .

DR. LACAN: What do you create? Because for you the word "to create" has a meaning.

MR. PRIMEAU: At the moment that it emerges from me, it is a creation. It is a little like that. One must not become intimate. The fact of speaking of these solitary circles and of living without boundaries; there is no contradiction. In my mind I do not see a contradiction. How can I explain that? I am in a solitary circle because I am broken off from reality. It is for that that I speak of a solitary circle. But that does not prevent living at an imaginative level, without boundaries. It is precisely because I have no boundaries that I have a tendency to explode a little, to live without boundaries, and if one does not have boundaries to put a stop to this, you can no longer struggle. There is no more struggle.

DR. LACAN: Before, you distinguished the world from reality, and you said that reality is things like this table, this chair. Good. You seemed to indicate that you think of it like everyone does and that you apprehend it through common sense. Let us then bring the question to bear on this point. Do you create other worlds? The word "create"...

MR. PRIMEAU: I create worlds through my poetry, through my poetic speech.

DR. LACAN: Yes, and the imposed speeches create worlds?

MR. PRIMEAU: Yes.

DR. LACAN: That was a question.

MR. PRIMEAU: Yes, they create worlds. They create worlds, and the proof is that...

DR. LACAN: The proof is that...?

MR. PRIMEAU: I just told you that *They want to kill me the bluebirds* implies a world where I am without boundaries. One comes back, I come back into my solitary circle where I live without boundaries. It is confused, I know, but I am very tired.

DR. LACAN: I just pointed out to you that the solitary circle does not imply living without boundaries, since you are bounded by this solitary circle.

MR. PRIMEAU: Yes, but in relation to the solitary circle, I live without boundaries. But in relation to the real, I live *with* boundaries, if only because of my body.

DR. LACAN: Yes, all that is very true, if we know that the solitary circle is bounded.

MR. PRIMEAU: It is bounded in relation to tangible reality, but that does not prevent the middle of this circle from living without boundaries. You think in geometrical terms.

DR. LACAN: I think in geometrical terms, this is true, and you, do you not think in geometrical terms? But living without boundaries produces anxiety. No? Doesn't that make you anxious?

MR. PRIMEAU: Yes, that makes me anxious. But I can't manage to get rid of this dream or this habit.

DR. LACAN: Good. That much said, you had a problem which determined your coming here. If I understood, a suicide attempt. What pushed you to that? Was it your friend Claude?

MR. PRIMEAU: No, no, no, no. It was because of telepathy.

DR. LACAN: Precisely. We have not yet touched on this word. What is telepathy?

MR. PRIMEAU: It is the transmission of thought. I am a transmitting telepath.

DR. LACAN: You are a transmitter?

MR. PRIMEAU: Perhaps you can't hear me.

DR. LACAN: No, I hear you very well. You are a transmitting telepath. In general, telepathy concerns reception, no? Telepathy warns you of what has happened?

MR. PRIMEAU: No, that is clairvoyance. Telepathy is the transmission of thoughts.

DR. LACAN: Then to whom do you transmit?

MR. PRIMEAU: I don't transmit any message to anyone. What passes through my brain is heard by certain receiving telepaths.

DR. LACAN: For example, am I a receptor?

MR. PRIMEAU: I do not know.

DR. LACAN: I am not very receptive, since I am showing you that I flounder in your system. The questions that I asked you prove that it was precisely from you that I wanted to hear your explanations. I have thus not received the important part of what we will call provisionally "your world."

MR. PRIMEAU: A world in my image.

DR. LACAN: Do these images exist?

MR. PRIMEAU: Yes.

DR. LACAN: They are something that you receive, since you see them.

MR. PRIMEAU: Telepathy concerns speech. The emerging sentence and the reflections that I can have, because I have some from time to time . . .

DR. LACAN: Yes, you reflect all the time about your sentences.

MR. PRIMEAU: No, I do not reflect all the time on the sentences, but I have reflections on diverse subjects. I do not know what is given by telepathy, but these images are not transmitted by telepathy. Finally, I suppose so, because I am not at the same time me and an other.

DR. LACAN: Yes, but how do you see that the other receives them?

MR. PRIMEAU: By his reactions. If I ever aggress them, if I ever say things which do not seem to me . . . The physicians have often asked me the question. It is a reasoning that I make. When I go to see someone, I see if his face is frozen or if there are different expressions, but I do not have a perfectly objective or scientific notion that certain persons receive me.

DR. LACAN: For example, have I received you?

MR. PRIMEAU: I don't think so.

DR. LACAN: No?

MR. PRIMEAU: No.

DR. LACAN: Because the questions I asked you showed that I was floundering. Who here has received, aside from me?

MR. PRIMEAU: I don't know, I have not had the time to look at the people. On the other hand, these are psychiatrists who habitually concentrate and do not react. . . . It is especially with the patients that I see.

DR. LACAN: Your friends in the hospital?

MR. PRIMEAU: That's right.

DR. LACAN: How long has this been going on, this telepathy, this frozen expression in which you note that someone has received something?

MR. PRIMEAU: It started in March 1974, when G—— diagnosed my paranoid delusions.

DR. LACAN: Do you believe in this paranoid delusion? I do not find you delusional.

MR. PRIMEAU: At the time it was there. At the time I was very excited, I wanted . . .

DR. LACAN: You wanted . . . ?

MR. PRIMEAU: I wanted to save France from fascism.

DR. LACAN: Yes, go ahead.

MR. PRIMEAU: I was listening to a radio program on *France-Inter* at 10:00, and I was speaking at the same time. Pierre Boutellier said, during his program, "I did not know that I had listeners who have those gifts." That was when I became conscious of the fact that I could be heard through the radio.

DR. LACAN: You had, at that moment, the feeling that you could be heard through the radio?

MR. PRIMEAU: Yes. And I have another anecdote, when I made my suicide attempt. There was a program called "Radioscopie." I was reflecting . . . They talked for a moment, and they laughed together as though they understood something, and I was talking, I no longer remember what I was saying, but finally, they said, "That is what I want to say to an anonymous poet." It wasn't exactly that, it was an indifference which is not indifferent; indifference did not exist. They spoke of an anonymous poet. Another time on "Radioscopie" there was another guest who was Roger Fressoz, the editor of *Canard Enchaîné*. [7] It was after my suicide attempt. Just at the end of the interview they were talking of anticlericalism, and I said "Roger Fressoz is a saint." [8] They burst out laughing, both of them, on the radio, in a way that had no relation with what they were saying, and I heard, somewhat softer, "He could work at *Canard Enchaîné*." Is that the pure fruit of my imagination, or did they really hear me? Were they both

7. [A satirical political newspaper.]
8. [In French the word *saint* is feminine.]

receptor telepaths, or is it pure imagination, a creation?

DR. LACAN: You can't make up your mind?

MR. PRIMEAU: I can't make up my mind.

DR. LACAN: Thus it was because of this telepathy, clearly distinguished from clairvoyance, that you made this attempt?

MR. PRIMEAU: No, it was not because . . . I was abusing my neighbors, I was very aggressive.

DR. LACAN: You were abusing them?

MR. PRIMEAU: Because there were often family squabbles. One afternoon, I was coming back from O——, and. . . .

DR. LACAN: And what?

MR. PRIMEAU: I had a lot of medicine.

DR. LACAN: Yes.

MR. PRIMEAU: I had a lot of anxiety already about people hearing certain of my thoughts.

DR. LACAN: Yes. Because these abuses happened through your thoughts?

MR. PRIMEAU: Yes, through thoughts. It was not face to face. It was the apartment above ours. I was aggressing them. I heard them cry out, "Mr. Primeau is mad, he should be put in an asylum," and so on.

DR. LACAN: That was what determined your . . . ?

MR. PRIMEAU: I was very depressive. I was already very anxious from seeing that certain persons could perceive certain of your thoughts or certain of your more or less baroque fantasies. I was listening at the same time to the radio, and I was saying things that were insignificant and banal. On the radio I had the impression that someone was listening to me, was making fun of me. I was really at the end of my rope, because with this telepathy, which had been going on for a while, I had other neighbors who I had abused and who looked at me strangely. All of a sudden I wanted to commit suicide and I took . . .

DR. LACAN: No, but what does that resolve, your committing suicide?

MR. PRIMEAU: It's an escape. . . . To escape my anxiety. Intellectually I was against the suicidal mind. I had a sentence: "Life as a means of knowing." Every time I was in despair after I fell ill at fifteen, I have this sentence which came back: "If I die, there are things that I cannot know." I believe in reincarnation, but I do not believe in heaven.

DR. LACAN: You believe in reincarnation?

MR. PRIMEAU: I believe in metempsychosis. There was a time, when I was about eighteen, when I believed I was the reincarnation of Nietzsche.

DR. LACAN: You thought you were the reincarnation of Nietzsche? Yes, . . . why not?

MR. PRIMEAU: Yes, and when I was twenty I discovered Artaud. When I was seventeen I read *L'Ombilic des limbes*, and I bought the complete works of Artaud. And when I was around twenty I had the impression that I was the reincarnation of Artaud. Artaud died March 4, 1948. I was born September 10, 1948. He was born September 4, 1896; we were both born under the sign of Virgo. Since I knew the length of time between March and September, I had the impression that his mind and soul had emigrated for six months and that this soul, this mind, were reincarnated in me, when I was born, September 10, 1948.

DR. LACAN: You really believe that?

MR. PRIMEAU: Now I no longer think I am the reincarnation of Artaud or Nietzsche, but I still believe in reincarnation, because when I was very young, I had a dream which was kind of a double reincarnation, a dream at night, a nocturnal dream. I was seven or eight. At this age one has not read books on metempsychosis. In this dream, I found myself in the Middle Ages, and I had the impression that I had already lived in the Middle Ages. At the same time, in this dream, I found myself in a run-down castle, and in my dream, I was also dreaming.

DR. LACAN: A dream within a dream, yes.

MR. PRIMEAU: And I thought I had known this castle before, when I had another life, before the Middle Ages. I remember that I knew this castle, even though it was a little run-down.

DR. LACAN: Then this castle dated from before the Middle Ages.

MR. PRIMEAU: Perhaps during the Middle Ages the life span was no more than thirty-five or fifty years. The dream of the dream was perhaps from the time of the Middle Ages also, and perhaps it took fifty or one hundred years for the castle to become a little run-down. But that is a hypothesis that I formulate but which was not formulated in my dream.

DR. LACAN: It is a hypothesis that you have emitted.

MR. PRIMEAU: I had experiences of levitation. I developed[9] very young, when I was eleven. One day . . .

DR. LACAN: What you call "developing," what is that? Having erections?

MR. PRIMEAU: That's right.

DR. LACAN: Then?

MR. PRIMEAU: I had a levitation dream.

DR. LACAN: Yes, tell me.

MR. PRIMEAU: I was masturbating, and I felt an extreme *jouissance*. I had the sensation of rising into the air. Did I really rise, or is it an illusion of orgasm? From the point of view of thought, I really think that I levitated.

9. [The French expression *être formé* refers generally to a girl's attaining puberty.]

DR. LACAN: Yes, one does hope. (silence) Tell me, what are you going to do now?

MR. PRIMEAU: I am going to continue to try to get well. Now? Long- or short-term?

DR. LACAN: Long-term.

MR. PRIMEAU: I have no idea. I do not formulate into the future.

DR. LACAN: Are you following a course of study?

MR. PRIMEAU: No, I am no longer a student.

DR. LACAN: Right now you are not working?

MR. PRIMEAU: No, I am not working.

DR. LACAN: One day you will have to leave the hospital. How do you envisage pulling yourself together?

MR. PRIMEAU: If I succeed in overcoming my anxiety, in finding a possibility for a dialogue . . . There will always be this phenomenon of telepathy which will harm me, because I will not be able to act, all my actions will be immediately recognized by telepathy by those who hear me, without my even hearing it . . . I will not be able to live in society as long as this telepathy exists. I will not be able to have a social life without being the prisoner of this telepathy. People hear my thoughts, I will not be able to work, it is not possible. What tortures me the most . . .

DR. LACAN: Since when have you been feeling a little better?

MR. PRIMEAU: Since two weeks ago. I had numerous discussions with the psychiatrists, and that has loosened me up a little. But the fact that my secret garden is perceived by certain persons, that my thoughts and my reflections are . . .

DR. LACAN: Your secret garden, is that the solitary circle?

MR. PRIMEAU: A secret garden where the reflections, the images or the reflections that I can have on different subjects, and so on . . . How can you have a professional activity if some of those around you perceive your reflection and are short-circuited? Even if one lives in a completely direct manner, there are things . . . If I was in a study group and I had to direct people, and they heard me, it would be unlivable. A month ago I was really very sick. I stayed on my bed constantly sleeping. I was very broken up. I had thought of committing suicide once, because one cannot live with this telepathy, which has not always existed, which was born at the moment. . . .

DR. LACAN: Which has not always existed? Imposed speech came first?

MR. PRIMEAU: Imposed speech and telepathy began in March 1974 . . ., at the moment of the paranoid delusion, when I wanted to fight the fascists and so forth, with thoughts.

DR. LACAN: At the time you were seeing H——.

MR. PRIMEAU: I only saw him once.

DR. LACAN: At this time, did you have anything like the imposed speech or the telepathy?

MR. PRIMEAU: No, that's not right. Besides, when I saw my psychiatrist G——again, when I returned from O——, he said to me: "Your telepathy..." I had twenty-five electroshocks, thirteen at N—— and twelve at O——. I am more and more anxious. I can't manage to concentrate. With electroshocks they attain the cells.

DR. LACAN: That is what you think. The drama of being ill, for you, is the electroshock.

MR. PRIMEAU: These electroshocks were made to heal me, because I was really delusional. I have taken a lot of tests in my life. When they took me to the clinic at M——, I was so delusional. . . . Intellectually I was hearing voices which asked me questions about fascist France. I had the impression that I was studying philosophy or elementary math—I do not know, I can no longer concentrate. I was thinking that the fascists had taken power, that they had taken by force the radio and television communications center. Using thoughts, I made Jean-Claude Bourret and Jean Ristat[10] kill each other, strangling each other. At that time I was also obsessed with fraternity. . . . I was responding with mathematical symbols. I had the impression that they were posing questions. It was necessary that I answer in order to save France from fascism. They asked me questions, and these responses, I gave them very openly, they were mathematical series or poetic symbols. I cannot remember that. That is why they said I was delusional.

DR. LACAN: Finally, who is right, the physicians or you?

MR. PRIMEAU: I don't know...

DR. LACAN: You put yourself in the hands of the physicians.

MR. PRIMEAU: I put myself in their hands, trying to conserve my free will.

DR. LACAN: You have the feeling that free will is important in your life? In what you have just told me, you are undergoing certain things which you don't understand.

MR. PRIMEAU: Yes, but...

DR. LACAN: Yes, but...?

MR. PRIMEAU: I have a hope, a hope of finding my power of judgment again, my power of dialogue, a power to get hold of the personality. I think that that is the most crucial problem. Like I had told you at the beginning, I can't manage to get hold of myself.

10. [Well-known television personalities.]

DR. LACAN: Good, my friend, good-bye. (Dr. Lacan shakes his hand) I would be happy to have some samples of your...
MR. PRIMEAU: Of my writings [*écrits*]?
DR. LACAN: We'll get together in a few days.
MR. PRIMEAU: Thank you, sir. (He leaves the room)

DR. LACAN: When we get into details, we see that the classical treatises do not exhaust the question.

A few months ago I examined someone who had been labeled a Freudian psychosis. Today we have seen a "Lacanian" psychosis... very clearly marked. With these "imposed speeches," the imaginary, the symbolic, and the real. It is because of that very fact that I am not very optimistic for this young man. He has the feeling that the imposed speech has been getting worse. The feeling that he calls "telepathy" is one more step. Besides, this feeling of being seen puts him in despair.

I don't see how he is going to get out of it. There are suicide attempts which end up succeeding. Yes.

This is a clinical picture which you will not find described, even by good clinicians like Chaslin. It is to be studied.

2 Teachings of the Case Presentation

BY JACQUES-ALAIN MILLER

Never—oh, how I wish that this "never" were true and that routine had not numbed me—I never attend Lacan's case presentations at Henri Rousselle Hospital without dreading what will take place there. To put it simply: a man, a patient, an unfortunate soul, will encounter through Lacan the cipher of his destiny and will do so without knowing it. For one or two hours he will be heard, questioned, sounded, maneuvered, and finally sized up; the few words Lacan pronounces will weigh heavily on the scales of his fate, even more so, since Lacan is frequently called upon to interview a difficult case.

Lacan does not teach here. What we learn we grasp in flight, from the patient or the analyst, and we are never sure whether we have been taught something or nothing. There are, however, two or three things that appear to me more certain than the rest, and it is these that I will discuss. These are impressions from which I would begin teaching.

Often Lacan's last question to his patient is the following: how do you see the future? A young paranoiac responded that she was sure now that a page had been turned and that things would get better and better. Lacan approved. She had hardly left the room when he added: "She got off on the wrong foot; she won't get out of it."

Those in attendance were moved by this about-face. During the interview we had not been leaning in this direction, and thus we had been taken in or deceived by the attitude of the questioner no less than by that of the patient.

As a member of the audience, I would say that its function of looking on or overhearing is necessarily dumb. We are there in large numbers as apprentices, and Lacan does nothing to raise us from this abjection. Like a psychiatrist he lets an atmosphere of complicity be created, and this extends to the relation between master and students. Lacan works at this and at the same time protects the element of risk in the exercise. There is no physical barrier in the room, and yet

Jacques-Alain Miller is co-chairman of the Department of Psychoanalysis at the University of Paris VIII. He is the general editor of Lacan's seminars, forthcoming in book form from Editions du Seuil. He is also a member of the governing board of the Ecole Freudienne de Paris. This article was first published as "Enseignements de la présentation de malades," in Ornicar? 10 (July 1977), pp. 13–24.

we could just as well be behind a two-way mirror. One has the impression that Lacan and his patient are enclosed in a transparent capsule; the patient is enveloped by a steady and unvarying attention, by the almost total immobility of the questioner.

Those in attendance are silent, but one guesses that if they spoke they would speak like a Greek chorus. When we are there, we form the *doxa* of public opinion or of modern civilization, and there is, curiously enough, a secret agreement between us and the patient. When the patient evokes "formula ones," we know that he is talking about racing cars, but Lacan does not know, does not understand, and he makes the patient repeat, explain. . . .

The audience awaits a diagnosis that the hospital has not found or on which there is a difference of opinion. The diagnosis will permit the staff to place the problem in a nomenclature and to direct the treatment and the therapeutic strategy. We await a name or label that will fall from the master's lips and will be destiny itself. The audience, waiting for this, is always disappointed; the questioner, the expert, more often than not responds like a Zen master, with a kick in the pants.

It is not that he goes into hiding, that he refuses to pronounce the words "paraphrenia" or "retardation" for fear of labeling, but the labels are pronounced ironically, so that they are annulled. We have learned despite ourselves that the sentence for which there is no remedy is this one: "But he's normal." Thus even when the clinical picture is revealed unambiguously, and even when a diagnosis can be stated in the most classical terms, something of the sense remains suspended. Strangely enough, even when the name or label is spoken, there is deception. The answer we are waiting for is never really given. And nothing shows this better than the fact that for a year some of us have wanted to get together to talk over each of these sessions and to retrace the path of the questions opened by this singular practice. What the patient said was enigmatic, and we were waiting for Lacan to decipher it. And then the deciphering itself was enigmatic and demanded another deciphering. Perhaps there is no better deciphering than by an enigma—especially if it is true that there is no metalanguage.

Is recognizing and classifying mental patients a deciphering? There is a grid that permits us to do it. The grid was developed by psychiatrists in the last century and at the beginning of our own. Doubtless the grid is not absolutely consistent for different psychiatrists—the dividing lines of the one are not those of another, and a symptom described here is neglected there. Some of the clinical forms are marked by the names of their discoverers. But we will not scrutinize this closely; the knowledge of classical psychiatry is designed for manuals and forms a simple, solid corpus that responds in the large to the demands of everyday practice and, I would add, will not be replaced, if only because chemistry nowadays does not permit the symptom to follow its course as it did in the past.

Doubtless at Henri Rousselle this psychiatric corpus is the obligatory reference point; this doxa is the foundation of the place itself. But, to tell the truth, it seems to me to be no less present in the institutions that renounce it, simply because it is the element that determines and justifies any hospitalization. To renounce it, or purely and simply to deny it, is to fall even more under its sway. Breaking away from it requires more of a ruse than that.

Lacan's questions are sustained by this reference, which gives a sense to the "supposed" diagnosis that he will offer. But curiously, at the moment when this sense is going to be solidified or frozen, it is suspended, it becomes a question. Turning on the reference point that was its inspiration, it puts that point into question, suspending its certainty. When I see that, I cannot prevent myself from thinking of what Roland Barthes once wrote about Brecht: that he knew how to affirm and suspend a sense in the same gesture, to offer it and to disappoint the expectation. All of Brecht's plays, Barthes said, finish implicitly with a "Look for the way out!" addressed to the audience.

With Brecht we know immediately that the way out is there; the play is constructed to persuade us that it exists. With the case presentation, however, who would not be persuaded of the truth that Lacan has articulated, namely, that there is no place for hope? "Clinical work," he says, "is the real as impossible to support." Thus the clinical dimension is tragic. It is so for the patient, but also for the therapist. Is it not that which is verified every time—that this real is insupportable for therapists, and more so, the more they devote themselves to it? "Look for the way out." The way out: it is we who name it that; the way out, his way out, the mental patient has already found it—it is his illness. And if we seek the way out for him, in his place, well, that is perhaps our way of being ill.

If this is a truth that we grasp during Lacan's presentations, then clearly it cannot be the object of a dogmatic teaching. We would denature it by making it the only truth when it is only one among others. Nevertheless, this truth is sufficient to temper the spontaneous activism of those who devote themselves to psychotics.

"But," it is said, "can you ignore the fact that these presentations are one of the most traditional exercises in medicine; don't you see what happens when there is a public dissection of the mind where the master demonstrates his know-how for the sole benefit of an audience whose complicity you exemplify, and that in so doing he objectifies his patient? Do you not feel that you are thereby encouraging psychiatric racism and that the influence of psychoanalysis ought to move in a contrary direction, which is to restore to the madman his status as subject, by listening to him, but not by presenting him?"

I am not defending *the* case presentation; rather, I am talking about Lacan's. I bear witness to what is painful in it. Those who work in the hospital could speak of its beneficial effects on the patient, either because it has given access to speech or because it has led to a more just appreciation of the case. Surely enough, the procedure comes from the university, and this in itself is proof that being silent and listening do not suffice for entering into the discourse of analysis. But how can the interview—whose discipline you would not dream of eliminating and which you would agree is therapeutic in itself—not be profoundly transformed by the truth that Freud prevents us from ignoring—namely, that misunderstanding is the essence of communication? I see well enough that you are persuaded by its contrary and that for you, to speak is to make oneself understood.

We learn a great deal by reading Maud Mannoni here. She says the following about Lacan's presentations:

> Lacan has never felt himself obliged to ask questions about the practice of presenting patients at Sainte Anne Hospital Center, one of the bastions of French psychiatry. In the most classical manner, he has found there examples to justify his interpretation of cases and to show his students a pertinent form of interview. Certainly the student profits, but always within the framework of the dominant psychiatry. Thus Lacan has underwritten, despite himself, a traditional psychiatric practice in which the patient serves as the primary material of discourse and what is asked of the psychiatrist is to come and illustrate a point of theory without serving the patient's interests. A Laing or a Winnicott would never have been able to put himself in this position, which the psychiatric institution reserves for its most eminent physicians. With Laing the effect of his psychotic identification is to open the possibility of identifying with the patient. . . . This form of identification is completely different from that of identifying with an eminent psychiatrist.

That the passion to understand and to cure the psychotic give birth to the ambition to identify with him—this much makes logical sense. I would say of this ambition that it would be dangerous if it were not so vain, except for the hysteric. Mme Mannoni is wrong to oppose Lacan to Laing and Winnicott; one of the teachings of Lacan's so often decried presentations is precisely that there is a madness in understanding, a madness in communication. The psychotic has his voices to understand him and to communicate with him, and they suffice. As I have said, Lacan understands nothing.

I suppose that Laing hopes that the imaginary identification with the psychotic will become a transference and will lead the patient to enter into a discourse that makes for a social tie. And it seems to me that it is the psychotic absence of social ties that takes the therapist onto a path leading inevitably to social reform. The therapist renounces the project of adapting madness to society only where he can dream of adapting society to madness. From this dream microsocieties have been born, and they are in no way incompatible with modern liberal ideology. Each of them is attached to and organized around a strong personality. When patients' problems are forgotten, those of the members of the staff come to the surface, and the staff comes to share the segregation of those it heals. These new Pinels—do they not serve as underwriters, I ask you? I do not see the master's knees shaking.

There are those who think that anything that shakes the self-confidence of the psychiatrist is excellent. What is more human than for the psychiatrist to identify with his mad patient? Many things would be better, because this aping can only lead the therapist further into an imaginary dialectic where he will finally supplant the patient (who ought to mobilize his interest) by becoming impassioned only for his own condition. I believe these antipsychiatrists to be no less infatuated than their masters. Pretending to call the institution into question, they no longer talk of anything but themselves. And when they speak of rendering society psychotic, who cannot see that they are preparing it for "psychiatrization"?

How can one be a psychiatrist? We leave this tormenting question to those who are. But for those of us who are not, there is the old question: what is a madman? Lacan's presentations lead us back to it and to the response that he sometimes gives: "someone perfectly normal." This response surely discourages you from identifying with the madman. What I want you to see is that when Lacan says this, he is not making a joke.

To do so I pronounce a name that is no longer heard in our colloquia, that of de Clérambault, and I raise his "mental automatism" from the neglect to which the decadence of our clinical work has consigned it. Thus a return to de Clérambault—and why not, if we see that his work motivated Lacan to become a psychoanalyst.

"Clérambault, our only master in psychiatry," wrote Lacan, and I remind you that he added, "His mental automatism . . . appears to us . . . closer to what can be derived from a structural analysis than any other clinical effort in French psychiatry. . . ." Shall we say that this praise, given in 1966, has even more weight because it contradicts Lacan's thesis of 1932?

Mental automatism is de Clérambault's version of Occam's razor; and precisely because it is an instrument, he came to reduce it to the first letter of the word "syndrome."

The introduction of this S yields an extraordinary simplification in the clinical approach to psychoses. Attacking the old approach, de Clérambault deconstructed the well-established clinical entities like Magnan's psychosis and wiped the slate clean. French clinical psychiatry had always excelled in the description of the nomenclature of delusional states.

This S is not of the same order: de Clérambault proposed it as the initial form of all psychosis (excepting true paranoia and purely interpretative delusions, such as those isolated by Serieu and Capgras, which are most often mixed with mental automatism). As such, S is athematic and neuter, which is to say that contents and effective coloration come to it later, according to the "depths"— paranoiac, perverse, mythomaniacal, interpretative—on which it is produced or according to whether or not it is associated with a passion. S is autonomous; it does not depend on these passional givens but refracts itself and differentiates itself, thus giving the diverse clinical pictures.

"Delusion is a superstructure," declares de Clérambault, and this "ideation is secondary." The primal S of psychosis imposes itself as an irreducible fact of thought, an absolute fact, in relation to which I have no scruples about invoking the Kantian fact of reason, the categorical imperative. Also in question for Kant are the phenomena of enunciation.

What is the "echo of thought," which de Clérambault makes the original positive phenomenon of mental automatism, if not a disturbance between state- ment and enunciation that emancipates a parasitic source? The subject finds himself continually shadowed by a double that emancipates him, accompanies him, or follows him and cannot say anything. Fading, mute, empty, this double still has the power to suspend the subject in the position of receiver. De Cléram- bault calls this independent enunciation a "purely psychic phenomenon," and he names the play on words (signifiers) that it liberates "verbal phenomena." The terms that I substitute for those of de Clérambault indicate that it is not in some obscure "deviation of influx" that we can found the syndrome of mental auto- matism but rather in the grasp of intersubjective communication. It follows that the sender of a message becomes its receiver and that the psychotic disturbance consists only in his experiencing himself as such.

The construction is sufficiently Lacanian for us to take the S of de Cléram- bault and make it the first letter of the word "structure." The structure bared—by its celibates—is the subtitle that this dogma of mental automatism deserves. French psychiatry came to repudiate it in the name of sense and personality. Without a doubt de Clérambault thought in terms of mechanism. But this mechanism is metaphoric (Lacan in 1932 did not see this). De Clérambault did not in any way elaborate on this point, which remains entirely formal, but it was nevertheless no less decisive in instituting a break between psychology and the order of structure.

In a word, de Clérambault made his automatism into something mechanical, but he did this in order to hold on to its autonomy, leaving to Lacan the discovery of the symbolic order. Lacan sought to define the symbolic through a mechanism (certainly not that of de Clérambault, but that of Türing and Wiener), so as to distinguish it from Jung's. Lacan made the symbolic primal and neuter, instituting it thus as signifying and structural. And when he made it athematic, sustaining the point of view that the symbolic is produced first "in the ordinary form of thought, in an undifferentiated form, and not in a definite sensory form," he proposed an idea that is debatable from the point of view of observation but has a logical import that cannot be misconstrued. S means nothing, and this is implied in its name "echo." In question is a purely signifying effect that becomes mad when a delusional deciphering invests it with imaginary meaning.

This construct permits us to distinguish persecution as a delusional interpretation that does not entirely block the efforts of the physician—this because it preserves in the subject the capacities of "confidence, sympathy, tolerance, and expansion"—from true persecution, whose psychogenesis de Clérambault accepts. What is in question in this latter is the structure of knowing; in the former it is the structure of the enunciation. "Interpretative delusions" are another form of "ideogenetic imprint" and would lend themselves equally well to a structural rereading. I will content myself only with evoking this rereading, adding that de Clérambault's deconstruction of Magnan's progressively systematic hallucinatory psychosis seems to me to be epistemologically exemplary.

When the slight separation of the enunciation from itself is amplified until it engenders individualized and thematized voices that appear in the real, when the subject feels himself transpierced by bursts of messages, by a language that speaks of itself, when he feels himself spied on in his inner core and subjected to injunctions or inhibitions whose productions he cannot annex, we then have the great "xenophobia" that Lacan founded in the field of language with his matheme of the Other. Would it be too much to say that the discourse of the Other was already there, in the clinic of psychosis, before Lacan invented it and linked it to the prehistoric Other that Freud found in Fechner? Xenopathic emergences are founded on structure, if structure wants all speech to be formed in the Other. The question is no longer "What is a madman?" but "How can one not be mad?"

Why does the normal subject, who is no less affected by speech, who is no less xenopathic than the psychotic, not become aware of it? The question is more subversive than the identification proposed above. By what inversion do we misconstrue the fact that we are the puppets of a discourse whose syntax preexists all subjective inscription? What is normal is the xenopathia. A subject for whom the Other is no longer veiled is certainly not going to be attained through our imaginary manipulations.

This detour brings us back to the presentation of patients and precisely to the only one Lacan talked about in his seminar last year, the one he labeled a case of pure mental automatism or a "Lacanian psychosis."

The subject had in fact read the *Ecrits*, but this took nothing away from the authenticity of his experience: he was subjected to what he called "imposed speech," which intruded into the sphere of his private cogitation. He could not recognize himself as its speaker, even though the speech most often assigned him the place of grammatical subject of the statements. Each phrase he heard demanded that he complement it with a phrase of another kind, "reflexive," which he knew himself to be emitting. In contrast to the "imposed" statements, he did not figure as the subject of the "reflexive" statement. He witnessed in this way the emergence of the discourse of the Other, but directly, without this soothing misapprehension of the reversal that makes us believe that we speak, when in fact we are spoken. From there we move to the transformation that poses the question of madness. "How do we not sense," Lacan asked, "that the words we depend upon are imposed on us, that speech is an overlay, a parasite, the form of cancer with which human beings are afflicted?" If we identify ourselves with the psychotic, it is insofar as he is, like ourselves, prey to language, or better, that this is what he teaches us.

The teaching by the patient at Lacan's presentations—that is how it should be described—goes farther than a ratiocination on the idea that the norm is social, that one man's madman is not the other's, that normality is mad, and that madness is logical. There is no good usage of the word "normal" that is not antonymical, and Lacan uses it as a synonym of its contrary. Present him with someone slightly retarded, with a cultureless soul who was in the Italian campaign, or someone perhaps hit by a car on the Place d'Italie, someone asocial, a mythomaniacal nobody, even a bum, lazy, unconvincing in his xenopathia, and doubtless a little hysterical—there is a good chance that Lacan will label him normal. A strong personality will lead us closer to paranoia: paranoiac psychosis has no relation to personality; as Lacan corrected himself, it *is* personality.

The patients presented are not in fully delusional states: Lacan is not confronted with senile dementia; the chronic psychosis is rare. What do we see?

Some people representing elementary phenomena, about which the essential question is to give a prognosis of the evolution of the illness, and then others who in Lacan's sense are normal but are troublemakers whom the police or the courts have sent to the asylum and who may well spend a lot of their time coming and going because they have not been correctly grasped by the symbolic. They retain a defect, an inconsistency, and for that reason there is most often no way to hope to see a readaptation.

I recall a person presented last year whom Lacan counted as "one of these normal psychotics who make up our environment." "They want to give me validity," she said at the beginning, and she was right, because the large audience gave her a public. "I always have problems with my employers, I do not accept being given orders when there is a job to do, nor having a schedule imposed on me; I am neither a true or a false patient, I have identified myself with several people who do not resemble me, I would like to live like an article of clothing. . . ." Doubtless we note some beginnings of the creation of language; she had the fleeting idea that she was being hypnotized and that someone wanted to pull the strings, but there was nothing that took on any consistency. She was perpetually floating. As she said, in a remarkable formula, "I am my own part-time employee." A mother, she wanted to "resemble a mother," and when Lacan evoked her child, from whom she is separated, by showing a photograph, she did not respond.

From my notes I reconstruct when Lacan said: "It is difficult to think of the limits of mental illness. This person hasn't the least idea of the body that she is putting into this dress. There is no one to inhabit her clothing. She illustrates what I call 'seeming' [le semblant]. No one has been able to crystallize her. It is not one of the more marked forms of mental illness. What she says is without weight or articulation; to oversee her readaptation seems to me to be utopian and futile." Then, referring to Kraeplin, "We can call it a paraphrenia, and why not qualify it as of the imagination?" He continued, "It is an exemplary mental illness, the excellence of mental illness itself."

Doubtless this is teaching by enigma, but it makes us aware of what it is to suffer in having a "mentality." Every speaking being, gnawed by language, has a "mentality." Is hypnosis anything other than the effect of suggestion inherent in speech? Is the effect of mythomania not inherent in the subjective splitting induced by the signifier? What makes this patient excellent, demonstrative, is the fact that her being is pure seeming: her identifications, so to speak, have not formed the precipitate "me"; there is no crystallizer, no person, no one. She is retarded, if retardation consists in not being inscribed in a discourse. She was hypomaniacal, troubled, an imaginary without ego, a mirror attached everywhere but captivated by nothing, pure "mentality" out of control. No master-signifier, and at the same time nothing that gives her substance, no object *a* to fill her parentheses and give her validity. (The object *a* is a singular Lacanian substance, made of a lack, but a lack that is constant gives to a subject an illusion of synthesis.)

Perhaps belaboring Lacan's fleeting indications, I will say that our clinical work makes us distinguish between the illnesses of mentality and those of the Other. The former derive from the emancipation of the imaginary relationship, the reversibility of ego and object, troubled in no longer being submitted to symbolic scanning. These are illnesses of being that approach pure seeming. To illustrate the latter, I evoke another case, that of a delinquent (twenty years in prison) who for three years has been hearing himself think and who has the impression that the world hears him and hears obscenities.

What we sense most clearly is that he can speak perfectly correctly: "from my early childhood," he says of himself, with emotion. He is fifty-two and bears the name of a father he never knew. Of himself he says: "I am a dirty bastard." That is his conviction; he does not float, he is not confused, he knows what he is, and he is worth nothing: he is manure. He has attempted suicide. Could we without this simple letter O (for Other) make a series of the people in his history, from the highly placed person who pardoned him to the eminent psychiatrist who examined him, to his wife, so perfect that he has no reproaches to make against her. He says starkly that his wife replaces his mother.

Throughout his life he has been faced with a perfect Other who has left no place for him, and this is why the Other does not err: he himself has been identified with waste, he *is* manure, and he takes his subjective consistency from this incontrovertible certainty. This is how we understand what Lacan says at the end. "He is unsubmersible." And he adds: "He believes in his wife, his belief is unshakable."

He believes in his wife as he would believe in an apparition from the beyond. He believes in a complete Other who lacks nothing; there is nothing he can give her. And from this he knows his own truth. His certainty of being "shit" and his belief in his wife are the same thing and are the same as the intrusion of the vulgar voice of the Other, which hurts him.

Finally a physician asks Lacan a question that law and humanity dictate: "Is he dangerous for his wife? I fear he is, I believe. . . ." "No," answers Lacan, assured of the structure, "he is for himself. I am afraid he will try again to commit suicide."

If there is a teaching in the presentation of patients, it is this: "Look for the certainty." One imagines that Lacan has gone to look for knowledge and cer-

tainty in Descartes and Hegel—which is also true—but what he says derives
directly from concrete experience. If there is a clinical practice to be founded, it
is in using these terms.

Knowledge, that is all the paranoiac knows. His relation to knowledge
establishes his symptom. What persecutes him, if not a knowledge that ambles
around the world, a knowledge that becomes a world. The subject, most often, is
certain of the moment when he passes to the other side, of the moment of the
onset of psychosis that Marcel Czermak described this morning. [See chapter 12
of this book.]

And where is this function of certainty more in evidence than in
erotomania? This is what makes all psychotherapy so vain: it knocks its head
against an unattainable certainty that engenders its own proofs. De Clérambault
has made this into an entity whose validity is not questioned here. Instead of
"certainty" he used the word "postulate," whose logical accent is perfectly appropriate to this function.

Because the erotomaniac believes in the Other's love, he believes nothing
and no one, not even the Other who wants to tell him the truth. "He speaks to
me in contraries," says the erotomaniac of his Other, "he was speaking to me in
inverted parables."

The female erotomaniac elects an Object, in de Clérambault's sense, a
canonical figure of the Other, who has no place for her. She is constituted in her
delusions as its lack, passionately sought after. She is thus what is lacking in the
Other who lacks nothing, this Other who is benefactor, omniscient and, if
possible, asexual: the priest, the professor, the physician.

Mental illness is serious when the subject has a certainty: it is the illness of
the unbarred Other. How is one to "therapy" this with speech, when speech can
become idle talk? The illness of mentality, if it is not serious, does not take
speech seriously, since the dimension of the Other is deficient. Who will explain
the psychotic's transference?

PART TWO.   NEUROSIS

3 In Praise of Hysteria

BY MOUSTAPHA SAFOUAN

Psychoanalysis began with hysteria, and psychoanalytic knowledge will always be worth only what our knowledge of this structure is worth.

We can do our work, and well, without knowing what the transference is; and we can obtain appreciable modifications in the cure of an obsessional neurosis without being able to say exactly how we have obtained them; but it is out of the question to introduce significant modifications in a case of hysteria without *knowing*.

Is that too presumptuous? Let us turn our affirmation around: introducing significant modifications in a case of hysteria without ridding oneself of all knowledge is out of the question. This affirmation is nonetheless not believable, as everyone would agree. But then?

We take up this sentence, which we often hear from hysterics, in different forms, depending on style and temperament: "The positive transference, it will never happen!" or else: "It's incredible how you leave me indifferent," to which is sometimes added "It's beginning to worry me" or "It's impossible for me to love you" and so forth.

At first sight, it is a negative sentence. From having heard it repeated with insistence, however, one is obliged to conclude not simply that an intellectual negation is in question but that it derives from a denegation. Thus we have no doubt about its truth, which is easy to find: it is sufficient to deny the negation, which gives: "She loves me." But as—I was going to say: "as it is impossible"; let us rather say: as I did not give her, the analysand, any particular reasons to love me, this can only be an appearance of love. Not even that; for where has the appearance come from? Thus it can only be a reappearance of love, or better, a repetition.

Let us suppose now that we have this little thing called patience—which does not mean that we are going to resign ourselves to routine habits; let us

Moustapha Safouan practices psychoanalysis in Paris. This article is based on comments offered during a meeting of the Ecole Freudienne de Paris, held on June 24, 1973, to discuss hysteria. It was first published as "Eloge à l'hystérie," in Moustapha Safouan, *Etudes sur l'Oedipe* (Paris: Editions due Seuil, 1974), pp. 206–13.

suppose that we know how to suspend entirely a received knowledge, even if it is well founded. Then we finish by learning, sooner or later, that the issue was a sentence that finally was not particularly negative. I mean to say that its impact is not in the form of the negation. This sentence, like many others, is in fact only a half-sentence: the other half has remained repressed. The restitution of the repressed half would give very different results. For example, this one: "It is impossible to love you . . . because it is impossible to love shit." There one begins to know.

To clarify the oscillation that appeared at the beginning of this communication, let us say this: it is impossible to analyze a hysteric without knowing *what we are doing*. Besides, it is a known fact, but one that we cover with a prudish silence, that some of our colleagues are incontestably competent with all kinds of analyses, but when it comes to displacing a hysterical structure by one inch, for them there is no way: they do not know. Let us enter now into the quick of the subject.

One premise that we are going to pose at the departure, in our attempt to deduce hysteria, is this one: the form of the law, presented as a demand or commandment, is the source of a luring, which consists in *the law's appearing to be born out of the mouth of the one who proffers it* as a law that the will of the other imposes or wants to impose and not as a law to which the other is submitted. Besides, does the other submit himself to it? Here is the *hic*.

While waiting for the subject to find out, we see the possibility of his wishing to be the lawmaker. This wish, if it has no chance of being fulfilled, easily finds the means of being satisfied by believing in its object, which is to say, believing in this lure: that there is an Author of the Law.

What I have just said can be summarized in this formula: there would be no reason to believe in God if it were not for the role that Descartes expressly assigns him as creator of eternal verities.

Let us now suppose a subject who is settled into this belief in its sacred or profane form: we see, first, that the movement is not without a *reciprocal divinization*: both God's and the subject's. We can in the second place translate this movement into our language by saying that the subject in question demands *the symbolic father* and can be appeased by nothing less. In the third place, we conceive of the possibility that—by an obscure pathway not impossible to trace, which leads to a questioning of the paternity of this divine or symbolic father— something is produced that is worthy of being labeled "knowing too much about maternity."[1] And it is a fact that the hysteric ignores nothing that concerns motherhood.

We will keep present in our minds this constellation or this package of premises, and we ask what consequences it has for the subject we have just defined.

In order to appreciate the response fully, it is essential to recall here Lacan's thesis on the function of beauty. Lacan defined beauty as a brilliance that dazzles us and is interposed between us and the second death. Now, what is this *second death*?

Hegel says that the life of children is the death of parents. This is doubtful; most often we observe the contrary. What is not doubtful—but only analytic experience permits us to affirm this—is that the child (the subject) comes to be a parent only to the extent that he rids himself of the fantasy that Hegel describes, without knowing that it is a fantasy, which is to say, Hegel takes it for reality.

Knowing that it is a fantasy is the second death. It is precisely because all tools fail him, all tools that would permit him to accede to this knowledge, that the one we call the psychotic is sometimes pushed to realize the second death in a real death. And the *first*? If there is a second, there is also a first.

The first is that of narcissistic birth, of the birth of the subject into an image that, far from being able to give him the sense of life, is the model of all corpses.

Now, let us remember the pathetic moment when Dora spent two hours contemplating the Sixtine Madonna of Raphael in the museum of Dresden, a Madonna that is one of the images of beauty before which desire experiences itself in its intimate tenor of nostalgia and regret at the same time that its pain and sickness are veiled. In any case, this is not a reason for us in our turn to remain mute before it.

Let us imagine that the stomach of the Madonna begins to inflate, to round out, advancing into the real space, and imagine the effect that this unusual miracle would produce in the one contemplating it. This helps us arrive at an idea of the strange convulsions that—every time that her discourse, and not her vain curiosity, puts her closer to the *reality* of maternity—transport the body of the hysteric and make of it, not a dispossessed body in the imaginary or the real, as would be the case with a neurotic or psychotic, but—unique condition of the

1. The divinization of the father conceals the mystery of origins. The hysteric is going to be "too" interested, as in enigmas that "do not have solutions."

hysteric—a possessed body: a body that spits, vomits, bleeds, grows fat, and symptomatizes. Of all that she understands nothing.

There is nothing surprising in her understanding nothing: since it is this *too much* (she knows too much about maternity) in which resides, not the distance, but the formal hiatus between this knowledge—which, however real it may be, is no less marked by denegation—and truth. But what truth?

Several formulas are usable here, but we are going to propose—as we did with the second death—the one that puts us closest to the thing. Here it is: *only the law* makes jouissance condescend to desire. But the hysteric does not hear it that way. She wants—it would be better to say that she dreams, for this can only be a dream—she dreams, then, of *a desire that would be born of love*: and this in turn can only sharpen the antinomy between love and desire.

Let us be clear. In a sense, such an antinomy does not exist: desire always brings along with it a certain quantum of love; a little or a lot, repressed or not, it is not important. But the inverse is not true: despite all the praise that has been addressed to the little god of love, he has remained completely incapable of engendering the least little bit of desire.

But what is love, if not the fibers of being tending toward an object. Would this lack be a lack of desire? Yes, for there are lacks and there are lacks.

Philosophers have defined the concept of lacking as privation or as a real lack. Analytic experience has brought forth, to the point where it is impossible to misconstrue it, another kind of lack, which is distinguished from the first in that the recovery of the missing object brings no plenitude and no satisfaction; this is frustration. Love is this frustration—I mean pure love, as we say pure oxygen, love as it is almost never isolated in practice, except in some socially institutionalized forms, the most exemplary example of which is courtly love—or else in poetry, specifically, in the English metaphysics or in certain Arab mystics. Love is frustration in this sense, that at the root of love there is annulment and abandonment, to say nothing of destruction by the object. Of this object one retains only a sign, a look or a salutation, its simple presence, its portrait, we might say, or its photo. This affinity between love and object loss or mourning has been noted by many analysts, beginning with Freud;[2] they have asked themselves questions about it, but without ever dreaming of finding the lost object in the object itself: the object of the erotic aim.[3]

2. See Robert C. Bak, "Being in Love and Object Loss," *International Journal of Psychoanalysis* 54:1 (1973), pp. 1–8.
3. Sören Kierkegaard, whose melancholy dispositions are well known, grasped this truth and gave it its most powerful expression.
The distinction between love and desire is necessary to our understanding of a fundamental trait of the phenomenology of the obsessional—his doubt, which Freud relates to the doubt that everyone

Desire is of another order, one that recalls our formula and about which we have said that the hysteric consents to it with difficulty. But then what does she do?

Tell a child the story of the stork that nips a mother or future mother on the leg. If the child has strong dispositions toward obsessional neurosis, he will begin to limp. This symptom will have been founded on the following reasoning: "The stork nipped me, thus I have a baby in my belly." The obsessional is a naïf; that is why we can work with him more or less well. But if the child's dispositions bear towards hysteria, he will also limp; there will be the same symptom, but not the same reasoning; he will be saying: "The stork nipped me, but I do not have a baby in my belly, you are lying!" Why does the hysteric hold on to this "you lie!"—what need, what compulsion (to tell the truth, we consider that the hysteric has a compulsion that is as specific as the obsessional neurotic's doubt), then, pushes her to conceive of the Other as a liar? The reason is that it is precisely in her detection of the Other's lie that her faith, or her little faith, in the phallus resides.

"The phallus, I have no idea what it is," a woman analysand said to me one day, adding, "except that it is something that never stays in its place." This sibylline sentence, let out by the analysand in a kind of sacred fright, is one that would have been appropriate for the oracle at Pythos. It only took a couple of seconds, but that is sufficient for us to know what to expect: the phallus, she wants it to be a wanderer. And this is why, wherever the hysteric goes, she brings war with her, ideological war, war of prestige, which we know has no object, but of which she makes herself the object.

It is only when the hysteric renounces being what men fight over—we will have to precede her there—that she will be ready to conquer the truth. This is to say that she has never demanded anything other than to be loved not for her perfections but for her imperfections, things with which she has always been reproached. It is then that we learn from her, from this mother in sufferance, that there is only one pertinent trauma: that of birth.

---

has about the extent and durability of his love. In fact, many obsessional symptoms are a "knowing" denunciation of the narcissistic structure of love.

Why does the subject stop himself with this denunciation? Because by stopping he can forget and repress the desire that presides over the enunciation of "I love you."

We are not thinking here of the obsessional's particular difficulty in giving or receiving love, but rather of the paradox inherent in the declaration of love. While it "misses" completely the "second person," at the same time it attains her more profoundly, in the sense that it "tickles" her at the root of her desire.

Let us note, finally, the different structure of this kind of love. The love is not "reciprocal" but knows that a response that is not a refusal can only be favorable; it does not require the idealization of the object.

How can we close this *praise of hysteria* without returning to our point of departure: transference love? But how can we add one iota to what Lacan said, that transference love is not a true love but also not a repetition, because what is in play in this not-true love is *the very truth of love*?

I say this in all knowledge of cause. God knows if I have had to interpret repressed wishes for love, as well turned, as concise, as powerfully poetic (let us not confuse poetic and sublime) as anything we can imagine consciously. Consciousness, we know, is hardly verbose.

Well, these wishes were most often addressed to a third party, called by name. Again, with Freud we find the principal example: the alembic formula that the Rat Man composed with the initials of several prayers [*Glejisamen*], in which the name of his cousin was included without his knowing it. In this formula Freud knew how to mark his patient's wish: to inundate her, Gisella, with his sperm [*Samen*]. All wishes of love are not to be found on the same axis; others are located on the axis of tenderness. To tell the truth, even this wish of the Rat Man was not without tenderness, if we think that Gisella had undergone an ablation of the ovaries.

Sometimes such wishes are addressed to me. Here is the simplest possible example: a woman analysand enters, with her face somber and veiled; she lies down and remains silent for a certain time, then she says, "I left the children at the house." Then she again becomes silent, and in a context that leaves no doubt about the part of the phrase that is repressed, adds, ". . . for you!" It is good to let such wishes go as they came; to formulate them would be to refuse them.

Why then does this repression strike the declaration of love, a declaration whose being spoken ravishes the purity of love but whose placement in the unconscious calls for an authentication that only a third party can bring? And what is the noun or pronoun to which the declaration is addressed? Here the two questions seem so intimately linked that a response to the one will be a response to the other. The reminder that it is much easier to make oneself loved by an interiorized other than by a real other is sufficient for us to be able to conclude, with this formula in the guise of a response: *love is always the love of a name, even as desire is always the desire of an organ.*

The hysteric knows it; and this is why Lacan's formula is verified in her most particularly: "Anxiety is the sensation of the desire of the Other;" and from there we can see the challenge that she presents for us: to name this desire.

It is not easy to respond to this challenge. If we name it, we lie; but silence, with nothing else, can only be a retreat. There must then be a third way, . . . which we have discussed in "Langage et Satisfaction," in *Etudes sur l'Oedipe*, pp. 183–205.

4 The Fable of the Blood

BY EUGÉNIE LEMOINE-LUCCIONI

A "fable" is what a subject tells to himself and to me. It is a story outside the time of the subject's history but not outside the time of the analysis, since the fable punctuates the transference. To the extent that facts and characters are brought into a story and are thus organized in reference to signifiers rather than to historical truth, they constitute a fable. The subject even believes that there is a moral to the fable, but this comes down to an "And that is why . . ." spoken in discouragement.

THE FABLE

Anne-Marie, whose analysis we will consider here, is twenty-three. She is happily married. She wanted her child, and her husband also wanted it. He had even accepted medical treatment and an operation for "hemorrhoids on his testicles." As for Anne-Marie—this is not very rare today—she was on the pill and had to wait three months before she could conceive the child. In short, there was time to make a decision before the moment of conception, and this couple wanted to have a child.

Anne-Marie became pregnant during her analysis. I was immediately informed of her pregnancy, in the same way that I had been informed of the decision. When the pregnancy was confirmed, she declared to me that she had nothing more to say to me. That was false, as we will see.

The essential elements of the fable assemble around the theme of blood. Not that this theme leads to abundant commentaries, but it does appear in this woman's biography and in her dreams with surprising clarity.

Anne-Marie suffered from an amenorrhea for two years when she was eighteen, accompanied by constipation, exactly as her mother had when she was

Eugénie Lemoine-Luccioni practices psychoanalysis in Paris. This article first appeared as "La Fable du sang," in Eugénie Lemoine-Luccioni, *Partage des femmes* (Paris: Editions du Seuil, 1976), pp. 13–30.

eighteen. I note that Anne-Marie's speech is very slow and reserved. Nothing "comes out."

But nothing "goes in" very easily, either, since she has anorexia. From the distance of many years a voice comes back to me; it is the monotonous and hesitating voice of Blanche, a girl of twenty, also anorectic and amenorrheic, *like her mother at the same age.*

Anne-Marie's maternal grandfather died of a cerebral hemorrhage, and her father, a naval officer and later a high school vice-principal, also died of a cerebral hemorrhage, quite suddenly. This strange coincidence immediately suggests to me that there is a displacement upward in the men of both sides of the family. These sanguinary accidents cause me to associate the story of Anne-Marie with that of a male analysand: "I was convinced I had blood clots in my brain," he repeated to me. Thus he explained the terrible migraines that he had had when he was twelve. Obviously blood takes another path in girls of this age.

"One year after my father's death," Anne-Marie explains, "I put on lipstick, as a physician had advised, and my periods came back." She adds, "I was engaged to be married."

The red lipstick reminds me of the first dream Blanche told me: she was playing tennis and was wearing something red, a dress, a skirt, or a vest. . . . Several months later she told me that she did not dream any more; she also said that when she dreamed, the dreams were gray, colorless, . . . while her mother dreamed in colors. . . . Yes, Blanche's mother described her dreams to Blanche and even now tells her daughter when she has her periods. "You are lucky," Blanche answers her ("to be able to say that you have your periods," if I may complete the sentence). Thus her mother must know in turn that Blanche does not eat, that she does not sleep, that she does not have her periods. And I, the analyst, must know that she does not dream. Periods and dreams can be substituted, the one for the other, as object refused, as a no addressed to mother.

In the same way Anne-Marie, whose mother "as usual understands nothing," judges that her mother, forewarned by her own experience, ought to have understood. She bears against this mother a bitter rancor. When her mother appears in her dreams, she is always either insane or dead. Yet Anne-Marie is the most deferential and docile of daughters; she is, in addition, the oldest daughter of a second marriage. She is perfect, and she succeeds in things that the first daughter of the first marriage does not. This other first daughter is not perfect in any way. The role of the eldest who succeeds is obviously only there for display. It prepares the acting out that will betray her exteriorized organization or the passage into action that will supposedly liberate her.

With men, "things are all right." Anne-Marie married a graduate of

Polytechnic [a highly prestigious university], the son of a general: the army after the navy, then—and we go up in rank. His name is Xavier. If he is late for dinner, she thinks he is dead. When she was little, it happened once that Anne-Marie did not recognize her father when he came to wait for her after school, so intensely had she been waiting for him. Doubtless her eyes, preoccupied with the image of her beloved, were distracted to the point of drowning her look in the crowd amassed at the exit. Beyond the father himself, there is no other representative of the paternal family in Anne-Marie's story. The maternal family, on the contrary, is inexhaustibly present: there is the young uncle who delightfully terrorized her by making her play in the big waves, despite her phobia about water, notorious in the families of sailors. She notes that water and blood threaten, each in its turn, to inundate her dreams. There is her mother's sister, unmarried, and who tried to take from her sister all her children, one by one, to raise them in her way. Now Anne-Marie has become a psychologist and takes care of children. Finally, Anne-Marie's youngest sister, Murial, is depressive. Anne-Marie is very preoccupied with Murial and reproaches herself for having had a "privileged status" and thus for having made her sister depressed. Besides, she establishes a link between the mental troubles of this sister and those that supposedly threaten her mother. Her mother appears to her to be so sick that she is afraid (she will tell me much later) of leaving her children with this mother.[1]

When she announces her first pregnancy, her discourse changes completely. It is now the analysis that makes her anxious: "Am I analyzable? I don't dream any more." (Surprising denegation, for she dreams a great deal, as we will see later.) "What am I doing here? I'm pregnant." It is thus, with this question, that she announced this news. Presented as it is, the pregnancy appears to me to be a resistance.

Slightly before her pregnancy she dreams that she "had 'engendered' (instead of "crossed") a dangerous footbridge."[2] A little after this she dreams that she gives birth prematurely to a girl, although she is awaiting a boy. The sea, very blue, is very close, threatening, invading. Her older brother says: "We must close the window, there is a risk that the baby will drown." Then the baby is put into a bathtub. "It's frightening." We might ask why there is so much fright, if this is only a dream.

Thus she dreams; later she also has a clearly homosexual dream. It is not the first. She is nonetheless very astonished. I do not understand, she says (like her

1. During the analysis she will have two daughters.
2. [In French the word "engender" (*engender*) is very close to the word "cross" (*enjamber*).]

mother who did not understand, doubtless!). The dream is as clear as it is short: "I have erotic sensations with a little girl." As the end of the month she has another dream that she says is "atrocious": a little girl on a bicycle; there is a race on a mountain; she falls, and at first there is nothing; then all at once from all sides blood splatters; she is covered with blood.

The amenorrhea can be seen as a reaction of fear; a fear of the blood that flows, of inundation, of the terrible sea, of the wave that submerges, and so forth.

The husband is a bit forgotten, she no longer has much desire to make love. The sexual relations are less frequent. He works too much; and in addition, he makes her nervous. Finally, he is too small. She dreamed one day that he was "smaller than normal" and that she would have abnormal children. She is attracted to other men. She who is so moral and even bourgeois begins to dream, without wanting to admit it, of life in a commune. There is a young man who pleases her, a friend recently married. She remembers also that there was another suitor when she knew Xavier. The pregnancy makes of her a kind of universal woman, a woman for everyone—almost.

Finally she has another dream that recalls the first anxiety dreams: a car that follows right behind theirs is swallowed by an enormous wave; the sea is threatening; there is a dangerous bridge that must be crossed to attain the family home, which is on the lake. This summer she had a terrible anxiety attack because her husband left to go fishing on the sea: "I was really panicked," she says. When the baby does not move, she is afraid that he is dead. He must move all the time.

A new theme appears, that of the gift. "My mother received gifts; she barely responded."

She does not say it openly, but these dreams say in her place that she dreads giving birth as she dreads a tidal wave or a wave of blood. During the two years when her periods stopped, Anne-Marie made the very sign of femininity disappear (in comparison, the most obvious symptom with Marie Cardinal is the continuous flow of blood, without periodicity).[3] For Anne-Marie, woman is guilty. *Her mother stole her father from a dead woman.* She had in fact married a widower who had also lost one son from his first marriage. Not to have children is a punishment, Anne-Marie tells me. But once she has one promised to her, she is panicked. Death threatens. *Anne-Marie is balanced between not being a woman and dying in blood because woman is guilty of theft and murder.* The gifts she offers to her mother in dreams appear like the propitiary gifts offered to a terrible goddess.

The return to the mother leads us here to something very archaic. Anne-

3. [The reference is to a recent book by Marie Cardinal, *Les Mots pour le dire.*]

Marie has come into analysis to be saved from her mother: my presence erases her fear. At least, this is what she believes, despite her dreams. When she is pregnant, it is not to her mother that she announces it first. Yet a little before Anne-Marie's pregnancy, her mother had brought her "a child": in a delusional episode the mother believed herself pregnant—even though, she said, she had not made love. Anne-Marie was very shaken by this premonitory event. But finally: "That is all over; it is I who am pregnant, not my mother; and it is not my mother's child, even though she asked me if she could keep the child after its birth, to free me. But I will not let her take care of it. Besides, I would be too afraid." "Afraid of what?" I asked her. "She forgets things, she is not well; I would fear for the child."

Xavier is very happy; he takes care of everything. He dreams of the baby every night. We should add to the above that Anne-Marie herself dreams that being pregnant is like being asleep. In one of her dreams, waking up is the same as giving birth. But when she dreams of awakening, the baby is still not there. Anxiety. Then she wakes up, and in the real awakening she realizes that she is pregnant and that the baby is still in her womb.

She used me and she used analysis to get around the difficulty: She says that I am in some sense the Holy Spirit, and Xavier is St. Joseph. As for her, I will not say that she is the Virgin, because actually she has the feeling of never having been a virgin and of never having required deflowering. But especially her "I am no longer afraid" bears witness to a state of permanent denegation: she wants to sleep. With me as go-between, it was with her father that she as eldest daughter, sure of her prerogatives (she is "privileged") and to the detriment of her mother, crazy but omnipotent, made the child.

PREGNANCY

After this presentation of the fable—which I have made as brief as possible—I am going to examine a certain number of points that seem worthy of consideration:

1. Conceiving the child is here an acting out within the treatment. The child is placed like a stopper, to close the question: if I do not have periods, am I nonetheless a woman? It is also a means of putting the analyst up against the wall: are you—yes or no?—going to intervene?

2. When a woman becomes pregnant during an analysis, we can say that in the imaginary the child is the analyst's. "The analyst's child," is a way of expressing this idea, as we say "child of the Oedipus complex," given that the Oedipus

complex is not Oedipus and cannot really have a child. The analyst can do everything, but it is not as real progenitor that he is said to be the parent. Besides, it happens that I am a woman. If the analyst were a man, the problematic would in no way be changed.

3. There is a crisis concerning homosexuality and a return to the mother.

4. The child of fantasy is a penis stolen from the progenitor.

5. There is a changing of sexes between husband and wife, and I play on the word "changing" in order not to say "change," which would signify a real modification (which is evidently not in question, even though it does make its appearance sometimes; the breasts of Tiresias are the echo of this). I say "changing" in order not to say "sexual exchange" and to evoke the idea of leading someone to take one thing for another [donner le change]. This sex changing makes of the woman a father-mother; she becomes virile. As for the man, he becomes maternal and feminine. For each there is one identification with the other's sex, and this to palliate, I have said, the failure of the exchange.[4]

6. All these phenomena are held together by a strong resistance to analysis.

These six remarks order the reflections that follow.

Resistance and Passage into Action
(points 6 and 1)

I begin with the first and last points because the resistance to analysis was expressed clearly by this young woman and others at first, as soon as they were certain of being pregnant. "I have nothing more to say. . . . Everything is fine. . . . I want to stop the analysis. . . . And I would willingly leave you with a slap in the face. . . .[5] I am afraid of continuing to speak. . . . Pregnancy is a reserved domain. . . ." This is what I have been able to hear, here and there. But naturally the analysis has been pursued, and dreams have contradicted these deliberately pronounced speeches. "I do not stop dreaming of you," said one. Another wants to make me "witness" the birth of the child. One regrets leaving to go on vacation, because when the child moves, I will not be there, and she cannot tell me. One tells me she is pregnant after telling her husband but before telling her mother. Another woman who is afraid of being hysterically pregnant, as she has already been, tells me about the missed period, not without trembling

4. [In French the play here is between the word *change*, which I have translated "changing," and *changement*, which I have translated "change." As I see the distinction, *changement* refers to what we would call a "sex change." Changing sexes relates to the context of changing clothes. The difference is thus between a real and an imaginary change.]

5. When she was sixteen, Anne-Marie slapped her mother and then left the house.

at having to avow her disappointment. Anne-Marie dreams that I take hold of her; I have a bottle of red liquid in my hand, and I persecute her.

Another declares more specifically: "I had already had fantasies about the person I saw in the hallway, whom I took to be your daughter. Then I saw your grandson, and as though by chance, it was immediately afterward that we conceived the child." Another said: "You have been present since the beginning of the analysis. . . . I did everything during the analysis: my divorce, the child, my upcoming remarriage. You are someone who contains me and whom I contain. It is melted together. It makes me think a little of a mirror, but that has a volume."

The contradiction between the acuteness of the transference and the expressed desire to put an end to the analysis is only apparent. If the analysis stops, it is necessary that the link with the analyst be in some way preserved in the real. What better way than to make of him a *spiritual parent*? This is the form taken by the transference in this case.

The Return to the Mother
(point 3)

In this transference phenomenon, I the analyst am (first) confused with the character of *the mother*.

From the beginning of the pregnancy, I hear words like these: "I think ceaselessly of my mother. What could her love-life have been like?" One woman had a hysterical pregnancy like her mother's: "And I was born six years later," she adds, as though she were already there in the hysterical pregnancy. The other (Anne-Marie) had an amenorrhea for two years, like her mother.

She has a dream at the beginning of her pregnancy (as we have said) where she "experiences erotic sensations with a little girl"—dreams where we can note the return of the feelings that the girl had with her own mother. Anne-Marie does not understand; she has never been homosexual; she has never even had the idea. Another says: "I do not want to get married just to get married. I want to be a married mother for my mother." We must listen to this *for*; the mother is frigid, according to her daughter; she is thus a married mother and not a wife. Anne-Marie cannot think of her parents as a couple. Another, who is homosexual, dreams that she takes a shit (these are her terms) with her mother-in-law and that her husband is looking on: everybody is happy.

I have kept for last the following memory. Anne-Marie found it during the second month of her pregnancy, when she announced her remarriage and her forthcoming name change (for she, also like her mother, had two husbands; but

she divorced the first time). "I am about to find a violent memory. . . . I had
cheated in school; I was six. The teacher made me copy: *I will never cheat
again.* . . . I signed the punishment with my mother's name. That got me into a
lot of trouble. . . . Something else: I was sleeping in a converted attic. One day on
the door that led to the landing where my room was, I saw written in pencil the
name of my mother. I told her. She said, 'I don't understand; but I am sure it's
true.'" Aside from that, a novel could be written about the connection between
the maiden name of Anne-Marie and my name.

In the return to the mother, homosexuality and transference are thus
strongly articulated.

Stolen Penis and Changing of Sexes
(points 4 and 5)

The phenomena I have just spoken of led to a certain distancing of the husband. . . . "I was frigid just after I thought I was pregnant," Anne-Marie declares,
having been very affectionate toward her spouse until then; and she avows that he
makes her nervous; he works too much, and he is too small; her father worked too
much; he was always gone somewhere, and he was small. Another woman says,
"In relation to my husband, I am now very drawn into myself." Another woman
dreams that she is sucking the sex of a male homosexual and that something
remains in her mouth—"a chicken skin or something like it"; she also speaks
about a goose neck, then about testicles and a fetus. Another woman speaks to
me about the first man she loved and declares that she will never again have the
same feeling: obviously she is not talking about her husband.

Soon I hear tell of a husband who wants to become a midwife, who dreams
of the baby every night and wants to carry it; he attends all the childbearing
classes without any pain; he even says that he would like "to change places with
his wife." A man in a psychodrama group mimics the scene of his wife's
therapeutic abortion and says he cannot get over it; he cannot want a child; it is as
though he himself had had the abortion; his depression is a lasting one.[6]

"It's incredible how I can dream about the phallus not being in its place,"
says a young woman just before giving birth ("phallus" for "penis"). And another
woman says, "My mother offered me a penis detached from a body; a flying penis
and testicles." This is a dream that the analysand had forgotten, she claims.

All the remarks say that the husband is left aside; that he feels himself

---

6. For everything that touches on paternity and the "psychoses of paternity," I refer to R. Ebtinger
and M. Renoux, "Aspects psychopathologiques de la paternité," *Lettres de l'Ecole Freudienne* 4
(Paris, 1970), pp. 42–49, and to their remarks elsewhere in the same issue.

becoming a woman; that the woman is self-sufficient now. The penis that the frigid mother had stolen from the father is now given to the daughter to the detriment of the husband. That appears to be a bit forced here, because I am obliged to summarize a lot and to leave out many other remarks. But the following will, I believe, clarify this beginning.

A NEW READING

If the child is the analyst's, there must have been a *fertile moment* when it was conceived. At this moment, the analyst must have let something happen or let something pass by, even by his silence; I looked back through my notes for the fertile moment.

In fact I was absent during the conception in the case of Anne-Marie. Absent also when she made her decision, three months earlier. The conception happened in the provinces far from Paris, during a short vacation. As for the decision, it is even more laden with meaning, since it had to have been maintained for three months, at the end of which the child was conceived.

Also, something important happened for Anne-Marie during the month that preceded the decision and in the two months that followed: the couple had a ravishing young woman friend as a house guest. Immediately a ménage à trois was constituted: at first, the friend preferred the wife (Anne-Marie), who for her part said she was attracted by the friend. The friend thus refused to make love with the husband, declaring that she preferred Anne-Marie. But Anne-Marie did not make up her mind, and what was to happen happened. The friend and the husband made love in the conjugal bed, and Anne-Marie, lying near them, fell asleep. It was necessary, she said of Xavier, that he earn his wings, which signified that she did not consider him yet entirely a man.

Hearing this, I remembered that one day she had dreamed a situation very similar to this one. She was sleeping with her father and mother, who could not make love; and she put her hands between her mother's thighs. Her father then withdrew. Telling the dream she added, "They ought to have divorced before I was born," then, in the same session, "I do not understand how 2 and 2 make 4," then, "The couple was between my mother and me." Who was *between* the couple she would like to have formed with her girl friend?

In another dream in the same series, she was teaching a boy of fourteen, who is in therapy with her, to make love. She held him on her knees, in her arms.

If we return to this trio, there were two possible solutions. The first, which we could have expected, is that the women constituted a homosexual couple with the complicity of the husband. The second is that a ménage à trois became organized, in which the husband made love to the friend in front of his wife. This was doubtless the husband's hope. But Anne-Marie fell asleep. She had wanted to help her husband, in her dream. Besides, she describes her husband as a boy, with the appearance of a juvenile. Her first husband was also smaller than she and sickly; and he was a drug addict.

When she is not maternal, Anne-Marie becomes a man: I am a man with women, she says, and a woman with men. This is one way of saying it. Her only chance of feeling like a woman is with black men, big and bearded (she knows a certain number who always attract her), but then nothing happens because she feels herself to be a little girl. The gist is that between little girl and mother/father, there is no longer any place for the woman. From this statement it follows that Anne-Marie told me that she never had a "demystifier who could speak about her father"; these are her words; one may well imagine that I was not this demystifier either. [7]

I had not given her this signifier. Until then, as she told me at this time "I had considered you a censor, but that changed." [8] The analyst has become a mother "who makes one dead" if one commits certain "outrageous" acts. "Right or wrong," she says, "I have the sense that you would not agree to my drugging myself or my entering into a sexual commune. That would be to make my mother dead and you also. That I cannot do."

This makes me the one who has chosen with her the road called "normal" and who has put aside choices that are more "outrageous." I equally refused to receive her homosexual transference. She reminds me, on occasion, that I have never called her by her first name, and that had I done so, it would have pleased her; but she does not regret that I was cold and now declares this to have been helpful. The most evident turning point was the adventure with the girl friend as third person. *Not knowing any more—like a good hysteric—whether she was man or woman, she decided to force herself to be a woman by making a child.* Thus the question, she thought, did not pose itself any more. The father was evidently a man, and Anne-Marie was evidently a woman. This is what I call *taking one thing for another.* [9]

She also spoke of "provoking things to understand" and of "putting oneself up against the wall." These phrases betray the acting out.

7. [I translate the French *révélateur,* meaning "someone who brings about revelations," as "demystifier." The connotation of revelation should, however, be retained.]

8. We remember that her father was a vice-principal in a lycée [high school]. [The French *censeur* means both "censor" and "vice-principal," and I have translated it accordingly.]

9. [The French expression is *donner le change,* an idiom that plays on the distinctions heretofore established between change and changing.]

To summarize: Anne-Marie decided to make a child in order not to have to declare herself homosexual and to make herself become a woman without encountering a man. It is not a sexual encounter that decides the sexual identification or confirms it; she would moreover have needed this, since she sees herself as "not completely a woman." There is something that did not happen and would doubtless have been the revelation of her femininity; she says, "I did not have a demystifier who could speak of father." She does not know what is missing, what it is to be able to speak of the woman as a woman, so much is the lack missing. At least, this is what I propose, and this perhaps creates problems.

In any case, before becoming pregnant, she fantasized giving birth as a hemorrhage. I do not think we can say that she dreaded it and hoped for it, as she did the deflowering that did not come in its time—but again, why not?—rather, she saw birth as the expulsion of something that she had within her, which in leaving would empty her. I hypothesize, given the context, that it was the penis: the penis plugging the void, a stopper to prevent the body from emptying itself.

From the preliminary interviews she had told me that she took care of children and that she wanted to become an analyst. She even asked me to be reassuring; naturally, I did not give her these assurances. I should have done more and analyzed then a parallel that came to be evident later—to want to speak and not to be able to, to want to write and not to be able to, to want to be an analyst and not to be able to—all this because the analyst does not want it, because the mother does not want it. And I translate this into the form to want to be a woman and not be able to.

I do not permit her to be a woman any more than anyone else, doubtless. I do not render it possible; and what I do not give her she takes with force in making a child that she brings to me. She also says that I blocked her. I would thus have pushed her into the acting out. Besides, she imagined that if she revealed herself as mad, I would not let her become an analyst. The curious result of an analysis begun under the sign of health. For Anne-Marie the only question was to become an analyst, and the symptoms were put in the forefront manifestly to reinforce the demand.

If the child was conceived far from me, doubtless this served to confront me with an accomplished fact. But there is nothing irremediable, as it happens. The analysis continues.

A PARADIGM

She thus made a child because she did not know how to be a woman in any other way, and she made this child at a time when she had other choices: homosexuality and communal sex, on the one hand; on the other, the order I represented: order and not woman.

Besides, the child was not only wanted but programmed; we had all the time, during the three months of forced waiting, to enter into another discourse. But no, the child was conceived, and then this event was announced and offered to me. I have been confused with the refound mother. The husband is feminized. Anne-Marie becomes mother, not woman. The child will be the false guarantor of the sex of each parent and the symbol of their union.

But this also blocks the access to the symbolic, which cannot happen except by an encounter with the other, who appears as the other sex. We find here a remark made by Eliane Amado Lévy-Valensi, to wit, that man in the Christian couple is castrated; woman is magnified as mother; and the child is then made sacred as symbol, to the detriment of the couple. The woman gives herself the penis in the guise of the child, without having had to validate her demand for the penis as such. The woman makes a union that will benefit her by a kind of embezzlement.

It is not a question of my undoing the child after having let it be made. Besides, after a time of stasis where the analysand did a "dead man's float" on the couch with satisfaction, work began again and did not appear to be inhibited by the other labor, that of pregnancy. From time to time the analysand fell asleep, in conformity with the dream reported above. She rejoices in no longer having her major symptom, her death anxiety. The child has functioned well as a cork. But the euphoria (which made me think of the pregnant woman in Faulkner)[10] does not last. The disquietude and the analysis are taken up again. Anne-Marie reflects. She goes back to the moment of the decision and that of the conception to see what happened there.

In the guise of a conclusion, I propose the following fictive genealogy:

—mother; immortal goddess, omnipotent and crazy.

—father; not crazy, but sick, tainted, threatened with death.

—their daughter the analysand; takes care of children—usurpation.

—the husband: small and slim or young or sexually handicapped.

—the other man: powerful and bearded, never encountered by the analysand, for the good reason that she is afraid of this encounter.

—the analyst: woman (and/or man).

—their child: whose child?

10. In *Light in August*.

This genealogy has the value of a paradigm, even though not all pregnant women have had a crazy mother, a sick father, or a small husband, in the literal sense of the terms. But in one way or another we can say that they are those things (crazy, sick, bearded, and small). All little girls in elementary school sing a song that is significant in this context:

> My mother gave me a husband
> My God what a man, what a small man!
> My mother gave me a husband
> My God what a man, is he small!

The husband is in some way small, not a great man; the paradigm is only apparently contradicted. Doubtless the attributes could be distributed otherwise, but then the whole set would change. The child remains, in any case, the last on the list. Can one speak more harshly than Goethe did of a legitimate child conceived in love? Let us remember his words in *Elective Affinities*: "Let me," he says to his new love, Odile, "throw a veil on this fatal hour which will give being to this child. . . . Why would we not pronounce this harsh word: this child is the fruit of a double adultery. . . ." In fact they were four when the child was conceived, and no longer two.

We know the story of the four partners of the *Elective Affinities* and the chemical law that regulated their exchanges: if you put in the presence of A and B another couple equally united, C and D, there will be the fatal production of a crossing, where A is united with C and B with D. If a child is born of this, whose child is it?

Edward, Charlotte's husband, is neither sick or small, but he is older, and the marriage was not a union of love. The captain, since he is a captain, is necessarily the "bearded" lover, and potent. The young Odile takes the place of the ravishing friend in the couple Anne-Marie–Xavier. And the captain is the friend of Edward, like one of the potent men (analyst or lover) who subjugate Anne-Marie, and he has been and remains the friend and ideal of the husband.

The child that Charlotte brings into the world, after she and her husband had, respectively, renounced their passion for the captain and for Odile (but could we not also speak of the love of Charlotte for Odile and of Edward for the captain?)—this child physically resembles both Odile and the captain. "It is the fruit of double moral adultery," wrote Jeanne Ancelet-Hustache, after Goethe.[11]

---

11. Jeanne Ancelet-Hustache, *Goethe par lui-même*, Ecrivains de toujours 27 (Paris: Editions du Seuil, 1957), p. 73.

The epilogue is tragic: Odile lets the child fall in the lake and lets herself starve to death. Edward commits suicide.

In analysis, the child said to be the analyst's is only the fruit of transference and not the fruit of a moral incest, provided at least that the analyst has known how to mark in the transference that his own desire was not a desire for a child: only on this condition will the child be disengaged from all transferential alienation.

5 The Story of Louise

BY MICHÈLE MONTRELAY

PART 1

In the nineteenth century, books of natural history were illustrated with colored plates. The illustration was printed not on one sheet of paper but on ten or more transparent sheets, on each of which a part or an organ of an animal was drawn.

There were books like this in the library of Mr. X, the father of a little girl named Louise. This man was, as they said at the time, a "man of letters." He wrote plays and critical works.

Every evening, Louise's father, who loved his daughter a great deal but did not know what to say to her, led her into his library and leafed through these books while commenting upon the images. It was a risky thing to do. Louise could have torn them. At the time she was a lively, happy, energetic little girl of twenty months. But looking at these images, she was good. Very good.

Thirty years later Louise sees herself in a shadow, seated on her father's lap. She remembers the inflections of his voice, a very steady voice that showed some pain, sought its breath, and opened long silences.

Adults forget how a very young child looks at images. He sees them as things to touch, to eat, to destroy, things that provoke him and then steal away. Louise, who is a painter, says that she will never be able to grasp an angle, a trait, or a color with such an intensity. She took great pleasure in recognizing the silhouettes, but the elements of the drawing—lines, hatchmarks, granulations, and spots—were even more important. These touched a certain and familiar knowledge that had always been hers, even before she could talk.

At the beginning of her analysis, Louise retained few memories of her relationship with her mother during her early years. How can we distinguish true memories from what her mother told her later: that she was very happy when her daughter was born, but in the months that followed, when she again became

Michèle Montrelay is a psychologist practicing psychoanalysis in Paris. This article first appeared as "Histoire de Louise," in Michèle Montrelay, *L'Ombre et le nom* (Paris: Editions de Minuit, 1977), pp. 119–46.

pregnant, that things became more difficult and she more solitary? The mother had not measured the cost to her of abandoning her work. This woman was a pianist, an excellent musician, who had to give up competitions and work. Since there was very little money, she found employment, taking up worldly occupations, and in the little free time she had, she read her husband's writings and spoke to him about them. These exchanges were precious, even indispensable, to Mr. X, and they occurred at his suggestion.

These are the states that Louise relives in the anxiety that overwhelms her when she is pregnant. The same anxiety is evident in the transference. At least, it was in the "slice" of analysis that she did ten years after her first. For three years she oscillated between states of being beaten down and an acute suffering that seemed to be without a true object. As it was spoken and dreamt, this suffering brought back chains of associations and memories. Here are the fragments:

—memories of places: Mediterranean gardens, white with dust and light;
—a stroller, heavily laden;
—a fat body. We see the feet, the legs, the pelvis. It is as if this body were surrounded by a wall and a great tower. "It is not my mother, it's her body." In Louise's mother's face there is a generosity, a radiant quality that touches those who approach her, an intelligence "inseparable from that of the heart, inseparable from the happiness of being alive." And then the body—all the distress is contained in this body because it is so isolated, so fat, so walled in. Louise, who never cries, sheds torrents of tears. First this water destroys her—it is bitter; then it floods her like rain coming after years of drought;
—but again, always: solitude, the gaping silence of the garden. Somewhere, a great basin;[1]
—memories of caring for a little brother. His sexual organs are "wrinkled";
—mama is dirty, is all wet, is not well. Confirmed memory: Louise saw her mother lose her water.

As the memories appear, the depressive state gives way to anxiety. "A hole in space. Pockets of void. The body withdraws and dries up. The feet are especially threatened." Then dreams emerge that lead Louise to speak of frogs with gaping, devouring mouths. "Could I have had a phobia about frogs?" She asks her mother about it. Once she was playing in the garden, near the basin, when her grandfather arrived. "If you get too close, you will fall in, and the frogs will eat your feet."

1. [In French the word *bassin* means "basin" as well as "pelvis" (mentioned above).]

Difficult Circulations

What is wrong? What is she missing? What object could satisfy her?

"I find nothing. There is a hole in what is said of my mother's desire. This hole will devour me."

Such is the anxiety of little Hans, as Lacan described it in his seminar on object relations. Such is the anxiety of Louise. The two children cannot express it: the words are lacking—theirs and perhaps also those of their mothers. The gaping, terrifying hole of maternal castration—is it not the hole opened by the mother who cannot speak?

A phobia is not a symptom like others. This hole opened by the phobia is situated in space like a fault around which all roads would open, would cross, would permit an easy circulation, providing that the hole acts as a barrier on the road.

As though by accident, when Lacan commented on the case of little Hans, he was able to demonstrate things by using a map of Vienna. In a phobic space one can circulate without any great difficulty, except that all of a sudden the ground vanishes from under one's feet. The only solution is to stop short—like a statue.

How are things "going"? If they are not, most often it is not said; but the image is there of an arrested motion. Neither for Hans nor for Louise are things going very well. In the garden the bodies, the objects, are in a state of stupor. The mother's body, among others, is isolated, immobilized, both heavy and sad. All of which evokes another mass, an overloaded car or else the enormity of a body that Hans saw fall one day. The unsaid circulating in the streets of Vienna with the most perfect fluidity, can, all of a sudden—what a surprise—take on mass and fall.

Walks, flights, falls, drops. Happy and easy circulation. Intolerable, obscene traffic jams. In his first seminars, Lacan introduced metonymy as a progression, a displacement: language moves, slides. The signifiers are displaced to infinity. They take on body, form a carnal, elastic material. As limited as they are, these surfaces do not contain their limit, which seems to be outside of them. The surface has no hole.

In a phobia the surface that the set of signifiers forms is discovered, on the contrary, to have a hole. In a specific place someone wounded its infinity. Would the mother's castration be the wound causing the phobic object, in the set of possible trajectories, to be inscribed as a boundary marker and not as a limit?

Not only is the mother's body seen, immobile in the garden, but Louise—

and this makes her cry—must see that this body has no relationship with the face or the look; the latter communicate, give and receive. She sees her mother as split: on one side is her desire or what can be expressed of it: loves, music, maternity; on the other are these "jobs," which degrade and de-idealize. Perhaps the reason why Louise's mother does not tolerate her housework very well is that through it she finds her own mother, who was too much of a presence in her own history. Her marriage separated her from her work. Louise, considered by her grandmother as a love object, reactivates an old, passionate conflict between these two women (mother and grandmother).

Beyond the particular context of this story, the vision of the mother cut in two gives the image of feminine sexuality as heterogeneous, torn: the sublimation of drives leaves the real in the shadow. Is this the real so difficult to symbolize that a woman incarnates with her own body?

This fault that tears the woman—and thus the mother—does it have a relationship with the hole in phobic space?

The father looks with Louise at the drawings in a book of natural history. It is worth the trouble to come back to these scenes between father and daughter and to ask the question again: at this age, how does one look at images?

Louise insists on the materiality of the images: the colors, lines, granulations, hatchmarks, the transparency of the plates covering each other, the lightness and brilliance of the paper. She is sure she knew that whatever she was looking at was completely different from real things. It was fascinating for her to see a subtle, unreal world materialize from fragments, to see this world in such vivid and ethereal colors.

She speaks of a very old knowledge: it was as if her father were communicating fragments of his thoughts through the sound of his voice. These thoughts are perhaps those hallucinated by the child as "images," which form the network of infantile memory. Frayed, tangled, clouded networks that make for the substance of the "breast" and form this stuff from which the signifier takes on body.

Louise possessed a specular image. Now she possesses another, a half-symbolic, half-animal image of speech. And sustained by her father's voice, this metonymy begins where the mother's signifying chains fail. The images capture and at the same time displace the experiences of the most archaic jouissance; they are the same as those Melanie Klein discovered to be reified and fragmented. At this moment the mother is pregnant. There is every reason to think that Louise sees in these images a response to the question: where do babies come from? The fish in the images are "her babies." She is sure of that. They tell her the secret of life.

There is more. The images that her father looks at with Louise interest him a great deal. They interest him as the son and grandson of sailors, as an avid yachtsman himself. His own father collected seaweed and shells.

Thus he reveals to his daughter the insignia of the family. Let us count Louise as one more of these insignia, a little fish, a little girl sitting on his lap, eyes and ears wide open. Yes, Louise is surely one of the most beautiful prizes of the paternal collection. The child is most interested in one of the drawings. It represents a hatched crescent placed next to a round eye. The father calls it "hearing" [*l'ouïe*].

But the session is over. The books are closed. The father puts them back in their place with care, closes his bookcase, and takes the key with him.

Before following Louise as she leaves the library to go to the place where the phobia will be formed, can we not say with Lacan that in this library "there is a one"?[2] Isn't it stuffed with ones? Do we not see a swarm of them flying about? Because each of these traits, these names, these articulated contours can only signify itself. Each one is articulated for an other: not only the elements of the drawing, but the book chosen from among all those that other people have opened and leafed through.

The library is a reserve where books, pages, traits, and pronounced words are so many S_1s suspended, as Lacan says, in the half-saying. None of these signifiers taken in itself could signify itself. Each points to an enigma.[3]

The Fish Trope

Two or three months later, Louise refuses to enter the library. She no longer wants to look at the books and runs away when her father takes her on his knees. One day she is looking at her mother preparing his meal. The mother places a sole on the father's plate. Louise, who was watching the fish cooking without saying anything, begins to scream. Nameless terror. She refuses to eat. The fish phobia has declared itself.

Something happened just before the cooking of the fish. It happened on the beach. Louise is walking with her father. On the sand there is a black spot. An

2. Jacques Lacan, *Le Séminaire*, vol. 20, *Encore* (Paris: Editions du Seuil, 1975), p. 63.

3. [Lacan's S_1 refers to the master-signifier, which is linked to another signifier, S_2, which Lacan calls the "signifier of knowledge." The master-signifier confers mastery, and thus its utilization by a master makes his words imperative. Michèle Montrelay speaks of the half-saying (*mi-dire*) or half-telling, signifying that half of the story is not being told in the scene before us.]

observer could have believed that they would pass the object without stopping. But no. The father, interested, approaches the object. He moves it with his foot. He examines it and seeks to identify the species; he considers the head, the tail, and the scales. How could this kind of fish have gotten there? Did the sea reject it? No, a fisherman must have let it fall. Louise approaches and looks at it, for she is also very curious. It is a fish. Nothing extraordinary. Why, she asks thirty years later, was she then seized with a certain intense pleasure? She thinks that it has to do with "its matter." The fish had dried without decomposing. The scales, a nice deep color, were like dog-eared pages of a book. And also, the fish, very flat, had a form that Louise will never forget. This is the real image.

Louise wanted to handle it, to play, with her father. He does not agree. One must not touch the dead fish, he says. They go away. . . .

Now a phobia has declared itself. The parents are very concerned, and they tolerate especially badly the child's refusal to explain herself. Louise remains very lively and expansive, but about her phobia she can only say in a whisper: "Louise is afraid." "Of what?" How many days were necessary for the word "fish" to pass her lips! How much time before the fantasies were expressed: "The fish is in the garden. He bites. He has fallen."

The parents search the garden with Louise; they look into every nook and cranny. "You see that there is nothing there." In fact, the child cannot say that she may at any moment encounter, not a real fish, but a shadow, some stones, a plant, which suggest all or a part of the form of a fish.

Louise is haunted by the form. The house is at the seashore. In the sea there is a small island, or rather a large rock, whose form suggests a fish head rising straight up from the water. From the garden one can see this immobile form. There was no real fish in this place, but everywhere one runs the risk that there is "fish," if we can express it in this way. In any case, Louise examines her food as soon as it is put on her plate. If the fragments form the contour of the tabooed animal, she refuses to eat it. For the same reason again, it is important not to give a consistency to "fish" with sounds: its name must not be pronounced. One must not materialize the insignia when one may well devour them, or better, incorporate them.

Knowing Too Much

In the case of the Wolf Man, this knowing resulted from the uniting of two signifying chains that had been separated. In the case of little Hans and in the story of Louise, the same process occurred.

We had left the child alone in the library with her father and the "swarm" of

S_1 buzzing in the "half-saying."[4] An enigma presents itself. Which one? It captivates the child and then disquiets her more and more.

This enigma is not unrelated to sexuality. Remember how Louise evokes her father's voice: "It came out painfully from the interior of his body, . . . it came from the most secret recesses, . . . trembling, violent. One had the feeling that he was trying to catch his breath." Voice, breath, noises, violences contained or cried out: could Louise have found out, just before she became phobic, something about "them"?[5] Could she have heard her parents making love? No, this sudden discovery could not have taken place, for the simple reason that Louise slept in her parents' bedroom from birth.

Here again, knowing is contained not in the revelation of the "content" of a representation but in a new and impossible conjunction of signifiers. Two signifying chains created a cut or break. That is, they marked the place of an impossible passage. This cut took the place of a limit, and thus it closed the other. The chains, suddenly brought into proximity, created a short-circuit. The new sense, with lightning speed, opens the other where the subject fades.

In the history of Louise, we see these two chains very precisely. To distinguish them, we designate one "diurnal" and the other "nocturnal."

The latter is woven of the father's voice and body. Breathing, silence, sounds: Louise hears all that at night. She has always heard this jouissance, which transported her, since she was impotent to resist its terrible intensity when she was left alone. Louise was alone. One can say: she was even more exposed to her father's jouissance because her mother did not have any, at least in sexual experiences. Perhaps the child had orgasms while she was alone with her father? Suppositions. . . . We are not saying that her mother had no experience of jouissance. No doubt she did when she played the piano or when she was in the library, where many words were exchanged, many ideas. Or perhaps with Louise, her daughter.

There is a second chain of signifiers, concerning the library. It is made of all the S_1 that the diurnal voice of the father evoked. That voice designated, named, and prohibited.

For a certain time the two voices and the two motifs existed separately. Next Louise enters a more dangerous stage of her sexuality: she observes the sex of her brother, masturbates, and has orgasms, which are made of the stuff of a more archaic jouissance. Afterward this jouissance cannot be separated any longer from the voice of the father who tells stories. We can imagine the child in these

4. [The French *essaim* (swarm) is a homophone of S_1.]
5. The terrifying knowledge, revealed to the phobic individual as having the sense of primal scene, is one of the forms of knowledge designated by Lacan as S_2.

sessions in the library: the intimacy, the body-to-body, the position on the lap, Louise so close to her father's hidden penis. To her ears the whispered voice that encroaches on the land also encroaches on the different S_1 for the archaic jouissance. This latter is the same that the little bit of sense in the pages of a book was supposed to cause to slide.

Surely a primal scene is being played out in the library, and if the knowledge produced by the copulation of two chains terrifies, it is because this knowledge makes the limits of the subject (Louise) dissolve. This time the Other's hole is opened. And the child would have fallen into it if the fish had not taken her place.

The schema below figures the "true" primal scene, the linkage of two chains. The paternal diurnal chain is designated as imaginary (I) because, before the declaration of the phobia, it possesses the status of image-limit of the Other. The nocturnal symbolic chain S is traced as the x-axis: it is discontinuous because it is made of the stuff of a fragmented jouissance, filled with holes, where the real can be discovered. The real can be the breast petrified by the father's jouissance—but it is also Louise blown apart in the explosion of archaic orgasms. Where I crosses S there is a hole, and it is open. At this crossroads, designated as R (the real), we guess that there is an eye, and to the side is a place that is not very clear, where the fish hears. This "jumble" perhaps corresponds to the black spot around the horse's eyes in the case of Hans. . . . It signals a confusion.

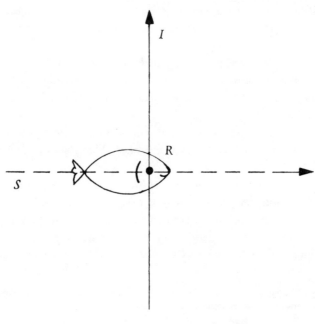

Confusion and coincidences: hearing is very close to the eye, which is seen by the child as an eye-ear, an open hole, which Louise says is "at the place of a human ear." The confusion is almost complete between Louise's first name and one of the organs designated on the drawings: hearing.[6] We should not forget that the mother is a musician and that the father, when he met her, was all ears when she played. We should know that an ancestor who died courageously at the helm of his boat was named Louis. We could find in this story many other coincidences. The confusion of organs gives us not only the image of the confusion of names but also their collusion with jouissance.

We have seen that a phobia is produced when a sense passes where it should not have. The impossible place appears for the moment like the one where several names get mixed up and lose their cutting edge.

"What gave you the right to make me see your voice," Louise asks on the couch, addressing herself to her father. Why does this man need to make his daughter see, with images, the first name he gave her? Why does the voice name, without there being the possibility of appealing its verdict; why must the voice's decision "That exists" be sustained by a sign? Why does the father of the phobic patient always invade the symbolic space of his child?

"Why did you make me see your voice?" In proposing to Louise images that gave sexual sense to this voice, her father threatened to destroy the first metaphor of his daughter Louise.

PART 2: THE SHADOW

The Bejahung[7]

The child coming into the world as the descendant of a lineage can do nothing other than describe the senses that are impressed upon him by a structure he knows nothing about.

How does he make his first move into the order that manipulates him, an order that is Other and omnipotent? How does he learn the rules of the game? Does he grasp them like a parcel of knowledge? On the contrary, everything

6. [In French, *Louise* is phonetically very close to *l'ouïe* ("hearing").]

7. [This term, which means "the affirmative judgment of existence," was used by Freud in his article "Denegation." Translated under the title "Negation," this article appears in Sigmund Freud, *The Standard Edition of the Complete Psychological Works of Sigmund Freud*, vol. 19 (London: Hogarth Press, 1953), pp. 235–39. Lacan has commented upon it in *Ecrits* (Paris: Editions du Seuil, 1966), pp. 369–401. The *Standard Edition* of Freud's works will hereafter be designated S.E. in the notes.]

begins when an index of these rules, through repetition, is detached and posed as an object that can only signify itself. An example, borrowed from Freud: the cry, he says, inscribes a trait and brings a being to life. Freud detaches the infant's pleasure or pain from the organic night to take them outside: toward the ear end thus toward the other who hears. This first condensation, sound-pain (or sound-pleasure), is called by Freud a "complex." What we see there is a manifestation of the Bejahung, where the life drawn from the shadows is concretized into "good" and "bad" objects. However much the child is dependent on the sensation he experiences, this object is no longer confused with the stupidity of the body. It has henceforth become Other: not an object of reality, but a hallucinated object, which as such places a being.

On the stage set by the Bejahung, no thought or judgment, in the current sense of the term, no effects of meaning, are legal tender. Only the jouissance of the primal representation is exercised for itself. Slidings, shocks, and condensations bear witness to the work of the hallucination, which is, as Freud says, seeking the "identity" of perception with the hallucination that was there at first.

Impossible to find it again, because this perception was condensed, embossed with another to form the object of the Bejahung. Thus the primal representation weaves its networks from this object, which is the navel and cuts the hallucination off from life.

The Breast and the Placenta

This hallucinated matter, never again equal to living matter, is the breast: not the real breast, but the breast as part object, sometimes "good," sometimes "bad," never possessed—woven of clouds of representations lacking limits, suspended out of time, sustained and contained by an ignored reality, that of the other. We know that hungry or sated, the child can no longer hallucinate.

For this reason, submitted to the good will of the other and to his desire, the substance of the breast is not homogeneous: in places it forms a tightly woven network, raveled; it can be hardened or have holes, be filled with crevices or abysses.

Lacan says that the breast as part object is detached from the body of the mother, that it is fastened onto her, as though suspended, even though it belongs to the child. There is a cut that passes between the breast and the maternal body. It is thus the mother who first loses the breast. What is this loss that is the condition of the primal hallucination and, consequently, of the Bejahung?

To permit the hallucinated breast to exist for the child is to open for him a place other than the one that concerns the satisfaction of need. His desire begins to take form, inseparable from an unspoken suffering that cries out. How can he support this suffering, which he can say nothing about? How can he not do everything in his power to annul it? The love for a child is doubled with an anxiety that is much more difficult to sustain, in that it repeats another anxiety, obscure, ungraspable, lived by the mother with her mother during the first months of life.

To give the hallucinated breast is to live and sustain the anxiety without being able to measure it. In the mother-child relationship, there is always this dimension of impotence; there is either acceptance or refusal.

A woman is also impotent to say something at the moment of giving birth. The loss of the breast reproduces the loss of the placenta. It repeats the way in which the mother lived the birth of her child and her own birth, which is replayed during that of her offspring, but not in the same way. It is as a speaking being that she experiences a real loss this time.

Men and women have fantasies about pregnancy. But pregnancy is a real state, lived as something new, unique in time.

When a woman in analysis expects a child, she has much to say: dreams, concerns, fantasies, and new sensations abound. Most often the unconscious keeps silent. One perceives that the woman's time disappears.. In the unfolding of the treatment, there is no longer an alternation of strong times, when the words move, strike each other, and break into fragments that pierce with each blow of anxiety, and weak times, when a provisional peace is made. The spoken word is there, but the rhythm of the transference disappears. It is as if the child's heart were beating in place of the pulsations of the transference, as though the unconscious left to itself had no way to manifest itself any more. It is as though the unconscious slept.

One is no longer alone: one inhabits a floating time, made of the future present, where the past cannot be, for the past is the finished and consequently is the counted. The state of pregnancy does not take into account the habitual mode of counting. When a woman expects a child, she cannot say that she is two. Even less that she is one. Except in the case where the fetus is experienced as a foreign body, the woman and her child are suspended together, disjoint, in the same life potency. Someone inhabits her, opens her, tears her, is inside her.[8] The mother carries the child, but she is also carried. Her relationship with the part object is modified. Her real state renders her drive organization partially useless.

8. [In French there is a play on words generated by spelling the word "inside" (*dedans*) as *deux-dans*, meaning "two-in."]

Giving birth the mother loses, not the child, with whom she will live, but the real state of pregnancy. Perhaps women who "retain" the child at birth want to keep, even more than the baby, this infinite placenta-time. The difference between them and the others who participate in the work of expulsion is even less important than it appears. Letting the pushing happen, relaxing yourself, and opening yourself to the head's labor make the child come out, but not yet the placenta.

Some mothers experience the loss as the loss of the child; others, as the loss of the placenta. One does not actively "make" the placenta. Another person gathers it up and pulls it from you. The tree of life, the velvety mass, is extirpated from the belly and is then thrown out. There is bleeding, a leaking of liquid that one does not feel. For the child the trace of the loss of the membranes is the navel. For the mother it is the child's cry when he is born. At the moment of birth the mother cries, then bleeds in expelling the placenta-time of pregnancy, hers and the child's. The one and the other lose some life; this is a fact.

The child cries, and his cry is a beacon for both of them, child and mother. But this cry opens on a night. . . . How can the overflow be contained? How can one say, and tell the child, everything real that is happening? Impossible. Infinite impotence.

After all, some will ask, since the real is not the symbolic, since this is a fact, why not hold onto it? One *does* hold onto it. Things cannot happen otherwise. But something else happens: an effusion of jouissance takes place when one gives birth. Sometimes it is recognized as such, very much like an orgasm. But there is also a limitless pain, falling, panic, the black hole. An unheard-of tearing of being. A rapture of anguish, dizziness, states of being in flux. Ecstasy of the encounter with the child, all of it drawn out in time. There are many forms of jouissance, but it is always there during childbirth.

The Shadow

This jouissance has been compared to an immense orgasm, where the mother is transported by the body of her child, as though by a penis. The jouissance would occur in the furrow opened by the child's phallic stroke. This interpretation derives from a view of orifices as eroticized. It does not take into account the diffuse forms of jouissance that women experience most frequently, and in addition it neglects this fact: jouissance during childbirth occurs where there is an experience of the immeasurable. Not only does it bring into play orifices and objects (especially the voice), but it takes place where none of the body's holes can any longer define an edge: no anatomical edge can define for the mother the loss of child and placenta.

Jouissance occurs in the space opened between the Imaginary and the Real. It does not resolve this space. But because this jouissance is itself of the order of the infinite, it contains the immeasurable, to which it gives body. The mother is no longer the one who enjoys [*jouit*]. "It" enjoys [*Ça jouit*] in a place where it can no longer think itself—in the Other, where one can only be absent.

When she loses herself as the substance of jouissance that exceeds, in containing them, the edges of the body and its objects; when she leaves herself, seized by the infinity of the Other, who is "not-whole"—at this moment a woman becomes a symbolic mother. The substance of jouissance to which she gives body, since it exceeds the symbolic operation of castration, envelops those substances that the child will encounter. The fragments that will fall from the signifying chains—the objects *a*—will always repeat elsewhere, life's first real loss, because on the mother's side, a jouissance subsists at the expense of these objects.

We know the story by Hofmannsthal entitled "The Woman without a Shadow"[9] and the truth that it postulates: the woman who does not have a shadow because her mother did not give her one cannot have children. This Shadow, what is it, if not the absolute Shadow within any detached and thus visible shadow: this feminine substance of jouissance that makes for the stuff of the Other, envelops it, and develops it to infinity? A double that, far from representing the placenta, on the contrary gives consistency to its loss. It is true that a woman cannot become a mother without letting the Shadow exist outside her. Without anything being said, this gives body to the Real in which the child participates, in her place. The Shadow contains the thing.

In the Shadow where a woman gets lost, there is also her own mother, "absent" and real. At the moment of giving birth, the real mother is encountered.

That is where we are, from mother to daughter, transported and lost in the Shadow. From mother to daughter, for one does not live the birth of a boy and a girl in the same way. The male child draws you at once out of the wave. He makes you emerge and reinsert yourself in the visible order, sure of reality and of objects. With the daughter, matters remain obscure. We are together maintained in some limbo that we cannot escape. . . .

9. See also Eugénie Lemoine-Luccioni, *Partage des femmes*, for a discussion of female sexual identification based on pregnancy.

The mother "loses" the breast, that is, she makes possible the detachment of the (hallucinated) objects from the organic night and from the Other that her jouissance contains. She loses *with* her jouissance. This loss, which happens before the child takes any signifying operation on his own account, is the condition of primary castration.

I lived in the land of this dream. I recognize its grain. I see it aglow with white and violet flowers, in March, as the snow melts. Long grasses covered the stiff slopes, then making them shudder in the wind. The summer comes all at once. It falls in a few days on the country and immobilizes it. The woods of beech trees, blued, seen from afar, seem to be humid. When we go there we see that the atmosphere is dry. The light passes through the leaves, warms the earth, the insects. The gray shadow does not suffice. The only true shadow is elsewhere: it falls from the trunks of the walnut trees, vertical, brief, intense, distributed, or better, measured like crotchets of a musical score.

In these regions the mountains are unproductive. Not only is the land poor, but the surface is eaten away by erosion and is thus kept in a savage, unrealized state. The views distract the eye as long as one does not hear them with the ear. Perhaps the excessive dryness, which makes the luminous vibrations visible across the craters and flanks of the mountain mass— yes, this secret rock, but off against its internal mass, its shadow, which stands up, the mute reason of light—perhaps that makes this boring country seize you like music? I also remember having looked, terrified, at the piled debris at the bottom of the ravine. I saw the great clash of stones, their empty and noisy silence.

Such are the associations of Louise concerning a painting and a dream.

The Initiation

The representations of the mother are henceforth illuminated differently: the walled-in body, "cut off against its internal mass," against its Shadow, is the reason for the rest: the rhythms of nature, the recurring periods of drought, of appeasement, of desire and need. "Musical" reason: for Louise as for many women, symbolization is first a question of the ear. But what kind of music is discovered in the ravines, deeply cut, that let Louise spy upon the great clash of stones? It is as though the mountain were wounded.

This wound attains neither the body nor the sex of the mother, but rather the Shadow, jouissance as something infinite. And it is an other jouissance, that of the father, which creates this wound.

A writer, he gains his jouissance through words and ideas. This is why he stages in his library the rediscovery of the breast. Doesn't he take pleasure in showing his daughter the prodigiously varied substance, colored and fragmented, of the words he is pronouncing? Yes, father and daughter travel together in a subtle space, which they know to be a space of nothing. They play at piercing the mystery of this space by making it concrete. Father and daughter: it is evident that she, Louise, does not play, that she identifies with the father's games. But this game is dangerous because it unveils the phallus.

Lacan writes that the phallus is the signifier whose veiling signifies "the latency with which all signifiable is struck from the time that it is raised to the function of the signifier."[10]

What is veiled? Perhaps a fragment that is not, in its carnality, without affinity with the part of life torn away by the Bejahung? For a man there is nothing more fascinating than the veiling of this object and the decoys that it brings into play. He approaches to see, all the time knowing that he will not see it all—knowing that if the veil is lifted, it will be elsewhere, diffused across a string of words. The transparent sheets of the illustrations show and at the same time veil the fragments, of which the animals that Louise calls her children are made. Perhaps these animals are also the children that the father would have wanted to bear and give birth to? In other words, this father uses his daughter to realize his own relationship with the phallus. His child's excitement and curiosity bear witness to the fact that the phallus is at once present and shrouded in mystery.

This very nice man is a pervert. His failure to sustain the law is manifest. Far from putting up a barrier against jouissance, he does everything he can to tear away a little more of its secret. This way of loving a daughter is not what we expect from a father.

His merit is to spread out in the light of day, more clearly than most men, his failings and his perversion. For we should not fool ourselves. The majority of fathers, unless indifferent to their daughters—which is worse—behave just like this one: they are at once perverse and disarmed.

Disarmed. A father is always disarmed before his daughter, whose body without a penis provokes him where a phallus and not a penis exists. He does not have this phallus that is not a penis (so he believes), but the Mother, the place where he confuses his own and his child's, does.

10. Jacques Lacan, "La Signification du phallus," in *Ecrits*, p. 692.

He does not have it, but somewhere he *is* it. The little girl, about whom he knows that she will not give his name to her child, obliges him to play for stakes other than those that unite father and son. Here this man is provoked not as the element of a descendance, but as an individual: the man of flesh, the son of his mother and, as such, the participant in her femininity.

Here he is being solicited into repeating his relationship with the most archaic jouissance under the sign of the archaic maternal phallus. The father relives his own feminine side with the body of his daughter. He delights in a prohibited jouissance, which comes savagely from the superego, since there is in our culture a censure of the boy's desires for maternity. It is difficult for him to say them, to "narcissize" them, to sublimate them. Nostalgia for a body hollowed out inside punctuates any analysis of a man.

Certain hysterical-perverse individuals, such as Louise's father, profoundly identify with their mother, remain familiar with her jouissance, and bathe in femininity. Others have repressed it more profoundly but have brought it into play with their daughters in the form of prohibitions and of sadism—or of "somatizations" where father and daughter are prisoners of the same impossible fantasy of pregnancy. For each of the many manifestations of paternal femininity, there are modulations of the symptoms and desires of the daughter.

Thus a father seduces his daughter not with the penis that he reserves for his son but by proxy, with a maternal phallus that he designates for her. And he succeeds only too well. The phallus around which he turns, thought to be veiled, is she, the little girl. It is made of her feminine substance, with which the father is identified.

If a woman is not everything in the phallic function, it is not because she ignores this phallus. She knows it only too well. Every woman knows about the phallus, with an acute violent knowledge that has been hers, attached to her, from eternity. Attached to her body as well, it is felt as a fragment of a lost life, but one that the father revivifies as the object of his jouissance. Thus this phallus becomes real.

The case of Louise illustrates the general rule according to which feminine sexuality is led back to the scene of jouissance by a perversion. Most often it is that of the father, but sometimes it is that of a homosexual woman of the family. From there, desire, in order to survive, must return to the mother's side, sustaining itself through the drive structures already in place. These are consequently very archaic drives, where breast and voice are privileged.

Perversion is played out in the unsaid, through silence and passion; this is the way it happens among women. The jouissance in which the little girl bathes is intense but diffuse. It opens a fixed and floating space where the trauma seems to melt into heaviness and sleep. But the analysis of these kinds of silent hysteria shows that the jouissance is in fact always there, marked by the paternal seal.

The father's jouissance, declaring itself with its insignia and objects, is the most decisive declaration of love that will ever be made to a woman. How does she hear it?

Louise knows that her father initiated her.

The Birth of the Name

About feminine jouissance nothing can be said because it exceeds all sense. To the same extent that feminine jouissance contains in its "folly" the symbolic order, the father's jouissance is finite, since it has an apparatus and plays on words and on the name.

That the one who experiences jouissance speaks and names is a fact that marks and traumatizes at the same time. The jouissance without a hole, all of a piece, being that of the father, assigns a place to the Other, "attacks" its infinity, and injures it. But in injuring the Other, the father inscribes on it his trace in real letters.

A strange sort of paternal metaphor that, rather than basing itself on the Law, breaks it; rather than turning the child away from the real, reveals it to her. At issue is an initiation: the insignia of the paternal perversion are inscribed on the Shadow and in injuring it open it up, revealing the thing and its rotten jouissance, which the girl for a brief moment can no longer distinguish from her life. "The fish," Louise says, "gives a glimpse of the filthy secret of life, which my body wanted to reject and to vomit."

The father's jouissance opened the sides of the mountain. Granite blocks were detached, debris. In the bottom of the ravines one sees the great crash of stones: the noisy silence of the thing; the deafening silence of music.

Louise's dream:

> In the garden. The fish emerges from the dead leaves that cover the soil. It jumps into a clearing, a flat space where the ashes should have been swept up. The fixed and black eye contrasts with the beating of the tail. I ought to take it in my hand and put it back in the water. This is impossible because the scales point upward.

We find the staging of the expulsion of an offspring: the fish emerging from the leaves, itself leafed over with scales, as if the earth, or better, its Shadow, had given birth to it. As if a piece of the thing had been expelled from the maternal hollow, stamped with the father's crest.

In the emergence of the fish from the leaves, there is a sliding of two elements that one would have believed to be the same. The one moves and gets out: the object is seen at the level of the surface, lifting the surface, raising itself up. We see the raising up—*Aufhebung,* say Freud and Lacan to designate sublimation, this moment when a substance that is differentiated is in the process of "elevating itself to the dignity of the signifier." The phobic object, like a piece of writing or a painting, is a signifier being born, but not by the effect of spontaneous generation or by parthenogenesis; its engendering is the father's doing. What emerges, drawn out of the Shadow, emerges stamped with his crest, palpitating and stupid: the Name.

She (the Shadow) has just given birth to the Name. It is neither Louise's mother nor her daughter. It comes from the place where they do not know that they get lost, where they are absent. A silent and mobile place, scattered with debris, swept by currents, where the elements are mixed up, to propagate, to divide themselves abruptly—traversed by what forces? They do not know. In this Shadow and its forgetting, there are contained the signifiers that are lost from generation to generation. Repressed in a primal repression.

"Repression" or, we might say, enveloping of the thing by the feminine jouissance that contains it and permits a fragment, but not all the real, to be expelled and to be born as Name. Only a fragment. The thing remains in the Shadow, not capable of being symbolized, but it is not dispersed, as happens in psychosis.

This possibility of containing the thing, at once threatened and confirmed in the phobia, defines primary narcissism. It appears to be as necessary to the engendering of the Name as the mark impressed by the father.

But why designate as Name the fragment of material that makes its way across the leaves of the dream? Isn't the object that rises up an archaic phallus that is erected in piercing its veils? The question is posed: is it known whether the distinction phallus/Name-of-the-Father has a place on the stage of sublimation? For the phallus operates veiled. Only under this condition does it sexualize jouissance. If it discovers itself unveiled, does it still initiate into desire, or into an Other order, a "divine" order, where the Name is revealed as that which the thing expels?

Periodically, shaken by the trauma that the father impressed on her, brought back by him to the scene of jouissance, the girl is confronted with the Name of the Father more than with the phallus. A Name of the Father is not given once and for all. It is given to destroy and to expel, to remake unceasingly.

This jouissance with which women are confronted is not theirs. It is Other, and it remains Other. Cut off from it by the father, man makes the best or worse of this loss that he projects as part objects. Woman herself is always forced to come back to it. Further, what terrifies her is less her relationship with infinity than the wound that can reach the envelope containing the thing. But she is a daughter. Daughter of a mother. With the Shadow that was opened at birth, where she and her mother exist, absent from themselves, she will again contain and restore the Infinite.

So when Louise begins to grasp, during the analysis, that the fish is not only a fixed and black look, that under the scales it is living, she sees that *it* concerns milk and voice. When the fish discovers the empty silence that is in the interior, when, revealing the Other's groove, which was hidden, it becomes a Name, then Louise begins to be absent. In the sexual act, a jouissance she knows nothing about erupts, suddenly and brutally, having more to do with possession than with voluptuousness. Its eruption puts the states of sudden emptiness into the background, creating a hole. Of this state nothing can be said, obviously.

And yet each time it seems that a stroke cuts—suddenly, violently, by itself. It is certain that it strikes the ear, but it is heard in the greatest silence, inside all noise: "Then it opens onto the night."

There, what does she hear in Shadow? What noise? Of that we know nothing. But it is certain that at these moments jouissance is deployed to contain the abyss of the Other. The mother, the musician, is called upon to destroy the sound of the thing with the night.

Is music made only of the cry and the voice?

Or is she going to seek it again in the interior: can she murmur something about the silence, from the night of the body that has escaped from the cry?

6 Jerome, or Death in the Life of the Obsessional

BY SERGE LECLAIRE

If there were even less snow than there is, and if I had pursued the task with more fervor, I could have presented you with a nice piece of work this evening, well constructed with the neat and clean lines of a temple portal, surrounded by grass and flowers. But you will excuse me, the work is still under construction and there is some rubbish on the lawn.

Already I think about the epigraph that will greet the visitor to this temple, and I will have to choose between the two texts that have been my guides.

"Above all, obsessionals need the possibility of death to resolve their conflicts," wrote Freud in the case of the Rat Man. And you will remember this delectable sentence that we find a few lines above it: ". . . and in his imagination he constantly killed people in order to be able to express his sincere sympathy to their relatives."

The other epigraph I extract arbitrarily from a seminar of May 1955. It begins with a question posed by Oedipus: "Is it when I am finally nothing that I become really a man?"

"It is there," J. Lacan tells us, "that the next chapter begins: beyond the pleasure principle."

Lacking an edifice, we need at least an outline. This is what I propose—a pencil mark on tracing paper, a blueprint. You be the judge.

In the first part of this report, we will talk of what we know, or at least of what we do. In the second I will try to reconstruct my dialogue with Jerome, taking care to replace my silences and my exclamations, my "yeahs" and my "hmms" with more elaborate formulas. In a third part I will propose an outline that can guide our future work, if at that time we have the least desire to undertake another project like this one.

Serge Leclaire is a psychiatrist practicing psychoanalysis in Paris. This paper was first read before the Société Française de Psychanalyse on May 28, 1956. It was first published as "La Mort dans la vie de l'obsédé," in the journal *La Psychanalyse* 2 (Paris: Presses Universitaires de France, 1956), pp. 111–40. It was republished as "Jérôme, ou la mort dans la vie de l'obsédé," in Serge Leclaire, *Démasquer le réel* (Paris: Editions du Seuil, 1971), pp. 121–46.

Our knowledge begins with a story—a bit simplistic, a bit stupid—of the kind we hear from the couch or read in the paper.

It concerns an analyst of great renown, who hour after hour is generous enough to receive and to listen to his illustrious clients. One day he was a little weary and did not get up from his easy chair. A charming secretary, used to this, ushered each patient out at the end of his session. It was five o'clock, and the obsessional who was lying there was speaking a great deal. When the session was over, the patient, particularly satisfied with himself, concluded with these words: "I think this has been a good session." Then, echoing the words habitually spoken by the analyst, he added, "We are going to leave things there." He looked at the therapist, who appeared to be colder than usual; he seemed to be asleep. But no, he was very pale, really cold. The patient was concerned and summoned the secretary, who became agitated. They called a colleague, who ran right over, listened, and said that the analyst had died three hours earlier.

This story, known as the story of the five o'clock patient (thus avoiding using a name that would refer to what is in question), has been used to attack psychoanalysis. But why disdain it? Let us stop for a moment and ask ourselves about its meaning.

I agree that there are more witty stories, but this one has the merit of being "striking." I do not know its origin for sure, but I would wager that it was born on the couch. Since its invention, I think that all the patients in the world have learned it or have reinvented it and told it as though it were theirs. I have heard that one day about five o'clock, while one of our master didacticians was relaxing, as one should at that time, cradled by the soft philosophical murmurings of his wise student, he stood up all of a sudden and, just at the punch line, scowled and said, "Aha, you find that funny?" to which the imperturbable student answered: "Yes, why?"

But enough of diversions. We know what it means to speak; let us analyze.

It is certain that the issue in the story is a particular form of the fantasy of the analyst's death, and this appears with a remarkable constancy in our patients. What does this innocent fantasy signify, if we can put it that way? You know the answer as well as I do and as well as the patient does, for he no less than we is fully informed of what is written in our now classic literature. I will remind you, then, of the different keys that we habitually use to understand—if in fact it is a question of understanding—what our patient is telling us when he speaks of death.

In the first place, it is clear enough that in imagining us dead, he wants to kill us. "You want to kill me" is the response of those who understand. Those who are more clever will ask, "Haven't you ever dreamed that your father had a fatal accident?" or else they will employ a ruse: "You were imagining the other day that I had a beard like your father!" It is certain that with this story our patient manifests his aggressiveness in the transference and that he wishes for our death as he did that of his father—unless, of course, he fears it. Any informed patient will explain this to you himself.

The story of the five o'clock patient confirms other elements of our knowledge: for example, that the analyst is a gentleman who is often taciturn, says very little, and from time to time maintains a deathly silence. Freud reminds us of this in "The Theme of the Three Caskets": in dreams, muteness is the usual representation of death. Certain patients whose wit is especially pointed even insinuate that the psychoanalyst sleeps while they speak, and the story reminds us, as does the canon of Haydn, that sleep is a brief death.

Often Jerome talks to me about that—about sleep, that is; I will tell you more later. But Jerome himself can fall asleep on the couch when, out of breath he renounces reason in order to stop his "echo chamber" from resonating. (That is his name for his *cavum*, whose permeability concerns him a great deal.) A long sigh and a pause suspend his vocalized commentary on his images. I sigh also, relieved (in silence), and I open my second ear: for the last two weeks he has been doing everything he can (monotonously droning on) to make me fall asleep. Then the word "crocodile" comes to him, like that, out of thin air; and he does not know why. Yes, it is crocodile leather, and he does not like it. He remembers a documentary film. In it there is a crocodile that seems to be asleep, floating like a dead tree trunk, and then in an instant it opens its jaws and swallows a black man in less time than we need to say it. . . . Naturally, Jerome did not see the scene of "incorporation"; it was cut out of the film. But he knows that the imperturbable filmmaker kept his camera fixed on this scene and ate it all up with his glass eye, not missing a morsel of the action.

The moral is: playing dead can permit one to eat the other.

Crocodile . . . , yes. Crocodile leather like that which is on your notebook; I do not like this leather.

So be it, perhaps I am the crocodile. But after all, and here we touch on identification, why should it not be he, the patient, who is the dead tree trunk, sagely lying down, sometimes silent, even asleep, like the analyst? Why would this inert and menacing thing not be he?

We know that the analyst keeps silent, but he also has patients who play dead . . . and who say so. This game can continue for a long time.

Happily, tradition says that the imperturbable analyst has the last word. To demonstrate this I will tell you another story that I think I was one of the first of our group to hear. It will be very instructive. An analyst, very experienced, has the technique of repeating the last word of his patient's phrase, until one day he echoes the "kerplunk" that concludes the ultimate acting out.

We seem to believe, rightly or wrongly, that the analyst should have the last word. The example of the crocodile is nonetheless interesting, for it conjures up around silence, sleep, and death a series of themes familiar to the interpreter: objectification, "anality" (I refer to the black man), ambivalence, identification, aggressiveness-passiveness, incorporation, and voyeurism. Each of these keys could guide us in formulating an interpretation that would retain the value of a mythic explanation.

Until now I have wanted to do nothing more than remind you of the frequency and banality of these fantasies of the death of the analyst—which patient has never put you in an auto accident?—and evoke at the same time our most common ways of understanding what relates to death.

It would seem that when the practicing analyst hears the word "death" or finds it symbolized in his patient's discourse, he appeals automatically to one of the following three keys: desire and fear of death, identification with the dead, or symbolic representation of death.

Then, according to his taste or his humor, he interprets it of necessity in one or the other of the three registers designated by the keys. Let us again look closely at each of these three perspectives.

First, desire and fear of death. What is principally in question is a desire to murder, desire to murder the father, that is to say, to bring about a death. Everyone nowadays knows, after the shortest period of analysis, that he has desired to kill his father and to sleep with his mother. We will return to this point, which is of major importance. Freud reminds us in *Totem and Taboo*[1] that in obsessional neurosis, "at the root of the prohibition there is invariably a hostile impulse—against someone the patient loves—wish that that person should die." He also tells us that the fear of one's own death and then of the death of others is only the consequence of this evil desire.

"We admit," he writes, "that this tendency to kill really exists."

Thus the tendency to kill, which was immediately confused with aggressiveness, constitutes the root of everything related to this perspective: murder of the father, fear of one's own and the other's death, neurotic fear of death, and guilt related to the evil desire.

Under a second heading we can group everything related to the theme of

1. Freud, *Totem and Taboo*, S.E. 13, p. 72.

identification with the dead. The Freudian source is *Totem and Taboo*, and especially "Mourning and Melancholy."[2] For the moment, however, what concerns us is best found in a text by Fenichel that summarizes the common psychoanalytic "knowledge": "All of this gives evidence of an identification with the dead person, subjectively perceived as an oral incorporation occurring on the same level as in psychotic depression but of lesser intensity." And "in summary it may be stated that mourning is characterized by an ambivalent introjection of the lost object. . . ." In this perspective we can surely probe the meaning of the concept of identification. We speak unhesitatingly of identification with a dead parent, a brother, or a sister. We could also study (beyond mythological illustration), everything that is covered by the notion of introjection: introjection and incorporation, partial introjection, alliance of the introjected object with the ego or the superego, a whole series of problems that we leave to one side today.

We will not stop, either, to question the work of mourning, on which D. Lagache has contributed an ethnological study that follows the Freudian tradition faithfully.[3] He has promised us the clinical complement very shortly.[4]

Finally, under a third heading, we gather everything that psychoanalytic experience has taught us about the symbolic equivalences for death: thus as we have already mentioned, there are silence, sleep, immobility, but there are also references to "the other side," to the "beyond" or "other shore" of the river, and to the kingdom of the dead. The dead are laid out, as corpses, more or less gnawed away at, and as we see in statues from the end of the fifteenth century, there are skeleton, skull, sickle, and chariot. We would add to this what we have learned about funeral rites. But again, we will not follow this path today.

If I neglect such enticing subjects, if I only make fleeting reference to what you were perhaps waiting to hear about, this is because psychoanalysts, with the exception of Freud, have been principally interested in the *theme* of death, as though what mattered was to veil death in thematizing it. But we propose this evening to reintroduce the *question* of death, as it is posed for the obsessional.

Some will think that this is a mere quibble over terms and that the question of death can only be the theme of a dissertation: this much is certainly evident. But it is precisely this veiling of the question that we want to avoid. I admit that the difficulty begins here.

We tend to use all our force to put death to the side, to eliminate it from our lives. We have tried to throw a *veil of silence* over it, and we have even imagined

2. Freud, "Mourning and Melancholy," *S.E.* 14, pp. 243–58.
3. "Le Travail du devil," in *Revue française de psychanalyse* 4 (1938), pp. 693–708.
4. ["Deuil pathologique," in *La Psychanalyse* 2 (Paris: Presses Universitaires de France, 1956), pp. 45–74.]

a proverb, "To think about something as though it were death" (which means that one does not think about it at all). Freud wrote this in 1915 in "Considerations on War and Death."

It was also Freud who a few years later introduced a concept that most analysts have reduced to the uselessness of a theoretical excrescence that can only disturb a nice and simple practice. Even today there are those who believe in the death drive only in the same way that they believed in Santa Claus, in reverence to the fancy and the obstinacy of the old man.

But here we arrive at a point beyond our knowledge.

Let us stop then and start on another tack.

We return to our everyday experience.

For a moment I thought I would follow a friend's suggestion and examine the clinical application of the function of the dummy in bridge.[5] I renounced this, first, because I feared it would not be a sufficiently "serious" subject for a scientific meeting, and second, because I am a terrible bridge player. This, I admit, is regrettable. Reflect for an instant on the exemplary function of this dummy: incontestably, to use the terms of J. Lacan, he is the fourth person, whose presence is blinding; he is laid out, entirely exposed, closed, finished, complete; he is the only person we see in such a state of nakedness. He is the dead, but it is precisely because he is seen as laid out and complete that the play is organized around him. He is the declarer's partner, and the defenders are situated in relation to him, playing on his strength or weakness—because he has strength and weakness, even when dead—depending on whether the living defender plays before or after him.

We will leave the bridge table and return to the couch.

One day Jerome was in good humor and was talking about the artful way the English had of ridding themselves of their assassins. In England they hang them. . . . You know the feelings that ordinarily accompany these capital themes, but most striking to Jerome are the judge's words when he passes sentence: ". . . is condemned to be hanged by the neck until dead."

"Well," Jerome adds, "for me it is as though someone had said to me one day, 'You will live until dead.'"

Jerome lives under the weight of this condemnation. If it is obvious that all of us will live until dead, it is no less strange to hear it recalled when we would rather forget about it. Hearing it as a death sentence is even more surprising, as though it had been addressed to Adam himself in the garden of Eden, when Eve

5. [In French the word for the dummy in bridge is *le mort*, which literally means "dead man."]

was the one who ate the apple. Then, the Bible says, "their eyes were opened, and they knew they were naked." And the Eternal in his anger said to man, "It is through work that you will draw your food all the days of your life . . . until you return to the soil from which you came. . . ." Adam knew it because God told him: "You will not eat of the tree of knowledge of good and evil, for the day you eat of it, that day you will die." Now why does Jerome think of himself as condemned like Adam: *You will live until dead?* And why does he live in a perpetual dungeon, expiating his life unto death? This is one question I have asked myself, and others who have been interested in the world of the obsessional have asked it, too.

Certainly we can find in Jerome the theme of the death of the father, fully developed. He lived his first years in the shadow of his father's absence. Jerome's father was fighting the Germans at the time. He killed in order not to be killed, and Jerome's mother feared for her husband's life, naturally enough. The father came back from the war, gassed, tired, and diminished, although alive enough to give Jerome a little sister three years later. His sister was born as black as a negress . . . or as black as something else. Her abundant black hair fascinated everyone. Jerome would have much preferred to see her dead; she was an object to put in a box or to burn, and he has reported numerous fantasies attesting to this. Later he killed her in his memory, purely and simply by forgetting her. This we found after a few months of analysis.

It is no less evident that Jerome's progress was marked by his taking the form, appearance, and voice of his father, this *instead of becoming his son, as he would surely have wished.* Thus he told of a particularly dramatic scene: he was twelve or thirteen and had found an old revolver. There was a discussion at dinner, a dispute with his father, who broke down in tears. That day Jerome swore to himself never to oppose his father for the rest of his life.

Finally, during the first year of analysis, Jerome lost his father, who had for a long time been dying of cancer. Jerome was resigned, sometimes anxious, as he awaited this end. Looking at his father on his deathbed, he noticed one last time how well he had succeeded in reproducing his father's image. The father was buried in the family crypt, which our patient had straightened up beforehand, by reducing the number of corpses there.

We will not stop here to draw a hasty conclusion.

I would rather like to take this opportunity to analyze the attitude of Jerome before the corpse, and to do so I will take a childhood dream that Jerome brought me during the first month of analysis. The dream had impressed him a great deal, and it seems that he has never forgotten it. During the rest of the treatment we had occasion to return to it several times, precisely as a touchstone or nodal point, which will always have an irreducibly mysterious aspect.

We find ourselves in a vast room surrounded by a covered gallery that leads to a loggia: the atmosphere is chiaroscuro. Borne by four men an open sarcophagus advances; up close we clearly see a perfectly conserved mummy in its wrappings. But suddenly, as the procession advances, *the mummy liquefies*. All that is left in the sarcophagus is a red juice whose horrifying aspect is veiled by the certainty that these are but the unguents that had served to embalm the body.

Such is the dream of the mummy.

We are going to linger a while with this dream, using it to pursue the analysis of the implacable condemnation to live.

Jerome says that this dream is very old. He brings it to me with all the objectivity and indifference of an impartial observer; has he dreamed it several times, or has he remembered it many times to feed his fantasies? He cannot say.

He does remember that this dream preceded or followed a visit to the department of Egyptian antiquities at the Louvre; he had for a long time desired to have a mummy. Moreover, Egyptian history interests him, as does anything else that can clarify the problem of *origins*. Jerome likes family trees and grand historical syntheses. He wants to know precisely of what lineage he is the final term, the result. He regrets not having a gallery of ancestors whose portraits he can see, so why not Ramses II, who is the mummy.

He also evokes the mysterious subterranean passages of the pyramids; we must add that when he was twelve he was very interested in walking through catacombs and grottoes. He always dreams of subterranean cities and tastes an anxiety born of perplexity when in his fantasy he finds himself at some subterranean crossroads where seven mysterious doors open.

But he has talked to me most often about the surprise and satisfaction he feels in contemplating the mummy in its human appearance; witness to a vertiginous past, immobile, protected, conserved, it is the very image of that which endures.

In another dream he represented the source of his fascination: in an enormous grotto he discovered a splendid black marble statue of a laid-out corpse, and he was ecstatic contemplating it. It was the very image of the perfection of a realized, definitive form, a form that ignores time. In another dream he saw a warrior who had found the ideal protection: he was transformed into a man covered with a tar, a perfect weather-resistant armor, and—what is sometimes more useful—he could resist murderous projectiles.

Jerome often asks himself about motion, and the image of the mummy animated by those who carry it represents for him the excellence of passive movement, where one is entirely submitted to others.

This would evidently be the place to talk about the complex movements of a man in a train, and especially of a man in his car; every automobile trip, Jerome says, represents the possibility of a fatal accident at the same time that it gives the satisfaction of finding oneself in an enclosed space. But it would take too long here to discuss man's motor complex or his motor. I prefer looking at the suggestive image that Jerome brings me: "For me to keep going, I must turn at 3,000 rpms." And when he says "for me to keep going," he expresses his concern that this coherence, the unity that he holds onto, will dissolve itself into a state that will not merely be fragmentation. Turning at 3,000 rpms is for him a vital necessity because he thinks that this rhythm gives him the appearance and properties of a solid. "If I stop for an instant," another patient told me, "*I am afraid I will turn to dust*," and he adds, "this dust that we are made of."

Whether it concerns the constraint of internal movement or the passivity of external motility, of one's displacement in space, this movement, which is called the image of life, is always suffered.

And so it goes for the rest of Jerome's life. He lives by proxy: he loves to organize—this is his job—and to activate the companies he visits, to organize meetings and trips, to stage events. He is ready for everything, providing he does not participate in the event itself. Like Iconepherous, whose fantasy of the enchanted city I reported elsewhere,[6] he is alive only when inside the walls of the city, and his horror before the real is sacred. "I was next to a lake," Jerome tells me one day. "The place was lovely, but I was insensitive to it. Believe me, I am more moved by a beautiful postcard or by the photos of my trip."

You might say, why remind us of what we know to exist in every obsessional: their taste for statues, their problems with cars, or their taking vacations with a Leica? It is precisely because we know this too well.

Thus on a hot day when the air is immobile, the water games of a sleepy park seem to be painted garlands. But if the wind rises, you will think, if only for an instant, that an indiscrete eraser has distorted the linear ordering of the drawing, before you remember that these games are an animated movement.

Nothing appears to be more immobile than Iconepherous's city of Jerome's subterranean passages. There is wall after wall with steel doors that open and close like clockwork. Nothing enters without being controlled, predigested, ready to be assimilated into this universe of forms. It is at the heart of this world that we

---

6. Serge Leclaire, "La fonction imaginaire du double dans la névrose obsessionelle," in *Entretiens psychiatriques* 4 (Paris: Editions de l'Arche, 1958), pp. 193–220.

find the sarcophagus as the ultimate jewel case; it is open, we see the mummy, the corpse that has retained its human appearance, and it is beautiful, reassuring, nicely enveloped in cloths.

Watch out, Jerome told me, we are at the edge of the unnamable; only a frail bag of skin separates him from horror. This is what he tells me even more clearly in a more recent dream that I offer to you without preanalysis:

> A man is standing, on the bridge of a ship, and he will be killed *'because he knows.'* I leave so as not to be seen. I am annoyed because the corpse will be discovered, and I will have said nothing; his datebook, similar to mine, remains with his things. Then his bloated corpse is found in the middle of a boat filled with water and mud. They try to get him out, but those who are carrying him are hampered by a labyrinth of wooden planks. They bring him from one side of the boat to the other. He is bloated, stiff, blackened, and very ugly to see, and he stinks. At any moment he may fall apart. Impossible to get out. The corpse blocks the way out of the labyrinth. I am nauseous and ready to vomit. I wake up with my body twisted.

At the heart of this world we find a fragile bag of skin, ready to fall apart.

Now, if we have reached this place, it is because we knew how to wait and because we did not try to understand too much on the way. We could have been diverted during long sessions by dreams and fantasies of scattered members, of hands and feet cut off, of ovens and rancid odors. There were plenty of penises, cut off by a father whom Jerome would have liked to see as menacing. All of this was intended for the psychoanalyst, who is supposed to find it terrific. For our part we talked about it courteously, correctly, indifferently; his anxiety was not there.

It erupted in another place, as you can guess. We were in the fifth month of analysis when one day he was speaking about "incommunicability," of the hiatus separating two bodies. The words we use to communicate are only vibrations of sounds: he feels himself isolated, void, cold, immured without anything truthful to say. To see his father die, he confided later, to see suffering flesh, even in the movies, to hear a cry (which is not speech) from someone complaining of his agony—all this is simply intolerable. This day he had spoken to me in a tone that was between reporting and confessing, emotionless. He was wishing to be entirely transformed through analysis so that he could accede to communication; this was his only true speech, and it was heard.

Leaving my office, he was going to see his wife, who had just been operated on for a spinal problem. But on the street he was literally thrown to the ground by an atrocious pain in his belly, in the middle of his intestines. He got up and collapsed on a bench, silent; his entire being was called into question, and for a brief instant he saw himself dying. Then, surmounting his pain, he split himself from it, according to a familiar technique, and dragged himself to the hospital where his wife was. The doctor examined him and concluded that he had had an attack of nephritic colic, all the time admiring the patient's courage. There was no antecedent, and the x rays showed nothing. There was no repetition of the incident.

He told me about this incident at the next session.

One day he was seized by horror after having almost fallen asleep during a session. The noise of a motorcycle passing under the window made him jump up; he felt it as a force breaking out of and tearing his stomach. He continued to evoke the times when he awoke by jumping in the air. If he does not feel reassembled, together, in one piece, he is invaded by panic.

In his dreams also, abandoning the traditional theme of castration, he saw an open coffin containing his dead father, who revived for an instant to say to him, "Look, it's you."

Nonetheless, as I have told you, Jerome was not "impressionable": he had devoted himself without hesitation to reducing the number of corpses in the family crypt. A corpse is nothing but a thing, an object like another, he tells me. Fresh corpse or dust, it is of no matter to him; but the intermediary stages are literally intolerable. When he felt himself captured, he saw them as frozen masses piled up like boards. "It left me cold," he added.

But the atrocity he imagines to be the worst is finding all of a sudden, in opening a closet, a formless thing, an unknown, unidentified object that surprises you before it can be named "corpse." He adds that he can look at a pyramid of corpses in full daylight, but discovering one of them in a cave or crypt, a nameless thing with an uncertain form suddenly revealed by the light of his lamp, is precisely what he must avoid at all costs.

I agree that these are not pleasant subjects, and you will excuse me for having quoted Jerome textually. Clinical work, for which we are so avid, is demanding!

So we find ourselves faced with the purple unguents that served to embalm Ramses II.

I will spare you more crude images after I have noted a time when Jerome stepped off a streetcar only to put his foot down and slip, not in what you think, but on a pile of tripe. For him this evoked the picture of a fetus soaking in a bottle. . . . We'll stop there.

Now we can understand a little better what is surrounded by the ramparts of the city and the steel doors of the subterranean galleries. *Perhaps it is not outside of these walls that the threat of a seductive creature or of a judge with giant scissors is to be found....* The pile of stones evokes well enough the sepulchre.

At the least, to express ourselves in a brief formula, remember this. If someone should ask you one day on your oral exams during the second stage of the third year of the seven-year course of study at the psychoanalytic institute—if someone should ask you, concerning defense mechanisms, "What is the function of the cloths that wrap a mummy?" you must respond without hesitation, "These cloths are the object of the obsessional's constant attention when he is afraid of being liquefied."

Now we are on familiar ground. You will tell me that we have known for a long time all the horror man feels when faced with the corpse of his counterpart. You are right, and I will add that Jerome knew it as well as you do before his analysis, and he knew it in the same way that someone else knows before his analysis that he was jealous of his brother and that he was passionately in love with his mother.

Perhaps you are thinking that we could have broached the question of death from another angle, without drawing on the corpse? Possibly, but I am not so sure as you, and in any case we must recognize that the path we follow is the one Jerome pointed out to us during his analysis.

A question now remains: why does this horror at the decomposition of the corpse—to us this seems to be a natural and common feeling—why is it invested with such particular interest at the heart of Jerome's fantasies, at the center of his analysis? We will leave this question open for the time being. But it is important to show by this fragment of an analysis the nature of the fright that inhabits someone who sees himself as condemned "to live until dead."

Freud has shown in his analysis of the "uncanny" that such a fright approaches anxiety. And we ought to recognize that in analytic literature the fundamental anxiety over death seems often to have been abandoned in favor of the "original" anxiety of the birth trauma.

Now we have uncovered a formative image, a pole of attraction or repulsion that Jerome discovers to be the knot of his being. That his image may be shown to have the same destiny as the mummy uncovered, exposed, and then dissolved—this is what the analyst can hope for. Now that it is exposed before us, let us learn from it.

We will go back to the familiar theme of the stone figure covering the tomb. Enormous masses of stone have been carved into great monoliths. The tomb, perfectly sealed, opens into a grotto that one enters through a subterranean passage with an opening in a vague landscape surrounded by waste.... To a certain extent this dream is associated by Jerome with the memory of an incomprehensible anger that seized him when he was prohibited from climbing for an instant on the altar of the black Virgin under the cathedral choir.

He is dreaming of being structured like this tomb. And nothing can be safe enough to protect him from the disquieting fragility of this "bag of skin" to which he sees himself reduced when, like Adam, *he sees that he is naked.* Shell of tar or armored room, closed field of his capture or subterranean chamber, the intimacy of the analyst's office, tomb, mausoleum, cathedral constructed on a crypt— nothing will ever be heavy enough, hermetic enough, well enough constructed, to hide what he must not see, to prevent the intrusion of what must be maintained and hidden.

Thus, bringing his tomb with him, Jerome lies down on my couch.

When he opens it enough to speak to me from beyond the tomb, he has only one ambition, which is to persuade me that *the die is cast.*

Is he not already in the tomb? or almost, imprisoned until death ensues? He does not cease to tell me that he has no future but a past to "liquidate," a lost time to catch up on. Listen to him: "I want for once to be up to date; I want to liquidate all the files that have piled up on the left side of my desk, finally to be able to breathe. When I succeed, anxiety grabs me and I have to find another unfinished task quickly. I exhaust myself in catching up on my lateness, the work that I undertake ought already to have been finished. I have no free time; *there are no Sundays for me."*

Whether or not it is a question of identification, it is certain that Jerome *wishes he were already dead,* and especially that *he lives as though he were already dead.*

He is the end of a line, he cannot have children, he is the finish, the conclusion, *already ended;* there is no future for him, and the life that remains is already filled with tasks to accomplish, files to classify, affairs to liquidate, problems to bring up to date. On his trips everything is paid in advance. The only time he feels himself alive is at night in his car, when he discovers in the opening created by his headlights a road that promises new and mortal perils . . . a little like analysis.

Iconepherous, even more categorically than Jerome, affirmed that "the die is cast," that his universe was closed, terminated, definitively organized. Aside from that, it is too late, and in any case he has nothing to add. On that he concludes, "And that's everything."

Happily, they all know that their presence on the couch affirms—very discreetly—the contrary, and signifies to us that a door is open and that their statement about the conclusion is an appeal to whoever knows how to hear it.

Jerome expresses his desire and his fear otherwise than by automobile imagery. Thus he says, in voyeuristic terms: "How do you want me to get out of this? I am like a man who cannot find his lost glasses, since without them he cannot see. . . . It is true that someone who is wearing them cannot see them either. . . ." Or he comments upon his waiting, "I am like a blind man who wants to know what he will see before he gets his sight back."

Or he expresses himself philosophically: "*I want to find the* possibility *of utilizing all my possibilities.*"

Perhaps I will have the opportunity at another meeting to tell you about Jerome's case in a more systematic fashion and to speak of its positive evolution. For today I limit myself to the central theme of death formulated in the "you will live until dead." I will close my case with this *desire* to find the possibility of utilizing all these possibilities.

With these words Jerome proposes the category of the possible to our analytic experience, and on that basis I will formulate the notion that the *obsessional structure can be conceived of as the repeated refusal of the possibility of one's own death.*

This refusal is equivalent to a falsely anticipated acceptance that would make the one who supports it into something already finished.

This is surely the place to look at our epigraph again ("above all, obsessionals need the possibility of death to resolve their conflicts") and to understand it against the backdrop of another of Freud's reflections. "Our unconscious does not believe in the possibility of its own death." Freud adds a remark we will return to, namely, that the *unconscious does not know negation.*

Finally, this would be the occasion to meditate in Heideggerean terms on "our possibility, absolutely own, unconditional, insurmountable," precisely the possibility of "the impossibility of existence as such," which can be summarized in these words: "The possibility of my death reveals to me my possible impossibility and even the possible impossibility of all human existence in general."

Perhaps you think that with these words we are leaving the realm of sound clinical work. It is . . . possible. I would simply hope that this brief glimpse will introduce you to the true dimension of the possible and of death for the obsessional.

For the moment I can do no better than to resituate the problem we confront. We know that through symptoms, questions are posed.

I will compare Jerome's dream with the fantasy of Isabelle, who is a hysteric. An anguishing, almost unbearable question emerges for Isabelle at the limit of a feeling of depersonalization through a strange and invading coenesthetic experience. She is like a ribbon of colored paper, like the ribbons at last night's party that she unrolled into a garland while she was throwing confetti. Instead of unrolling a disk of ribbon, someone pressed its center, and it became a fragile cone or crater that now moves as though advancing and retracting. Isabelle is submerged in her anxiety. An evening's ribbon, fragile colored paper, poses, through its inner hollow or its outer form, Isabelle's question.

Jerome is very different. His wrappings are his mummy. When he was four, while hiding himself at his mother's breast, he said to her, "Call me 'my pet.' "[7] Call me "my pet" and I will be happy, and to make "my pet's" happiness last, he became dead as my pet and as mummy.

Certainly, everyone knows that the mummy, in the dictionary of dreams, can also signify "penis" and can evoke the image of the bandaged organ of a late circumcision. I had previously found this sense in the analysis of Victor, a hysteric whose father lived his last months in a plaster cast. Victor was, at the age of seven, circumcised at the same time as his brother, under the eyes of his mother, an inconsolable widow.

I do not think that Jerome's mummy, the one in whose wrappings he tries to contain the waves of his anxiety, is equivalent to Victor's bandaged organ or that either of them is equivalent to Isabelle's ribbon.

The question Isabelle poses, through the inner hollow or the outer form, while spreading out her anxiety, can be formulated in our sober language: *am I a man or a woman?*

The question Jerome poses, while containing his fright as well as he can between the marble statue and the formless liquid, can be articulated: *am I dead or alive?*

I think you can see that while Isabelle speaks of her sexuality, Jerome speaks of his existence. This is the way that J. Lacan has defined the questions of the hysteric and the obsessional neurotic. We have in the mouths of Isabelle and Jerome two great questions that many other patients have asked: am I man or woman? am I subject or object?

These are questions, or if you prefer, *symptoms*. At the beginning of *Inhibitions, Symptoms, and Anxiety*, Freud tells us: "The main characteristic of the formation of symptoms has long since been studied and, I hope, established beyond dispute. The symptom is a sign of and a substitute for a [drive] satisfaction which has remained in abeyance; . . ."[8]

What are the drives that have remained unsatisfied?

---

7. [In French "my pet" (*ma mie*) is almost a homophone of "mummy" (*momie*).]
8. Freud, *Inhibitions, Symptoms and Anxiety* (1926), S.E. 20, p. 91.

> After long hesitancies and vacillations we have decided to assume the existence of only two basic [drives], Eros and the destructive [drive]. . . . The aim of the first of these is to establish ever greater unities and to preserve them thus. . . ; the aim of the second is, on the contrary, to undo connections and so to destroy things. In the case of the destructive [drive] we may suppose that its final aim is to lead what is living into an inorganic state. For this reason we call it the death [drive].

I am quoting Freud from the *Outline*; he continues:

> The analogy of our two basic [drives] extends from the sphere of living things to the pair of opposing forces—attraction and repulsion—which rule in the inorganic world, and he adds in a footnote, this picture of the basic forces or [drives] which still arouses so much opposition among analysts was already familiar to the philosopher Empedocles of Acragas.[9]

I have quoted you this text of 1938 in preference to others more Freudian, dating from 1920 and 1921, because it bears the mark of a resolve that eighteen years of struggle against so many analysts could only strengthen.

The history of psychoanalysis shows this struggle. Freud said, "There is no difficulty in finding a representative of Eros; but we must be grateful that we can find a representative of the elusive death [drive] in the [drive] of destruction, to which hate points the way."[10]

It seems to me that this is precisely where Jerome comes to help us gain a more or less concrete idea of the death drive and the dynamics of obsessional neurosis.

When Jerome amuses himself by making himself into a corpse, when he isolates and protects himself, when he annuls or fragments himself into a collection of members or bones, does he not show us this force that tends toward the stability of the inorganic, represented by the marble statue or, less surely, by "my pet mummy"? There is no need for a greater unity than this, since as a piece of stone, he will be conserved.

Jerome sees himself as a statue or a mummy because he wants to endure and even to be eternal. Time is like a landscape for him, like the one he contemplated during his vacation. He does not really see it, but he does rejoice when he sees the photo he has taken. He does not live in the present, and continually

---

9. Freud, *An Outline of Psychoanalysis* (1940 [1938]), *S.E.* 23, pp. 148–49.
10. Freud, *The Ego and the Id* (1923), *S.E.* 19, p. 42.

says so. What he does is to *mark time*. In this context you will understand that the past is easier to handle than a future that hardly ever exists as such. Jerome is convinced that his death will not arrest clock time, and that is what matters for him. He has a truly spatialized time that keeps life suspended or framed. Within this time, death is the marker of a frontier that has virtually already been attained.

The patient's eternal loves, stronger than death, are also enclosed in this space. How can we not mention in this context the religious attitude that resembles obsessional neurosis in more than one way?

Fear of death is their common horizon. If Freud is especially insistent on this point in *Totem and Taboo*, on the "Thou shalt not kill" as responding to some "natural" desire, we can consider that the two ways of accommodating death, that of the obsessional and that of religion, make it the end of a stage of an adventure that must be pursued in the beyond.

The clock time of Jerome's life is filled. All that remains is for him to finish the work that has accumulated; this does not leave him any free time. Like someone who sees his end approaching, Jerome has to put his life in order over and over again. This spatialized, rigorously ordered world sustains, extends, supports, and constitutes Jerome's body—as the pyramids contain mummies. He has many times told us as much unambiguously. And I am convinced that this spatialization of time, this *freezing of becoming*, is in part the work of the death drive. You will understand that in such an atmosphere the processes of identification acquire a sort of corpselike rigidity, with an animation that can only come from a perpetual play of mirrors.

One detail is striking here. Jerome, who lives in a great necropolis and passes his time measuring and ordering the living things he encounters, has one great preoccupation: he wants to bring life back into religious practices. He struggles against the sclerosis of part of the clergy; he participates in the movement to renew the liturgy and militates for these beliefs politically. It is important to make others live and draw some profit for himself by proxy, as a puppeteer would, to use his words.

Some are still surprised that the analysis of an obsessional neurotic takes such a long time. How could it be otherwise for those who are already in the eternity of perpetual motion?

You know how much this concern for perpetual motion touches the heart of the obsessional; it would be pleasant for us to stop there, but I prefer for the moment to take you through one of the subterranean secret passages that lead to the heart of the pyramid.

I told you that Jerome was putting his life in order; his analysis, according to him, was supposed to help him finally to arrange his affairs. But there is one question that has troubled him since he was ten. At this time he was afraid he would die in his sleep and tried to imagine how the world would continue to turn without him. This was the occasion for interminable, deliciously anguishing fantasies. but another question added itself to his daydreams: *and if I had never been born?*

If I had never been born, if I had never taken form and body, solidity and consistency, if I had remained merely an unsatisfied desire, a formless liquid. . . ? With this question, anxiety pressed upon him and vertigo seized him; it was difficult for him to pursue the representation of a world into which he had never been born. But, he asked himself suddenly, have I really been born? Am I really alive?

There again we are at the doorstep of the labyrinth, at the entrance of the pyramid. Or else, to use a more recent image, Jerome is like a general who knows perfectly the layout of the city he has under siege, the city he must take. He knows it all, all that he must do to succeed . . . but he remains immobile like a statue. Thus the death drive stops a general and prevents him from *act-tacking.*

Jerome's fundamental question and the "cosmic" anxiety that accompanies it permit us to reformulate the obsessional's question in a more lively light, *to be or not to be.*

Jerome was not a general, but more a second lieutenant, yet he was a good soldier. He had authority, he understood his men—a little too well, perhaps— and he paid with his own person. He was an excellent captive for five years and never thought of escaping. He organized lectures, put on shows, and was fully alive.

But one day, in a great disorder, Jerome was freed, and for a time he wandered on the road looking for an organized center. There he had a terrifying encounter. On the same road, walking from the other direction, *a man* came to meet him; he had a military air, with a composite uniform that designated him as neither friend nor foe. . . . Jerome had some food and a gun; the other man had the same. Jerome was thinking very quickly, as if in a whirlpool; he slowed down, stopped for a second, started up again; the other approached, he also seemed to hesitate. Around them the countryside was deserted. The other's face was bearded; is he human? They were barely five yards from each other, and the other opened his mouth: he was a German and he was in hiding. Good, he wants nothing. Each continued his journey. Now they were back to back, and Jerome was transfixed by his fright. He thought, Surely he will shoot me to prevent me from turning him in, to take my clothing, my food. He dared neither to turn around nor to run. . . . He waited and walked. . . .

Thus Jerome encountered a man alone.

He had many dreams about this incident. He found himself faced with a great hairy brute who got on his nerves by not paying attention. They were going to fight. They agreed to a fight to the death, but . . . it was for the fun of it. It's all right, he said to another German who threatened him with his gun. It's all right if you kill me, but be nice about it, don't get angry. And talking about another, similar incident, he specified, It wasn't his weapon that scared me but the angry expression on his face.

On this road Jerome discovered that he was alone, without protection, that he had not been able to bring his tomb along.

If it is horrible to see a corpse liquefy in an open coffin, it is no less frightening for Jerome to see a living man when he himself is outside his tomb.

It is perhaps not necessary for me to tell you that I was never able to lead Jerome into that open field where he did not speak from the grave but truly kept silent!

I think we have here the beginnings of a theory of the relation of the obsessional with his counterpart. For the time being we can summarize it with a few images. Here are three typical situations that can sometimes guide our practice.

First, Jerome's speech is always "deferred"—this is not his expression—from inside his pyramid. It is useless to answer him "directly," he can only receive what we say if it is deferred.

Second, Jerome transforms you into a dead tree trunk, he opens the boards of his coffin and speaks to you—but only if you play dead. If you speak, the prison closes up again.

Third, you encounter each other face to face because by accident he has forgotten to close up his prison after you have responded (as in the preceding instance). Even in this situation, it is useless for you to exert yourself; for him it is "for fun," not "for real."

If these images are too simple, I will attenuate their overly rigorous quality with another dream in which Jerome condensed his question. This is also an old nightmare; he kills someone by holding him affectionately by the neck and beating his skull in. But the victim does not die, and when he is in pretty bad shape, he asks to live. . . . Is it too late?

Our technical rules can often be formulated in pictures like this. Under the pretext of talking about technique, I would remind you also of the fantasy of the crocodile that I mentioned above. This permits me to say that practically, and in the concrete experience of the session, if the obsessional wants to be dead, the analyst, as Lacan recalls in his discourse at Vienna ("The Freudian Thing"), must himself play dead. In so doing and in knowing what he is doing, he uses the correct technique with the obsessional. This technique permits the patient to raise the cover of his tomb ever so slightly and *to risk an eye before risking a word*.

It is time to come to the point and to reconsider our discourse one last time before it slides into the abyss of reflective silence, to flourish or to be dissolved.

But in fact, to come to what point? That of neglected problems or of questions we have opened?

I have led you on a visit of our construction site and have told some stories about obsessionals. I have spoken of death, time, possibility, and negation. You have seen crocodiles, mummies, pyramids, and soaking fetuses.

Perhaps it was necessary or perhaps it was a sacrilege to lift the veil that Freud talks about, which covers death with silence.

Let us leave the disorder of the theater wings and stop for a while on the other side of the stage, on the side of the audience.

Let us lower the curtain.

And now, waiting for it to rise again on the show that we promised, which you have not seen, we will draw on its canvas the image of that which is being prepared on the other side, a kind of allegory that summarizes the drama being rehearsed. . . . Imagine what we have painted: *Oedipus, at the crossroads, plays the part of the sphinx.*

7 Philo, or the Obsessional and His Desire

BY SERGE LECLAIRE

*From the time that a passionate girl had cursed
and sanctified my lips (any consecration entails both) I had superstitiously kept myself
from kissing, lest maidens suffer fatal consequences.* —Goethe, *Dichtung und Wahrheit*

A veil, transparent and impenetrable, separates the obsessional subject from the object of his desire. Whatever he may call it—a wall of glass, of cotton, or of stone—he feels it to be (as he tells us) a *glass shell* isolating him from reality.

He will spend an evening with the one he loves without ever holding her in his arms. His hand, heavy as a rock, cannot be brought to encircle her waist; his garrulous lips will never reach hers; and if in an adventurous moment he holds her in any way, it will only be to see her charm vanish and his desire quickly fade away. More unpitying than a wall is the spell that has been cast. As with the curse evoked in the epigraph, a word has assuredly arisen from an abyss to consecrate. For the obsessional neurotic this word is always connected with desire. So it is with the grave obsessional, and with him we recognize more clearly the impasse of desire in the petrified speech of the symptom, speech frozen by the spell.

Here we will limit the field of our research to the obsessional neurotic, already known through his character and described in his world—a completed model of man in his essential prematuration.

In the eyes of his friends, nothing is particularly distinguishing about Philo—they are surprised to learn that he is seeing a psychoanalyst. "You," they say to him, "whose reflection and wisdom are exemplary; how can it be?" It is true that Philo appears to be wise, and people have great hopes for him. He is

Speech presented before the Group for the Evolution of Psychiatry, November 25, 1958, and first published as "Philon ou l'obsessionnel et son désir," in *Evolution psychiatrique* 3 (Paris: Privat Didier, 1959), pp. 383–411. Republished in Serge Leclaire, *Démasquer le réel* (Paris: Editions du Seuil, 1971), pp. 147–67.

close to thirty, a bachelor. I will say very little about his history, since I have only chosen to relate a fragment of his discourse here.

He is the middle child in a family of five children. His parents died almost fifteen years ago, one shortly after the other. His problem is deciding what to do with his life. To appreciate his dilemma, one must imagine all the options that an individual can weigh without making a choice. At the tenderest age, he tells me, wanting to appear witty, he already did not know which breast to choose.[1] Matters have not changed: teaching or the oil business, the priesthood or marriage—it does not matter as long as someone else makes the decision. He only retains the privilege of exposing his doubt (to whoever wants to listen) and also the privilege of contesting, annulling, the other's decision. It is one of his three great passions; the others were having someone love him and failing in a task.

From a long clinical observation, we report only a fragment of one session: it concerns the tie that joins Philo to his mother.

Did Philo hate his father, did he wish to share his mother's bed, was he jealous of his brothers? Yes, without a doubt. But how, in particular? Here analysis becomes more arduous.

Am I wrong to think that the fundamentals of the Oedipus complex have already become commonplace? The desire of the little boy for his mother, of the little girl for her father—the rivalries that are the correlates of these passions are invoked even outside psychiatric circles as arguments and no longer as questions.

And yet, if we stop to consider this idea of the little boy's desire for his mother, remembering that yesterday it was still a new idea, we find that questions emerge and that they are the same as those raised at a time when this idea was scandalous.

Freud's notion was quickly absorbed and accommodated to the needs of an actively expanding intellectual commerce. "Attachment to the mother" became its convenient conceptual formulation; the idea is a nice one, and no one deprives himself of its use. The homosexual, we know, remains attached to his mother; the schizophrenic is too attached; the obsessional was, unthinkingly; the pervert, too precociously; and so on. Too much or too little, positively or negatively, attachment to the mother is now commonly cited in case histories.

These were my reflections on the fascination of newly received ideas when Philo said to me recently that he had not succeeded in breaking off this attachment to his mother and that it had marked a recent attempt at a love relation.

---

1. [The French *sein* ("breast") is pronounced like *saint* ("saint"), so that when spoken, "which breast to choose" could also be understood as "which saint to follow."]

My ear, the true one, opened up.

Surely Philo had known for a long time, and well before he undertook his analysis, that wanting to enter the priesthood was characteristic of men who have not been able to resolve an excessive attachment to their mother. Once the question appeared to be resolved by this knowledge, he hardly ever posed it again. At most it was invoked as an argument or explanation.

On this occasion, I heard it differently, and I sent the word "attachment" back to him in an interrogative tone. "Yes," he continued, "I wanted to speak of the privileged character of everything that ties me to my mother." The idea of tying pleased me, and I reformulated my question: "How are you tied?"

Here is the sequence that my question elicited. I transcribed it on the spot—this is exceptional—because I was alerted by the exclamation he uttered before answering. There was a brief silence as he hesitated to tell me the thought that had just emerged. He excused himself for this thought and then added, "Shit! As though that were any of your business!"[2]

This is not Philo's habitual mode of expression. He continues: "It begins with the look; it's like a communion, a symbiosis. Yes, in her look there's a second look. It is as though she had found in me the satisfaction she did not find in my father. As though I had been necessary to her. . . . There was a secret agreement, a complicity. The word that comes to me is secret 'intimacy.'

"But"—and here the voice trembles with emotion—"it is above all a true relationship on both sides.

"This idea of being a priest, to the extent that I took it seriously, it was as though she had transmitted it. We were able to see how mad it was, she as well as I. Wasn't it the letter, where I questioned everything, that weakened her? Did she feel that her son was in perdition?"

He stops for a moment, as he often does, to say something that will subtly cut through this sequence: "I am saying just anything. . . . Perhaps this will permit me to end up by knowing what I am saying." And he continues: "This letter was like the announcement of my shipwreck, the confession of the failure of the common enterprise. I no longer have any goal. . . . Yes, I no longer have my unique goal of being the only thing necessary to my mother."

A brief passage follows that I cannot report; somewhat literary, its theme is the same: his mother as unique object. And he continues:

"I like speaking this way. Here I find myself pleasing, I enjoy, I feel myself, I listen to myself. It's sterile, this complacency. But that also pleases me: when I

2. [*Comme si ça te regardait* translates literally "As though that were looking at you." The importance of looking is manifest in what follows.]

reveal myself, I am concerned with pleasing. I wanted to please my mother, all of that comes back to me. To be my mother's lord and vassal; she loves me, I love her; we are secretly united in a passionate look. My beloved is mine, and I am all hers. It's the serpent who bites his own tail, I am turned back upon my own penis."

"Analysis pleases me," he finally adds, "because I have the opportunity to speak about my father, to reveal both of us. But what comes back to me is the phrase: 'Is that any of your business?' " Thus he closed this sequence with a more courteous variation of its opening sentence.

I propose this fragment of an analysis as a reference point. It is hardly edited, and I have added no interpretation for the moment. From a strictly technical point of view, it would be best to analyze the exclamation that began it. But this technical point will not concern us here. We will look first at the "content" of this fragment, since it articulates in a relatively clear and accessible way what I will now call the *nodal complex of the obsessional.*

Philo, like most obsessionals, was *his mother's favorite son.* He has maintained, through all the difficulties of his life, an unshakable and secret self-confidence. This is the Eden of some of his fantasies, the wondrous garden of imaginary voyages, the sanctuary in the middle of multiple fortifications. Anyone who violates this place is threatened with death. This is the nostalgia of an unspeakable happiness, of an exceptional and perfect jouissance. If today he is banished forever from this universe that lies at the heart of the mythical rose, then he must have committed some crime.

Who is Philo? A subject predestined to be distinguished from his counterparts, from his brothers, by some sign of destiny, this for his unhappiness as well as for his happiness. He is in one sense, as Goethe said, the gods' favorite. This is how the obsessional secretly sees himself; Philo is no exception.

If by malice or by ruse, as we read in fairy tales, we approach this sanctuary, under cover of a psychoanalysis, what do we find there? Philo said it: "She loves him, he loves her, they are secretly united in a passionate look." Let us not respond by saying that we are seeing here a mere figment of a fertile imagination. If we tell him that, he will break down in tears in the most unexpected way, so despairing and violent that we will be as much if not more surprised than he is. Our astonishment will make us stop short, as though faced with one of these miracles that create the dialectic of fairy tales. Philo insists, "It's totally true, on both sides." And then again, "It's none of your business."

The obsessional is most often a being of facade and decoy; he is secretive and we all know it. He reveals himself, discusses, and reasons without appearing to concern himself with how the other will respond, provided, of course, that this other does respond. Hearing a response, he is indifferent, an egoist, a lifeless being. And yet, how many times does he repeat to whoever wants to listen that his nerves are exposed, that he is very sensitive and more intuitive than the dullards around him? This we can see clearly in his fathomless chagrin, the ridiculous, puerile, unexpected sobbing that arises whenever someone doubts the sacred reality of his sanctuary.

Here we touch on the dimension of sacrilege. Of course, we all think that we have largely overcome these fears of the abyss and have left them to a few primitives, to the superstitious, and to dreamers. And yet if our enlightenment had so fully freed us from the fright of being sacrilegious, why—I ask myself—are we so interested in the idea of "attachment to the mother"? We even have the idea of the "mother-child relationship," more comforting with its glow of innocence than the incest of the tragic context. Let us nevertheless pursue our investigation.

When Philo speaks, he never considers the possibility of "sleeping with his mother." Why? I do not think that it is because the terms are too crude—he has often used these terms and many more vulgar—but more simply because this expression, which we believe designates the fact of incest, does not correspond to his experience.

What he does talk about is "a communion, the happy effusion of a look." Certainly we could pause here before the delightful picture of the infant looking intently at his mother holding him on her lap. But this would not suffice and would move us away from Philo's words. He speaks about a "second look" and tells us clearly that it is his father's.

Having already experienced it, I can imagine what passes through our knowledgeable minds: father, Oedipus, Oedipus complex, jealousy, aggressiveness, better to hide, and so forth. But I prefer to follow Philo's words to us: "It is as though she had found in me the satisfaction that she did not find in my father." The question explicit in this second look is what a mother expected from a father, literally, "what she did not find in my father."

Here we can find the true knot of the situation: (1) *Mama was waiting for something*, (2) *something that Papa can give her*, (3) *which he does not give*. The problem concerns a mother's disappointed expectation, which led her, he tells us clearly, to a turn toward her son, "as if she had found in me the *satisfaction*." As Philo formulates it, there is a defect in his mother's satisfaction with her husband, and it is from this defect that the rest follows: communion by the look, complicity, secret intimacy.

It appears to us now that what is primordially at the center of the sanctuary is the *unsatisfied desire* of the mother, as it appears in her communication with the child.

Finally, a major factor that constitutes the veritable key to the obsessional position is the remark *"As if I had been necessary to her."* We know that there is nothing in the obsessional's world that escapes from the constraint of necessity. There is no pleasure that is not necessary, from "needed" vacations to a constraining schedule. "It is necessary that" or "I must" constitute the common denominators of the obsessional's activity. "My unique goal," Philo says, "is to be the only thing necessary to my mother." More classically, there is in Racine's *Bérénice* the role of Titus, which Philo quotes:

> *I made it a necessary pleasure*
> *To see her every day, to love her,*
> *to please her.*

We could continue to analyze the other phrases from Philo's discourse, and we would find there other subjects for reflection: for example, the problem of vocation, the doubt with which he questions the secret pact, the image of the serpent who bites its tail. I believe, however, that our very sketchy remarks are sufficient for the time being to let us begin to articulate the nodal complex of the obsessional.

At the center we find *the mother as desiring.* This should never be forgotten, especially if one is intrigued by the treasure hunt that the obsessional proposes. There are dozens of reasons why a mother may not be satisfied, and if this dissatisfaction is not sufficient to make an obsessional, it is still essential. To make a really good obsessional, it is necessary that the child be *marked,* as Philo often told us, by the indelible seal of the mother's unsatisfied *desire.*

This is the first ineffable experience in the history of the obsessional. This is the moment when the history of the rest of the world stops for him. He leaves our time to enter into the indefinite duration that marks the time of his microcosm. After all, this is easily conceivable: it is quite gratifying to be the object of one's mother's interest, to be the elected object of her love even before the wish has been articulated. The obsessional is satisfied beyond all common measure, even before he has desired and languished.

Freud affirms that this history of the obsessional, contrary to that of the hysteric, begins with a precocious sexual satisfaction difficult to recall. Within the context we have just described, where the child is the chosen love object of his mother, all physical contact takes on an erotic sense, especially washing up, not to mention the specifically perineal and anal concerns. I am not inventing:

the obsessional on the analyst's couch can imagine the most exquisite rape and sees himself delivered into the arms of an attentive, young, and maternal nurse.

Such is the nature of the precocious sexual experience that marks the obsessional and is constantly found in him. Analysis cannot fail to discover this behind the alibis of secondary experiences, the denegation, and the protestations of disgust or repulsion. When I say "discover" I do not mean it in the sense of a forgotten event. No—with this secret the tabernacle dissolves, and the moment of ineffable grace rejoins the living flux of forgotten memories.

It is not easy to get there: you have to be as quick as you are tenacious, when an opening presents itself. In the session we have quoted, the first words show a fear and an anger that are not feigned: "Shit! As though that were any of your business!" Do not believe that these words are there by pure coincidence. What is literally in question is a look. Besides, the emergence of this familiar theme marks the beginning of most of our interviews. First, Philo feels that my look is open and reassuring, and this gives him the sense of being indebted to me. Second, he responds with a fixed and fleeting facial expression, of the kind he thinks an analyst should have. My greeting remains for him a question and an assurance but also a threat. His way of representing this situation is shown by a recurrent dream that he also daydreams about: "Someone approaches me, fixing me with his look. It's a man. Again and again I force myself to push him away, but he continues approaching. I begin to hit him repeatedly in the face; the more I hit him, the more he closes in on me, like a punching bag moved by a spring. He seems to be insensitive and he has a sarcastic smile. Anxiety invades me. . . ." At that moment he wakes, trembling.

Is this the scornful look of his older brother fixed on the good little boy, or better yet, the indefinable look of his father passing through a pleasant exterior and penetrating him as something cold and unpitying? I do not know; these are no doubt the two models of the look of an Other whom he cannot attain.

Without having made any effort to resolve things, I have only reported what Philo told me.

We will now attempt to account for this analytical fragment theoretically.

I am not sufficiently naive to pretend that this extract from a session contains in itself the entire theory of the obsessional's desire. I do believe that this example can clarify some matters for us. Also, I am not audacious enough to believe that my own clinical experience alone is the base for the theoretical articulation I am proposing. I remain convinced that clinical experience can be fertile only to the extent that it tests a working hypothesis.

Before continuing I will outline briefly the concept of Oedipal development on which I found my work. Not that this is very different from the one we all know, but certain nuances and precisions articulated by J. Lacan have opened the Oedipal schema to a larger and stricter clinical application.

The Oedipal complex, we may say, gives an account of the evolution that, little by little, *substitutes for the mother, taken as the central and primordial character, the father, as principal and ultimate reference*. Having thus defined the general movement of this evolution, we will distinguish three phases.

At first, the mother as desiring is the central character. The subject identifies with the *object* of the mother's *desire*. Being unable to grasp the complexity of such a desire, the child seems to retain a simplistic schema: "To please mother, it is necessary and sufficient, whether boy or girl, *to be the phallus*." I recall in passing that the phallus is not reduced to the physical aspect of a signified reality, but that it already has for the child, as it does for the mother, a signifying and symbolic value. Such is the situation at first: "To please mother, it is necessary and sufficient to be the phallus."

The next step is the most important and the most complex. It is at this stage that most of the accidents that generate neurosis occur. We will summarize it in its normal evolution. The subject rather quickly has the sense that the mother is not satisfied with the first solution, and he detaches himself from his identification (with the phallus), which appears to him to be unsatisfying. The dissatisfaction and persistence of the mother's desire point him toward *something else*. What is this *something else (otherness)*? This is the crucial enigma that the mother's desire poses for the child. Through it a reference or a symbol that has captured the mother's desire appears in the child's life, even before its nature is specified. In this way a *third person* presents himself to experience. Is this to say that this *third person* appears especially as a person? No. The most scrupulous analysis shows that this third person, this father, appears especially *as a being to whom one refers* (to honor or to scorn) and to whom one refers as to a law. In everyday practice, we hear "Papa said . . ." or "I am going to tell Papa," words that had been spoken by a mother having difficulty with authority. Now, this father, before being depriving or castrating or what have you, appears to the child as a reference and even as the mother's master. If it happens that the symbolic phallus, *signifier of desire*, is going to function in the mother's reference to her man, in the eyes of her child and in his imagination, then the father must appear as depriving and as castrating in regard to the mother and not to the child himself.

This is what we have to grasp in order to be at ease in relation to the castration complex. In this second stage of the Oedipus complex, the child should gain access to the father's law, defined as the place of the *symbolic* phallus, through the mediation of the mother's desire. The mother's desire appears to take this phallus away and to keep it. The father is revealed *as refusal and as reference*. This is also the moment when the object of desire appears in its complexity as an object submitted to the law of the other. J. Lacan says that this stage reveals "the relation of the mother to the father's word."

The third stage is simpler. The father is not only the bearer of the law; he also possesses a *real* penis. In a word, the father is the one who has the phallus and not the one who *is* it. For this stage to take place, it is assuredly necessary that the father be neither too impotent nor too neurotic. In this third stage the father is discovered to be the real possessor, and not merely the symbolic place, of a penis.

The evolution is completed with the formation of a new identification and the emergence of the ego ideal. For the boy as well as for the girl, this is the moment where one renounces all vestiges of the first identification with the "phallus that pleases Mama." The child becomes like a big person, either the one who has the phallus or else the one who does not and who thus will await it from a man.

Thus the father, as the place of the phallus, replaces the mother as the principal and normative subject in the evolution. The mother, no longer the central character she was, takes on the role of mediator. The child's question is not "to be or not to be" the phallus, but rather to have it or not to have it.

What was the fate of Philo during these stages, and how did he become the person we have come to know?

There is no doubt that he retains his deepest and dearest memories from the first stage; it is as though he is still living there. If he does not say, "To please my mother it is necessary and sufficient that I be the phallus," he is not very far off when he says, "My unique goal is to be the only thing necessary to my mother." All that matters is to please her, and that is how he finds his own pleasure.

Without even looking at his dreams for evidence of his total identification with the phallus, we listen as he describes himself reacting in certain situations by blushing in a kind of diffuse and warm congestion that makes him tighten and become totally stiff. This reaction, this way of being whole, like a monolith, is not limited to muscular activity. I do not have the time to go into everything in Philo's being that demonstrates the satisfaction inherent in this primal phase of identification with the object of his mother's desire; that would make a very long list.

Certainly this patient is nostalgic for this first stage, and his nostalgia maintains him in a dream that he cannot get rid of. It is no less certain that he has not attained the third stage where, released from this massive identification, he would possess a phallus. In a word, he does not feel himself to be a man. At thirty he is still a little boy, submissive, asking for things politely, always excusing himself, feeling sorry for his outbursts. He does not feel any resemblance between himself and those men who have women: he isn't there yet, and he almost hears a voice telling him, "when you are grown up." Thus he revolts, protests, and argues his superiority, his intelligence, but nothing is done; he feels good; he is not yet "grown up," and he feels himself to be neither the possessor nor the master of his sex.

What happened, then, during the second stage, when he ought to have been opened to desire and the law through his mother's mediation? It seems almost too obvious to need saying: instead of encountering dissatisfaction, the natural correlate of a primal identification with the phallus, instead of a dissatisfaction that could drive him to look at the relation between his mother and the enigma of the father, Philo encountered his mother's satisfaction.

Why? Very simply because his mother shifted her desire over to him, with all the unconscious and disturbing tenderness of a woman neurotically unsatisfied. It is hardly necessary to provide the details concerning the moral rigor of the father, his charm, his goodness, and his charity, all of which muffle a virility that is exercised parsimoniously and with regret because it is considered to be sinful. Philo summarized with these words: "It is as though she had found in me the satisfaction that she did not find in my father."

Thus I recall our hero's way of describing and evoking the privileged experience that fulfilled him beyond all measure and for which he retains the most profound nostalgia. Since then he has lived as though he were in a prison and as though he loved the prison. His mother, who ought to have been the mediator and have shown him the way, imposed herself on him as the goal and object. The circle was closed in an exquisite effusion just when the path of desire was beginning to open.

Within the perfect sphere inscribed by the maternal look, this path is unendingly sterile and exhausting. Everything will now have to pass through this protecting veil. Philo hears his father's word as an echo, and he grasps his father's look only in a photo.

We will find Philo's desire imprisoned in this small enchanted world.

We have to recall here the specificity of desire in relation to need and demand. If we say that the attainment of an object and the experience of satisfaction with it are proper to need and that demand aims at the defective being of the Other, then desire is proper to the imaginary and is conceived as the significant mediation of a fundamental antinomy.

Philo, like any other child, had mixed relations with his mother, in terms of his needs—for he is far from being autonomous at this point—as well as of his demands. The recognition of being is the fruit of a long patience. While Philo, like his counterparts, lived in this *double expectation,* he entered into the *imaginary field of the mediating, questioning, exacting desire* of his mother. She, trapped in the net of her child's desire, was solicited again, in secret, and felt the emergence of her own desire and her particular dissatisfaction.

These are the general conditions, easily recognizable, through which the developmental short-circuit that founds obsessional neurosis comes to pass. The mother answers her son's hope with a manifestation of her own desire. The burgeoning desire of the child, just barely emerging from the exactions of need or the awaiting of the demands, finds itself all at once disengaged, confirmed, and better yet, satisfied.

The obsessional's desire, precociously awakened and promptly satisfied, will bear, more than all other desire, the stigma of its prematuration. It will retain above all else the character of the elementary exactions of need. It will also bear the indelible mark of the dissatisfaction inherent in any demand.

So much for general terms; let us return to Philo's analysis. Like many other obsessionals he imagined all kinds of stories when he was young; his dream life and his desire were nourished either by events in his experience or by the still obscure laws of the world of "grown-ups." A hero's exploits or a humiliated captive's suffering excited more than just his imagination. In his games he exhibited on the one hand all sorts of prowess, and on the other he liked to be stepped on by his young friends, vaguely conscious of surpassing the limits of innocence that are proper to children.

Thus he spoke to me one day of an edifying tale about which I had, in my floating attention, some difficulty in figuring out whether it came from some commonplace picture book or from the first book he read. It was the history of Gonzago-who-died-a-martyr-among-the-barbarians. I will not tell more of this marvelous and terrifying story, because I understood quickly that the happy Gonzago was a venerated ancestor who had really lived, suffered, and died some six score years ago.

Since he had spoken very little about this, I asked him. Responding, he recognized that Gonzago was secretly his hero. When he was five he thought naively that he would have to travel by foot to these faraway countries where barbarians live and where one can be martyred. He thus forced himself into long walks to prepare for this trip. At first the long walks astonished the family, but later, after the secret was revealed, everyone was rather amused.

Philo, the chosen, did he not have a calling?

Let us look at the sources of this childhood dream. Philo's father was an honest man, wise and reasonable when need be, but he was also the ancestor and devotee of this hero. Remembering his hero, this man named his last son Gonzago. Was he also in his youth attracted by the risk of adventures in faraway lands? Several indications permit us to believe this. In any case, he became a husband and a father who followed above all else the cult of virtue.

This was what Philo's mother loved in him. Through her husband she knew and venerated the descendant of the martyr. To the very estimable and honest "contingency" that her husband was for her, she added the dream of a Gonzago of light and death. From this conjuncture children were born. The parents accepted this virtuously, and each of the children compensated in his or her own way for this hybrid paternity.

Thus little Philo, who was the most gifted of the children, knew through the myths of the tribe and through family albums how to recognize the true object of the passion of such a reasonable and modest mother. His instinct did not deceive him. And this mother could recognize in her little Philo the true son of her desire. The secret complicity is to be found there.

Through his beloved mother, Philo had always sought happiness if not pleasure. He was, first, her "thing"; he was there to please her, "everything a mother could want." We will say abstractly that this is the phallus, or more concretely, something that should be found on the father's side. But he discovered soon, with the intuitive certainty of a child, the dream that his mother employed to make her law and to nourish her life: that of the martyred hero.

And then, to please mama by trying to find the *paternal reference*, Philo made the martyr his imaginary companion. His burgeoning desire found an immediate profit in the occasion. He found it even more so in living *the same dream* as his mother. United in this same dream, they soon became the true spouses of this honest family: they shared the same ideal; their desires, like their dreams, were the same. Philo, borne on by a blessing, entered into the great fantasy that is the life of the obsessional: model child and incestuous son, *he realized his desire in sharing his mother's*—both of them were satisfied.

It remains for us to question the fate of the *demand* for Philo. Sharing the dream, the desire and, in a way, the bed of his mother, was he for all that *recognized* as a subject in the eyes of others? Certainly not; at the most he was recognized in the eyes of his mother, so blind when it came to other things!

He was certainly a satisfied child, relatively happy, although profoundly anxious. The recognition accorded by a blind mother could not suffice. Little by little he began to take notice. The esteem of teachers for the good pupil that he was long deceived him, and he wished to be always a good pupil. But the time came when this situation was difficult to maintain: the teachers could not share in the desire of Philo and his mother, and they left him to make his way, to make a choice.

Philo asks questions and seeks at any price to be recognized and guided. Hardly does he find a counselor—and he finds a lot of them because he tries to make everyone into one—than he scornfully reproaches the counselor's ignorance of his fantasy. But if, on the contrary, the perspicacious counselor tells him to get out on his own, he becomes disquieted. He is finally satisfied if he succeeds in seducing the counselor, for he knows very well the power of his charm.

Here we should remember (to understand something of this inexhaustible ploy that we see in other Philos) that in dreaming of Gonzago, *Philo did not expect that his mother would dream with him,* but on the contrary, that she would reveal to him what she had *found that was better than this dream.*

The one who should have recognized Philo—to help him to disengage himself from the first traps of his desire, to make of him, after all, a little man—was his father (the living martyr). His mother, however, did not make this very easy; rather, she opposed it with much well-intentioned zeal! Instead of this recourse, this truly vital opening, the response Philo knew was only the luster of his mother's desire. This desire is a dream in which to commune in the sterile satisfaction of a shared wish.

So much so that since this first privileged experience, he can no longer pretend to be recognized without evoking the pleasure that followed the first recourse. He can no longer demand without having desire emerge. No aspect of the demand escapes the fantasmatic exuberance of the most violent desire, the one that was prematurely fulfilled.

Thus we can say that for Philo, *the demand,* the fundamental movement of a being toward recognition, *is lived exclusively by him in a mode proper to desire.* It follows naturally that desire—become the fantasmatic substitute for the quest after being—is condemned by this confusion to be eternally inaccessible. Finally, desire thus confounded is strongly marked by the natural component of need, and it is manifested in the obsessional with the character of necessity, impatience, and insistence, all of them bearing the character of need.

Here we find the ambiguity of the obsessional's desire; captive of the existential questioning that is below the surface, his desire is impotent to recover its autonomy and its value as mediator between need and demand; sterile, it proliferates in the great dream that is his life. It is manifested in the wild search for an other who *can recognize him and at the same time free his desire.* This we perceive through his passions and his symptoms. Philo doubts, fails passionately; this surprises us, it draws attention and makes the one who is trapped in the interest he wants to evoke ask himself questions; it is there that pleasure and hope are hidden. It would seem that he has no other way to break his enchanted sphere, the glass ball of his dream, than to reveal himself constantly: to show himself (buttocks or sexual organ) as a doubter, an unfortunate, a subtle dialectician, a paradoxical failure, in the secret hope that finally an *other,* man or god, but a true one, will manifest himself, will intervene to recognize, wake him from his dream, render him free to desire, even if this is in punishing him.

But, if it is true that hope exists, the wish that says so cannot be entirely sincere. Philo is too cunning. He already knows that there is a perfect Master, uncontested, the one and only, Death, and yet, even though he knows that in recognizing him he will be saved, he wavers on that too, and to escape, *he plays dead,* offering himself hypocritically even before having lived: "Why would you take me," he says to him in his dream, "when I am already dead?"

This is not all. To live solely on desire is not unthinkable, on the contrary; it is simply a little trying. Philo sometimes wants, like all these happy funnymen, and he wants to bring forth, to live and to exhaust the adventure of a nice desire, certain then to find another, even more interesting. But this is out of the question. Living such an adventure presupposes above all the possibility of approaching—however weakly—another warm and living being.

And this is precisely what the world of the obsessional cannot sustain. Philo and his mother, mythically united in Gonzago, have given birth to a people of docile shadows, of couples endlessly repeated. But they have separated themselves (this is the very reason for their union) from every other subject, from all the other beings of desire. Philo has never left the orbit of his mother's desire; it has not crossed his mind that his father or any other subject can live with desire, can nourish dreams different from his.

But there is no desire that can sustain itself in the isolation of a solitary daydream. Thus the masochist feeds his passion with the dream of what his sadistic partner will do to him, even if he is disappointed. More simply, someone who wants a woman will wish to be the object of her dreams; if the two dreams only rarely coincide, they are no less necessary to the life of the desire. At a time when men were gallant, passionate courting was conceivable only where the lover was assured that the object of his flame was playing the role of a frightfully reticent woman. Do we imagine today gallantly courting a liberated woman?

This is the way we should understand the formula that *the other is necessary to sustain desire.* Philo, on the other hand, is captive of his unique passion and is *fundamentally ignorant of the other as desiring.* And yet, in order for his own desire to live, the other is necessary. In this impasse he will make use of anything at all to create a *fancied other, the illusory support of a sterile desire. To give to the*

*inanimate object the appearance of life, to make it live and die, to care for it, then
to destroy it, such is the derisory game* to which Philo is reduced. *The obsessional's object is invested with this essential function of otherness.*

Without an industrious activity to sustain it, the dream may well evaporate,
and Death then threatens to bear witness to the truth. *In order to avoid this ruin,
the obsessional ceaselessly takes up the exhausting work of reducing the living to
nothing and of giving to others the impression of an ephemeral life.*

This impossible quest for the other remains the most notable characteristic of
the obsessional's desire.

Thus the circle is closed: the desire that was prematurely satisfied is substituted for the demand; it remains isolated in a solitary daydream peopled with
shadows, calling ceaselessly to the other, excluded yet necessary.

This is how Philo's desire manifests itself in the analysis.

We will have to conclude now.

Someone may ask, what advantages are there in formulating these things as
you have done? I answer that for me there are two advantages, one theoretical,
the other practical.

Theoretically, there is great value in taking up the problems of libido and
desire in a specifically psychoanalytic way.

From the perspective of research, the analysis of such a case permits us to
specify and to confirm the fundamental problems of obsessional neurosis. The
precocious "disintrication" of the drives in the obsessional's history is confirmed
and illustrated by the premature libidinal satisfaction that blocks the circuit of the
demand, where this circuit is the only rational support for that which comes from
the death drive. Doubtless if we followed this path, we would be able to articulate
the enigma of the obsessional's time, a time captivated by desire. The study of the
obsessional's desire has in passing shed light on the question of death.

In a more immediate theoretical perspective, the reference to and progressive elucidation of the fundamental concepts of desire and libido ought to permit
us to situate better some notions in current usage: whether it is a question of
topographical references, to specify the *constitutive relations of the ego and
desire,* or whether it is a question of the dynamic references in the properly
libidinal dimension of *transference.*

From the point of view of practice, and I suppose that this is what interests
us most immediately, the formulation of our central theoretical questions in
terms of desire can be very useful.

This situates us firmly on the level of neurosis and renders us attentive to the
mixed field of desire and demand that constitutes the obsessional's transference.
An appeal to "desire" is better than a reference to the theory of transference or to
the structure of the ego, since these latter are abstract and will make us have

recourse to book knowledge. Desire is there, living, disquieting or seductive, present in the tension of the therapeutic exchange; it is the weave of discourse, the substance of fantasy and dream, the essence of transference.

In concerning ourselves with desire, we are on the level of a specifically therapeutic problematic.

Now—as is well known—if every neurotic patient poses a question of his therapist, if he addresses him fundamentally with an implicit demand for recognition, the obsessional does it in his own way. His demand is particularly difficult to resolve because it is intentionally confused. Our analysis gives the therapist the means to orient himself in the field of this demand for help. He ought to be attentive to the fact that for the obsessional there is no demand that is not marked with *the seal of desire*. In vulgar parlance—but also literally—wanting to be recognized has become for him wanting to be screwed. And he invests everything in his effort to make it happen.

For the therapist to avoid being duped, is it sufficient never to respond or to respond obliquely, as the experienced psychiatrist and psychoanalyst do instinctively? If this attitude is essential, I do not believe it to be sufficient.

The psychoanalyst must also bear witness [to desire] in the guise of a response. He must be the one who greets the demand serenely and who can support this appeal to being without at the same time compulsively annulling it by an imperative reduction to some secondary reason. Finally, he must use his talent for discrimination and know how to introduce a cleavage between demand and desire, between the world of the law and that of the dream. For this he must have a sharpened instrument that is sturdy and responsive in following the contour of the joints that tradition speaks of, prosaically, evoking the art of meat cutting.

Around the *phallic symbol, the signifier of desire, the central reference and mediator in the practice of our art,* we must distinguish without fail the *real phallus* of Philo's father from the *imaginary phallus* of Gonzago, to distinguish the *negativity* of the absence of the martyred hero from the *negation* of the paternal presence, to distinguish *being it* from *having it,* all the while being cognizant of their linkage, not confounding the demand for recognition with the desire to sleep with someone.

This distinction is essential—and not only that, of course—if we are to avoid believing that it is necessary to open the doors of the prison where the unhappy Philo is crouched. If we believed in the image of the prison, we would enter into the game of his desire and his dream. Knowing how to discriminate helps us, on the contrary, never to forget that this *glass shell* is only an oneiric egg.

8 On Obsessional Neurosis

BY CHARLES MELMAN

With obsessional neurosis we are first confronted by a problem of method. If a clinical study had to present a clinical picture, that of obsessional neurosis would pose a singular difficulty, because it presents a confused collection of traits each of which when taken alone is nevertheless perfectly clear. This picture has in common with others the fact that the most minute dividing and subdividing of its space—in the most obsessional fashion—would not permit us to discover the cause of the neurosis. Even if we stopped to ponder the elements that suggest an inexhaustible quest for a return or an impossible desire to see something again, we would still not have the cause.

In other words, we will not allow ourselves to be fascinated by the picture, and thus we have only one recourse—to refer to structure, that is, to the structure of language. We will put this course of action to the test here, and ourselves with it.

If we set the picture aside and take hold of the neurosis as we would a ball of string, our first test is to choose the strand that will guide us in the unraveling. For that purpose, we will make use of the question that the Rat Man poses at the beginning of his observations, when he tells of the genesis of his obsession, of his infantile neurosis. And this question can be articulated as follows: what could he have seen one special evening under his governess's skirt for him to refer to that date as the origin of his obsessive compulsion to see the feminine sex? Freud will say that this compulsion and two other characteristics assure the signature, the constitution of the neurosis. These are: the fear that something horrible will happen—for example, that his father will die—and his delusional impression that his parents know his thoughts. This latter is connected to an eminently clinical note—psychoanalytically clinical, at least—that his parents knew his thoughts, as though he had spoken them out loud, but without having heard them himself.

Charles Melman is a member of the governing board of the Ecole Freudienne de Paris and is in charge of education at the Ecole. He is also co-chairman of the Department of Psychoanalysis at the University of Paris VIII. A psychiatrist, he practices psychoanalysis in Paris. This article was first published as "A propos de la névrose obsessionnelle," in *Lettres de l'Ecole Freudienne* 16 (November 1975), pp. 346–57.

The enigma does not merely concern the way in which these three traits are associated with each other. Even more it concerns the seeing of the feminine sex. Before he became obsessed with the idea of seeing this sex again, he had seen as much and more: according to family custom, children of both sexes and their governess all took their baths together, and there was no reason to stop this domestic ritual.

Let us propose, then, that what he saw on this fateful evening when he sneaked a look under Miss Robert's skirt was, in a lightning instant, the lack of the object as such, the lack itself, its want. It is perhaps disturbing that this experience does have consequences. From it the young boy gains a concept of the lack or want of an object, and this, the lack, is transformed into an object that designates the lack as such: this is to say that the lack is transformed into a signifier. The patient will now be tormented by the task of refinding it, and this torment will increase each time he approaches the discovery that what he saw clearly for an instant is now dead or destroyed or has disappeared forever. The feeling of an immanent irremediable catastrophe represented by the death of his father appears to be the just perception of the disaster that occurs in structure when the real is found to be obscured or blocked by the signifier. The obsessional's banal fear of having committed some ultimate crime, unbeknown to himself or while asleep, can be related to this effect of the signifier. We will hardly be surprised when we later discover that the obsessional is convinced of the omnipotence of his thoughts.

Another effect of this adventure is that a signifier thus understood is transformed into a sign, a sign of the missing object. That this missing object is found to be marked, tattooed, or imprinted with a sign has a decisive bearing on the construction of the obsessional fantasy. But I think that here we ought to be a little more precise. It is clear that no surface can receive such a tattooing; therefore nothing other than the letter itself will be embodied or incorporated through the fantasy.

From then on, desire will be sustained in relation to an object that can only be maintained when placed at a distance from the subject. And in addition, there is a mortal risk for the subject when the fantasy concerns the raising of a simple veil rather than a screen. When the veil is raised, there is a jouissance in horror, a jouissance in the committing of a crime. But also, whether or not it is fantasized as a veil, the object will come to make itself known in another way, strongly and insistently, without the subject's hearing a thing through either ear.

We propose to enter into what will be—why not?—a phenomenology of obsessions. This aspect of the neurosis has not aroused any particular interest, and I will not attempt to explain this lack. The only thing I will remark is that the

English word "obsession" is not a very good translation of the German term *Zwang*. Where "obsession" means "to lay siege to," *zwängen* means "to penetrate by force into the interior of." The difference is not irrelevant.

Back to our phenomenology of obsessions. The first characteristic, which does not appear to me to be entirely banal, is this: for a long time the patient does not consider his obsession to be a symptom. For years it was easily tolerated, like a familiar and natural object with which the patient was able to accommodate himself. Often enough he comes to a consultation because the obsession has imposed limitations on his activities or because his friends have become concerned or worried. Otherwise it does not seem to be experienced by him as a symptom.

The second characteristic is that the patient does not question the origin of an obsessive idea that comes to him, nor does he suppose that a subject exists who is the support of this idea. Even if it is addressed to him in the form of an imperative "thou," there is no speculation about the nature of the "I" who is supposed to be sending this idea.

The third characteristic is that he tells us that he becomes cognizant of the obsession as of an idea. There is nothing in it that touches the senses or that resembles a hallucinatory phenomenon. Here again, it is not easy to differentiate, because we know that there are authentic hallucinations that classical clinical studies have called aperceptive, which do not touch the senses and which the affected patient can distinguish perfectly from those that do.

In any case we can say that this obsessive idea is imposed on the subject as an idea, and we can add that ideas do not come to us very frequently or very easily. In general, I would say that most of the time we do not have ideas. We do have them when we take pen in hand and try to write. Then something akin to the idea is produced.

It would be necessary, if I were to pursue this narrow path, to conceive of something like a typography in the unconscious, working unbeknown to the subject, producing his ideas. We may note one elementary point here without risk, that the unity of these ideational phenomena is assuredly the letter. In the obsessional we see that the unconscious writes its messages letter by letter, exactly as a typographer would. At the least, this is troubling, but it permits us to characterize the obsessional idea by saying that it does not impose itself on the subject as a spoken word. If it did, there would be a time for its enunciation, a punctuation, which would generate ambiguity. On the contrary, the obsessional idea imposes itself like a statement [*énoncé*], being grasped all at once; its sense is impeccably clear, definite, whole. It is on the order of what is "said" rather than of the "saying."

Another characteristic is that this "said" always bears the sign of the imperative. Of course, it may well appear to be enigmatic. For the moment we will not address the question of the functioning of the signifier as master-signifier.

If we had to keep to the sense of this obsession, we could easily schematize it by saying that it is always—or almost always—the manifestation of something that functions simultaneously as a prohibition and a command. A prohibition is expressed as a "don't" applied to just about anything. We know that in certain cases this can extend to "don't get up," "don't eat," and so forth.

The command manifests itself as ferociously as the prohibition. It imposes on the subject, as our patients tell us, often the most cruel and obscene acts, and this despite the fact that the subject rebels. The least we can say is that the subject is split in relation to his obsessional ideas.

Presenting things in terms of the contradiction between a ferocious prohibition and a no less ferocious command permits us to refer to something we know only too well. This is the fact that desire and its prohibition originate with the same movement, which we call castration. The ferociousness and the excess with which the imperative of desire is exercised are particular to the obsessional. Nothing seems to control it, and nothing seems to say no to it.

It happens in some cases that these obsessions finish by becoming senseless. Concerning this loss of sense, there is an interesting compulsion in the case of the Rat Man that Freud did well to name a *Verstehzwang*, a compulsion to understand. There came a time when the patient could no longer understand anything people were saying to him, and he was constantly asking them to repeat themselves: "What are you telling me, what are you saying?" Evidently this was very annoying to the people around him, understandably so.

But this compulsion ought to put us on the right track for grasping the obsessional's relation with sense. If we were to ask ourselves, "What did he hear that he did not understand?" we would say that he heard music and that it did not make any sense. In certain cases the patient will eventually hear a pure play of letters. One of these in the case of the Rat Man is particularly remarkable. The patient's unconscious had succeeded in forging the neologism "Glejisamen," in which he coupled the holiness of the woman Gisela, whom he called his lady, with his semen, in German *Samen*. And as we know, this enabled him to screw her all the same. This is certainly a good example of psychic equilibrium.

Freud does not hesitate to give a brilliant interpretation of this Glejisamen. We note, however, that this word seems to contain vowels that serve only to permit the word to be pronounced. Even in Freud's analysis of the neologism, there is a hesitation concerning the way the word is written, and then there are vowels that don't make sense.

After Freud has brilliantly interpreted this Glejisamen, the patient returns and says, "I had a terrific dream; there was a map on which I was able to read *WLK*." Let us imagine that at this moment he is waiting for Freud to interpret *WLK*. Freud does not hesitate to do so. His interpretation is mistaken, however, because he has taken these letters as standing for *Wielks*, a Polish name that he translates as meaning "grand," I think, or "old." It appears that this is not the word's meaning, but that is not very important. What is more interesting in *WLK* is the fact that it is unpronounceable. It is a pure play of letters, a pure play of the symbolic, without any voice, without any link to the imaginary.

In this attempt to write a phenomenology of the obsessional idea, I am also bothered that no matter what sense the idea has or can take on, it seems always to conserve the same form, and this form, even when it prohibits all sense, can be noted as follows:

First, propositions are placed one after the other and are linked by the copula of conjunction ("and"). We can observe this most particularly in the obsessive ritual.

Second, another particularly common predicate is that of disjunction, the "either . . . or." This is also designated by the suggestive name "the excluded third" or "the excluded middle." I can marry either this one or that one, but if I marry this one, I lose that one. Either . . . or. And I must limit myself to the two terms of the "either . . . or," thus excluding any third party.

Third, a predicate connected with disjunction is that of implication. In the Rat Man we find it everywhere, and Freud analyzed it particularly well. His theory states that obsessional ideas are presented in the hypothetical mode. The obsessional hears: "If you do this, then that will happen."

The last of these logical signs is evidently that of negation, and we know that it can go as far as to be the negation of the negation of the negation. With this the obsessional may end up in a slightly confused state, especially since he does not always keep a count of the negations.

In proposing this presentation of the obsessional idea, we are borrowing, as you no doubt noticed, something that has been isolated in another field as propositional logic. Propositional logic is a closed system containing essentially two elements and two values; the elements are habitually called p and q, and the values, true and false.

If, as we have said, in obsessional neurosis the sign has become the sign of a lack or want, we can imagine that we will be faced with something presenting itself as a system with two elements and two values based on the exclusion of a third.

This much said, does such a proposal have any interest? Is it a coincidence, what is specifically called an analogy, or can it significantly clarify the mechanism of the obsessional idea?

If we apply the rules of this propositional logic, we note the following: at the level of conjunction, we find something that may be useful, namely, the fact that a proposition is true only if each of its elements is itself true.

Certainly we know that the obsessional may be constrained to go back over something he has written to verify that he has not made a mistake about one of the elements. For him any one mistake can destroy everything.

This necessity felt by the obsessional to backtrack, to check and double-check his work, has been noted in the literature. But when we ask why this is so, the analytic authors can do no better than to answer that this is because "shit comes out the back." Evidently, this is not very satisfactory, any more than it would be to say that because we have lateral ears, we are always slightly tilted to the side.

In any case, we see the usefulness of our reference in terms of conjunction.

With disjunction we are interested in a way of functioning in terms of the principle of the excluded middle or excluded third. In this case the obsessional cannot decide between one or another opposing choices. Thus he hesitates and vacillates. The Rat Man's solution suggests that for him the third is not really excluded. After all, as he says, because he is undecided, he will let God decide for him, and he waits for a sign that will come to him and make him decide one way or the other.

As for implication, the possibilities are even more rich, because implication, besides being a transformation of disjunction, has the property that a proposition is true if its second term is true and that in this case it does not matter whether the first is true or false. It is slightly troubling to notice that for the obsessional this is exactly how matters stand. In the case of the Rat Man, there is the command of the Cruel Captain: Pay back the money to Lieutenant A. This presents itself as an obsessive idea: If you don't pay back the money, something will happen to your father and the lady. And then another idea: If you do pay back the money, something will happen to your father and the lady. It seems to me that this contradiction is particularly striking.

Evidently it is very troubling to see in the unconscious a pure play of writings. But here we are talking about this kind of logic. It is troubling that all the possibilities are conditioned only by the way they are written.

If we go back to the case of the Rat Man, we see that the obsession retains the sense of a propitiary act, an act that would commemorate an event resembling an original crime or disaster. The act reminds the patient ceaselessly of his debt in regard to being.

The annoying consequence of looking at things in this way is that some aspect of the crime that contracted the debt renders the debt unpayable, regardless of detours and intermediaries, regardless of the number of monthly payments. No absolution is possible. It seems that the obsessional does not know if the other essential to his equilibrium is characterized by a fullness that would testify to the effectiveness of his integrity or, on the contrary, by a lack that is supposed to exist and is then taken to be no longer supportable in reality, except as a deprivation essential to the survival of the other. The two contradictory imperatives—If you do or if you don't pay back the money to Lieutenant A, something will happen to your father and the lady—seem to owe their violent and turbulent effect to the fact of their relation to the Cruel Captain. This fact encounters in Freud's patient (who has come into the army prepared to pay his debt with his blood) a knowledge that reimbursing Lieutenant A is impossible because it was not Lieutenant A who paid the debt. As the entire story points out, the patient knew it from the beginning.

Assuredly the debt has not been paid for him, and that is why the Rat Man, like a good neurotic, has his future behind him. I am tempted to say that it is here that the figure of his father emerges. This father is explicitly present in the history and is always a good guy for having been able to sell out his obligations cleverly, in regard to his own father and a religion that he camouflages and abjures as well as in regard to a marriage that he contracted to get hold of his wife's dowry (called in German *Mitgift*, which also means "poison included") and in regard to his children, whom he considers to be deficits and charges and to whom he feels that he owes nothing. On top of that he is a bad gambler, avid for the number that will break the bank on a small wager, cheating and stealing when fate goes against him.

Thus the origin of the infantile neurosis, the scene that introduced our report and posed the question of what the patient could have seen under his governess's skirt, is not to be conceived as the fortuitous product of bad guidance nor as an unfortunate accident occurring because the senses were overheated one evening, but rather as an effect of structure inscribed for him, for this neurotic—as we see in every case—well before his birth.

If the other is maintained in a state of completeness by the inheritance money that the patient lets his mother manage, this other is also maintained by a real deprivation. In this case the Rat Man imposes a deprivation upon himself in regard to the lady who is the object and support of his only love. In another context deprivation will be imposed on him by destiny when his father dies. It is not so much that the lady and the dead father come to occupy the same place, but rather that the patient behaves toward the lady with all the veneration one ought to have for the dead, and at the same time he celebrates his dead father as though he were alive. Nothing here is delusional; this is just the way his world is organized.

The impossibility of reimbursing a debt will find a solution that is obsessional in its style. In place of the alternative—to pay or not to pay, prodigality or avarice, enema or anal retention—something of accountancy and law will be established. Thanks to his neurosis, the Rat Man learned to count. In response to an obsessional idea that comes to him when he is with his girl friend ("for every coitus, a rat for the lady"), Freud makes this remark in his journal: "*Dies zeigt dass eine Ratte etwas Zählbares ist.*" ("This shows that a rat is something countable.") The meaning must have caused some problems for the translators of the *Standard Edition*, where the word *Zählbares* was rendered as though there were no umlaut on the *a*, which made it mean "payable."

I would say off the top of my head, without having read too many authors, that what we see here is the genesis of One, of a unity whose counting begins with the lost object. From this moment on, the Rat Man behaves according to the most strict legality and respect in regard to the other. We will call this "one for me, one for you."

It happens that in his dreams we can interpret in a similar way the obscene fantasy of an object hanging from his anus, with which he copulated with a girl lying on her back.

When the Rat Man prepares for his exams, he is controlled by this imperative, so frequent in the obsessional, not to study everything and to take the exams before he is ready. We can see there, among other things, what it is to renounce the possession of the other's knowledge, which Lacan has called S_2. The patient's own defect functions as a witness to and guarantor of the completeness of the other.

This is why we find that the obsessional wants to collect all knowledge. His idea is that it is all valuable, since it all serves the same function. But, after doing the work that he feels he must effectuate for the post mortem jouissance of his father, when the hour that marks this death comes, there is a masturbatory celebration of the right he has gained to phallic jouissance, and this jouissance, as we know, is sustained by a renouncing of the lady who tolerates his love.

If something prevents him from having any sexual relations, this something will assuredly function in the mode of the imperative.

The distancing permits the Rat Man during his analysis to enjoy a more proximate object, seamstresses. In German "seamstress" is written *Näherin*, which we can translate, by barely forcing the phonetics (forcing the phonetics would read the word without the umlaut), as someone who, to exercise his profession, has to be close by, in French, *proxénète*, in English, "a pimp."

During his analysis the Rat Man gets better, and as Freud notes, he even becomes more and more joyous. The more Freud insists on interpreting his neurosis according to the Oedipus myth, giving a sense to the irritating senselessness of the obsessions, the more the Rat Man insists that for him none of that is true, that his father was a good friend and that in his opinion everything was played out with his mother. And the more Freud sticks to his guns, forcing his interpretations of the obsessions to make them fit his theory, doing what he describes as "filling in the blanks of the ellipses," the more the patient is joyous. Freud says that the obsession must be interpreted, that it is produced in the same way as the dream and the joke, and that finally its most essential rhetorical play is the ellipsis. In any case Freud twists this ellipsis to agree with his Oedipal interpretation. And the more he does so, the more the Rat Man says that that poses some questions for him, that he asks himself now, and so on, . . . and at the same time he is getting better and he is joyous.

We will note in conclusion that this amelioration seems to have been due to the Rat Man's ability to see and put to the test the fact that the famous Professor Freud (with all that it meant to be a famous professor) was finding his knowledge particularly ineffectual in this case.

9 The Dream and Its Interpretation in the Direction of the Psychoanalytic Treatment

BY MOUSTAPHA SAFOUAN

If psychoanalysts are unanimous in considering the dream as the "royal road to the unconscious," this unanimity does not extend to the question of the use of dreams in directing the treatment. Some are not far from extending the rule of abstinence to the dream and suggest avoiding any communication with the patient concerning the interpretation of his dreams. Such a communication risks, according to them, leading the patient to use the telling of his dreams as a privileged means of resistance, thus aggravating the latter. Others, countering this view, do not fail to underscore the beneficial effects that they draw from this procedure and affirm that as far as they are aware, their patients do not dream more than those of their colleagues. A third position adds nothing to the debate, since it defines itself as eclectic; it is adopted by those who agree with both sides: "it all depends on the case." Implicitly this position sustains an impression we have in listening to the first two: that the first group works with patients unknown to the second.[1]

In truth, if analysts do not have the same experience, we must conclude that they do not have the same object, or more exactly, that they do not have a conception of this object that can found a common experience. We will thus begin by asking the question, what is our object? or better yet, what do we analyze?

The basic fact that strictly speaking founds the psychoanalytic experience has been defined by D. Lagache in terms that we can do no better than to quote: "Take the words of the patient. Clearly I as the analyst am not only interested in the objective meaning of what he wants to tell me; I am also and most of all interested, not in what he does not want to tell me but in what eludes both his intended communications and his conscious refusals."[2]

This article first appeared in *La Psychanalyse* 8 (Paris: Presses Universitaires de France, 1964). The text was revised by the author and was republished as "Le rêve et son interprétation dans la conduite de la cure psychanalytique," in Moustapha Safouan, *Etudes sur l'Oedipe* (Paris: Editions du Seuil, 1974), pp. 15–43.
1. This divergence is evident in the articles collected in *Revue française de psychanalyse* 23: 1 (1959).
2. Daniel Lagache, "Analysis and Behavior," in *Drives, Affects, Behavior: Essays in Honor of Marie Bonaparte*, ed. Rudolph Loewenstein (New York: International Universities Press, 1953), p. 121.

One conclusion seems to impose itself here: since what interests us is not in the patient's speech, we seek it outside or, in other terms, in his conduct—a category that can even encompass that of discourse, considered as a "concrete action" rather than as "abstract meanings"—as well as in his mimicry, his movements, his visceral reactions, and so forth. Such is D. Lagache's conclusion.

While it is certain that our experience begins at the moment when we "neutralize" or "bracket" what the patient wants or does not want to say to us, however, it is not certain that in doing so we dispense with the category of *discourse*. For when the patient tells us one thing and we hear another, this other thing is also something that we grasp within his discourse. Or else we find a connection between his discourse and another segment of discourse; for example, Trimethylamin, in the dream of the injection of Irma, is attached to the theories of Fleiss about sexual metabolism.[3] We grasp this something else because of the ambiguity to which this discourse lends itself, often because of its phonematic texture—thus *ananas*, which Freud notes as being assonant with the patient's family name. This principle is yet more evident in the case of denegation: there we see the proof that the patient's speech is mere words, but this is no reason to forget that the affirmation that interests us is included literally in a negative sentence. An example from the same dream is "Otto is guilty, not me . . .," as a result of which Freud identifies his own sense of guilt.

It is thus not by accident that Freud, in the first scene of this inaugural dream, takes Irma "aside, as though to answer her *letter.*"[4] The neutralization of the "objective meanings" or the abstract ones should not be taken as a neutralization of the category of language. Far from it, these meanings appear in analytic experience as the aspect of common discourse that the patient can reproduce in combining a certain number of unities whose significance, going beyond the produced meaning, remains for him unintelligible. There is a margin between the meaning that is the pretext and the text. It is true that we are not interested in the patient's discourse insofar as it covers such or such an abstract meaning. On the contrary, it is there that we begin to break the patient's illusion concerning this subject. But does this illusion not maintain for the patient precisely that which common opinion confuses, the difference between discourse and meaning? Analytic experience shows, on the contrary—and its rupture with common

3. Freud, *The Interpretation of Dreams* (1900), S.E. 4, pp. 106–21.
4. In underlining the word "letter" we have involuntarily effectuated the kind of listening whose importance we are attempting to explicate here. A detailed examination of this first case (which is not Freud's self-analysis but the birth of psychoanalysis) would give to Freud's phrase the value of an anticipation of a discovery and would show more amply than we can here the function of the signifier in the manifestations of the unconscious.

opinion in this area can be considered radical—that the discourse poses an enigma for the subject himself to the extent that it appears to him to be marked with the sign of nonsense, introducing thus the exigency of sense.

This distinction in discourse, between the meaningful or closed and the "letter" or pure significance, makes movement return. This distinction, manifested in analytic experience before it was formulated by modern linguistics, justifies the step taken by J. Lacan in underlining the kingship, if not the direct influence, that links analysis to the progress of linguistics, even though the formulations of this same linguistic science are responsible for the possibility of maintaining analytic experience in its true dimension as an experience of discourse.

Once we come to affirm analytic experience as an experience of discourse, and of a discourse whose statable meanings do not exhaust its significance, another conclusion imposes itself: we find ourselves in this experience faced with a significance that sustains itself by itself, faced with a discourse that is the discourse of "no one," in which the subject can only signify himself on the condition of being hidden from view. If maintaining analytic experience in its true dimension is so difficult that it necessitates the detour through modern linguistics, does this not confirm the conclusion that the discourse can do without the person, providing that we consent fully to this experience? Now this conclusion is in one sense unthinkable. It is not without doing violence to the mind that the Freudian view of the dream imposes the distinction between the subject who speaks *veritably* (the one who does the "dream work") and the one whom we can call the "locutor" or the "word machine," that is to say, the one who is awake and who brings us this same dream.[5]

One difficulty always gives rise to an other. This perspective, recalled by Lacan, is not without problems. But at least we are repaid by the certainty that these are problems and difficulties of psychoanalysis and that the essential facts of its experience are not altered or lost from sight. The virtue of cognizance [*connaissance*] is that it permits one to know how to measure oneself in relation to such facts, while the momentary benefit that can accrue from their being forgotten will quickly lead into an impasse.

In fact, as soon as we change our perspective and take for object not discourse but "behavior," as one consequence the subject will have to situate himself in relation to something that will always be outside him. Only in relation to the objects that people his world can our subject or our object—it matters little

5. This modification concerning the sense of the word "subject" did not fail to bring about another modification concerning the signifier, which J. Lacan defines as representing a *subject* for an other signifier.

how we name him, since we only suppose his movement—be said to be near or far. Certainly these are value-objects. But this means that they all have the same value; these are the objects of need. No term is more important than an other. The father, for example, will be an object among others, and the subject will either approach him in rivalry or else will distance himself to avoid the return blows that he dreads. All measurement and all value other than that of the object will then pass for arbitrary fancy.

I do not mean to say that the expressions called to mind here, such as the "ego's strength" or the "becoming conscious" or the "disalienation," correspond to nothing. They correspond exactly, in one sense or another, to something that is supposed to be realized in the subject's "behavior" after a certain amount of analytic work. But if we do not take into account a second movement, which is the movement of the treatment, the one through which the patient is not exactly the same after as before, how could we respond to the question: where was he before, and where is he now? If we base our conceptualization on "behavior," that which is and should only be the *result* is declared to be the goal: this implies that it has been chosen as such. And in this choice the analyst's ideals will inevitably intervene: such and such a result (for example, the ego's strength or becoming conscious) will be taken as a measure according to which the analyst will judge independence or authenticity. And the goal will dictate the means: the analyst will counsel the interpretation of the patient's dreams or will not counsel it, according to whether he aims at "becoming conscious" or at conquering a resistance. Now not only does any choice imply a limitation, but one chooses because one is already limited. And no one is able to measure fully the extent of the effects of such a limitation. The position of the analyst becomes attached to an irresolvable discontent about the conditions in which he works, and this makes itself felt each time he treats a question of technique.

The situation will not be the same *if* we can find in the subject himself a term that, without being a "concrete" object, still retains its importance. The term can serve as a standard of measurement without our having recourse to our ideals. This hypothesis can apply to the analytic experience envisaged as an experience of discourse. Finally, it leads us to declare that *the relationship between the subject and the world can be regulated by his relationship with a signifier:*[6] let me say parenthetically that it is through this relationship that he will be a subject. It is certainly not an accident that Lacan, the author who has most insisted on the character of the analytic experience as experience of discourse, is

---

6. It is understood that the opposition between the signified and the signifier is substituted for the classical opposition between the particular and the universal. Nominalists and realists, whatever their differences, maintain the same dyadic relationship between the word and the sense.

the one who promoted the function in the human psyche of the particular signifier, *the name of the father.*

But why this signifier and not another? Are we not here victims of a choice, what we wanted to avoid? Not at all. We will see that we can deduce a response to this question. If we retain this response until the end of the present chapter, this is because in fact such a deduction cannot be formulated without referring to the experience in question. This experience will first attract our attention to the conclusion we will have to deduce. It is necessary to see it first, before seeing its rationality.

Let us begin with an example. Mrs. Z——— is a young woman who was sent to me for psychotherapy. When she discovered her husband's infidelity, she tried to commit suicide by taking a large dose of sleeping pills, and she was saved with little time to spare. It was after this attempt that she came to consult with me, on the advice of her physician.

After a first session devoted to the telling of her story, she spoke for a long time, during the second, of the conflict between her and her mother-in-law, concluding with these words: "Finally, I cannot say that I am very jealous of her; for after all I never do anything to separate them."

I answer that a certain way of looking at things appears to be dominant, according to which her husband is always coupled, sometimes with her, sometimes with her mother-in-law, the one or the other being excluded in turn. Despite this, one can say that the possibility of a third solution permitting the coexistence of the three is excluded.

At the next, third session—we are thus only at the beginning of the analysis—she declares: "I had a lot of dreams this week."

In fact she tells me three, which she says she had on the same night:

1. I was in a room, a kitchen. I was afraid. I tried to flee a black cow that wanted to look at me. There were two openings in the room: on one side a window that was closed and on the other side a door that was not closed. And I remember that I pushed with all my strength against this door to prevent the cow from coming in. Yet the cow did nothing to force it. She kept turning around from one side to the other. She simply wanted to look at me with her good cow eyes, her brown eyes. It was not really wicked, and yet I felt that I was terribly afraid!

Here are the associations that the patient gives for the dream:

The room in the dream resembles her kitchen. Yet since her apartment is on the fourth floor, it is impossible for the cow to come look at her. In her parents' house, however, the kitchen is on the ground floor.

2. We were in a hotel with my father-in-law. My husband and another woman, a blonde, were embracing before me uninhibitedly. I could not tolerate that, but I saw that they did not acknowledge my presence, and I was incapable of chasing this woman or of catching my husband's attention; I no longer knew what I wanted. I did not even have a voice. Then all at once, I began to scream, calling my father-in-law so that he would intervene. At this moment I woke up terribly anxious. I was very agitated. I believe that I even threw off my sheets.

Associations:

the hotel. She had in fact spent the last winter vacation with her husband and in-laws in this very hotel.

The blonde woman. She knows that her husband's mistress is blonde.

3. An animal on the water: a kind of swamp. It was a frightening animal, flat and large, with short horrid paws and a long neck that was attached to a flat head like the head of a snake except that it was large, squared. It was covered with green scales. I was very afraid, but someone reassured me and said that I could touch it. I touched it, but I was disgusted, the scales were so sticky. Then the beast was transformed. Now it is a little girl with a pretty face, smiling and radiant. But she had paws that looked like palm leaves in place of hands and feet. It was pitiful to see this pretty child having paws like that instead of being like us.

Associations:

The beast. It is a fictive animal. Doubtless it has a long neck, because Mrs. Z—— saw, the night before, on a lake in the Bois de Boulogne, a swan that stretched out its neck, and she was surprised to see that swans had such long necks.

Someone reassured me. No one was there. It was simply a voice.

The child. Mrs. Z—— thinks of her niece, the daughter of her only brother, two years older than she, even though she finds no resemblance between this niece and the child in the dream.

A first glance shows that these three dreams are concerned with three themes: the mother-child relation, an appeal to a paternal character, and the theme of birth. If we agree that this succession should not be considered accidental, we may ask how these themes are related.

It is doubtless legitimate to take the cow as an object in which, in the mother, the patient's oral demand can find satisfaction. It is the mother who responds to the demand, but at the moment of encounter, when there ought to be satisfaction, there is an emergence of anxiety. Why?

We can suppose that the "good" in the "good cow eyes" means "bad" in the latent content of the dream. This badness may cover the memory of some maternal brutality, of a prohibition by a superego—or else, perhaps in projected form, the badness of the child herself? Impossible to decide. We can see that in formulating these hypotheses we have detached ourselves a little too quickly from the text of the dream and that this has not gotten us very far.

The text of the dream told us that the cow did not want to do anything other than look at the patient and that that was sufficient to render her anxious. In telling this she is astonished, even more so because the look in question was not especially wicked; this is a further elaboration that the patient offers. Instead of taking this astonishment as a secondary effect resulting from the discord between the manifest text of the dream and the affect, we are going to consider it an integral part of the narrative: in this sense we can expect to find in the latent content of the dream an astonishment.[7]

In fact the question implied in this astonishment (*but what was I afraid of?*) implies another question: *what did the cow want, with such a desire to look at me?* We can qualify this question as "latent" but only in the sense of "preconscious." It is very probable that the patient herself would have admitted, or at least would not have hesitated to admit, that this second question is implied in the first. What seems on the contrary to escape her entirely is the response that is necessarily implied not only in her question but also in the very place from which she asks herself the question—what does the cow want? If she sees the cow as wanting to look at her, this is because she has already taken *herself as representing something for the cow.* But what? If the cow represents the mother, she doubtless represents the child. Certainly this is a valid response, but again we cannot qualify it as latent except in the sense of being preconscious, and for the same reasons. But what is she for the cow, being its child? The answer to this question, or more exactly, the astonishment concerning this point of the response doubtless constitutes the true latent content of the dream that happens in the "Other Scene." What then is this answer? And why is the patient unable to approach this answer without setting off the signal of anxiety? Her dream, if we consider the text as rigorous, permits us at least to isolate her difficulty.

She simply wanted to look at me, with her good cow eyes, her brown eyes. It was not really wicked, and yet I felt that I was terribly afraid!

It is difficult to miss the tone of wonderment but also of tenderness with which Mrs. Z—— pronounces these phrases. She loves this cow who loves her so

7. Freud, *The Interpretation of Dreams* (1900), S.E. 5, pp. 452–55.

much. And in truth we have to agree that this cow is "poor" in the Platonic sense of the term, in the sense in which Diotima speaks to us of Love as the son of Poverty. Despite all the milk that she has, this cow still needs something else. What? Nothing other than the presence of this child whom she wants perpetually but in vain (how could this child be present without *alternately* being absent?)[8] in the field of her look. *This demand is a demand for love.* Is it that of the patient or that of her mother? Doubtless a conversion has taken place? "I ask her" has become "She asks me." But we can also say that the demand in question is that of any being who speaks. If it derives from a lack, it is a lack that no object, milk or sh—— can fill. Doubtless this extreme penury of the demand—manifesting itself as a demand for love and for nothing else, leaving no escape hatch in something like the satisfaction of a need, even oral—makes for the patient's inability to face it without feeling anxiety. This is also the interesting element in the dream; and if we wanted to invent alibis, we would dull the cutting edge of the question instead of maintaining the confrontation at the level where in fact it is placed, according to the dream text. The patient has difficulty responding, not to the need, but to the appeal for love.

We have no doubt that such an appeal poses a problem for the one to whom it is addressed. In fact a question is hinted at despite (or rather *because of*) the extreme symbolization of the demand as demand for love, and this question is the same as that to which our first analysis conducted us: what does she want in wanting the child that I am? Questioning the Other's desire defines the space where the difficulty is played out, the field where fantasy wards off anxiety, but anxiety is ready to emerge each time that the subject is called to "give" the fantasy.

It remains to be seen what this fantasy is. On that, our patient's first dream (we could also say: the first part of her dream) remains rather silent. But what this dream does not tell us has been taught to us through years of questioning the unconscious in our experience. And since we invoke this experience, let us cite from our own another example that in illustrating the response will best clarify the elasticity of the anxiety in question.

This example concerns another patient, Mrs. Y——, who in a particularly marked way analyzes her own movements in relation to the "analyst" in an ambiguous attitude of rivalry and complicity and nevertheless does not succeed in hiding from the person who listens to her the extent to which she dreads and

---

8. The text of the dream underscores this alternation: *She* (the cow) *kept turning around, from one side to the other.*

postpones any intervention from him, as one dreads and postpones that thing that we must call the "due date." After a certain number of sessions during which she analyzed her relationship with her mother, she remembers how, one day, she spoke the following phrase to her mother, a phrase that seemed to her to be "ridiculous": "I am ready to do anything for you, except one thing, to become a whore." In this context Mrs. Y—— brings me the following dream:

> She is trying on a wig, but after each trying on the wig becomes shorter until the moment when she notices that she is in danger of seeming to be bald. She has an anxiety attack.

As an association concerning the wig, she quotes *La Peau* by Malaparte, in which the whores of Naples dye their hair and pubic hair to trick the blacks who want blondes. I also know that a wig was not an object that left the patient's mother in a state of indifference.

We will not go too far astray in interpreting the dream in the following terms: in going to this extreme to comply with my mother's desire, do I not run the risk of finding out that I can only deceive this desire, without ever satisfying it.

From that, the anxiety. Anxiety, because if the identification with the phallus (the wig) can be taken to be a response before the question—a response that can be formulated in the following way: "To please mother, it is necessary and sufficient to be the phallus"[9]—this response can only maintain itself as repressed. All ulterior astonishment is already the signal of a knowledge in which repression runs the risk of being undone; any question is a calling into question.

Our first patient, Mrs. Z——, found herself implicitly invited to such a questioning by being in a psychotherapeutic situation. In speaking, what does she want? Questioning the Other about what he wants is also questioning herself about what she wants, this deriving from the fact that she too is speaking. Where is she at the precise moment when she confronts the demand for love in its extreme symbolization? She is at a limit where she can only imagine that this demand, which touches her in the fantasmatic core of her being, is going to fall back on her, to consume itself in a consummation: her mother will satisfy herself with her, and she with her mother, while she at the same time is unsatisfied. The "good" look of the cow is then, also, a "devouring" look. The patient barricades herself in her *kitchen*. We come back, then, to the hypothesis of wickedness that we would have been hasty to accept at the beginning; but the detour has not been useless. For now we see that if there is wickedness, then it is a wickedness that the giving of what one has will not be able to deceive or would only deceive. The

9. See Jacques Lacan, "Les Formations de l'inconscient," unpublished seminar, 1957–58.

patient loves the cow, and she loves it for its poverty—"for what it does not have," as Lacan would say. She could have noticed this herself. Her "error" (is she alone in making this error?) is in not noticing that the cow also loves her for what she does not have, and not for what she has. Since the cow did nothing to force the door, it was not seeking what it could find in the kitchen but rather . . . simply to see her? The foreignness that derives from how close she is to grasping her being in the dream is the element of latent content that corresponds to the patient's naive astonishment in telling the dream.

To pursue the analysis of the second of these dreams, let us remember that the patient during the next session described the conflict between her and her mother-in-law as generational. "We do not understand each other," she said, "perhaps because we are not of the same generation." Of this we can say that she was certainly right, if we understand by "conflict" the impossibility of joining two terms. She next described how she had felt that she was entirely incapable of making the least remark to her husband about this: "I would have the impression of seeking to separate a son from his mother, something for which I would reproach myself terribly, perhaps because I am myself very attached to my mother." We note finally that she associated the hotel where the second dream took place with one where she spent her vacation with her husband and her in-laws. Of her mother-in-law the dream says nothing: we do, however, find a blonde woman there.

All this shows at what point the relation "husband–mother-in-law" reflects the relation of the patient to her own mother. It is very possible that the husband also represents the patient's older brother (compare the child who reminds her of her niece in the third part of the dream). Perhaps, even more profoundly, we could have found the father in this connection. This gives us three terms—husband, brother, and father—that have the same value. What value? The value of one who deprives her and is substituted for her in the relationship with the mother—the mother who remains, in this game, the true master.

Through the subject's identification with the depriver, the mother is at the same time joined and rendered inaccessible. Things are joined again in the imaginary—which does not simply mean "in the patient's imagination": it is "reality" itself that appears impregnated by the solder-point that joins her husband and mother-in-law. Joined in the imaginary, we would say, by a depriver who serves at the same time as an alibi. But through the same movement, it is "in the real" that the patient finds herself *repulsed* beyond this circle of perfect accord, in a sympathetic jealousy: what is more difficult for a subject than to realize that his counterparts are really his counterparts, which is to say that none of them possesses what he believes himself deprived of?[10]

Under these conditions, we can ask ourselves how there could have been any genital realization. Our patient's dream gives us the response—we formulate it as follows: she has only to surmount all the fear and pity that prevent her from denouncing the "depriver."

The dreamer finds her voice. Until now the dream was concerned with an imaginary other: her husband was a reflection of her own fixation. Now she manifests herself as a voice.

She calls her father-in-law. The imaginary structure of the depriver leads to a necessary third term *that also cannot be identified with the person of the father.* In fact, if we suppose that the husband in the dream represents the father, and it is certain that he does, then he is the *imaginary father.* The relation to him remains that of substitution-exclusion *where there is no place for speech.* Conclusion: the father-in-law is only called on to the extent that his *symbolic position* has an effect on Mrs. Z—— and qualifies her to tolerate the function of the third party, to give weight and reality to this function, to render it effective and operative. *The name of the father, and not his "person," is the root of the Oedipal triangulation.*

The patient wakes in a terrible anxiety. The anxiety experience in her first dream was, to explain briefly, anxiety for her incapacity to palliate her mother's insufficiency. At its beginning the second dream realizes what the first did not realize, the mutual envelopment of the two terms of mother and child: husband and mistress embrace. This moment, opposed to the first, is no less the source of a profound anxiety. To escape it (*to wake, throwing off the sheets*), the patient had no other recourse than to call a third person, who presents himself as a *paternal* character. In other words, here the dreamer overcomes the fear of castration and of the couple's separation. But we can say with equal justice that what is found on *her path* in the dream surprises her at the moment when ("all of a sudden") she cries out. That is the truth, which is ordinarily repressed and is never approached in a dream without bringing an awakening! This awakening marks in some way the end of a world whose structure was profoundly illusory.

We should not be surprised if we find in our patient's third dream the symbolization of a phallus that will become a little girl. The relationship through

10. We see how much such a view is in harmony with all that our experience reveals to us about the ego as the locus of all misapprehensions and of all resistances, and not because this ego is "weak." If "to be strong" is to know how to hold onto one's place, we ought certainly to talk about a "strong" ego in this case.

which the child is substituted for the lost identification with the phallus is translated in the dream by a transformation: this transformation took place each time that she touched the thing most disgusting to her, a voice that had summoned her to that place, telling her that she could touch the beast.

But to the extent that the girl with the "luminous" face remains attached to her phallic origin as the object of a gift, to the extent that "without resembling her" she is the daughter of the brother's desire responding to his mother's, she remains marked by animality and is not entirely "like us"—like us other humans.

We recall the reply we received one day from a little girl six years old whom we treated during a few sessions for character disorders that were not very serious. She had made a drawing—in truth, a simple scribble—and she wanted to throw it away immediately. We stopped her to ask what it was. She answered: "Oh, it's nothing, a mother and her baby, two little animals. Animals! Yes, there is no Daddy."

To summarize this discussion, we will say, then, that everything has happened as if, beginning with our remark about the absence of a third solution, made to the patient during the preceding session, something had begun to resonate from the place occupied by this signifier of the name of the father, a term that reveals a decisive function, whose misapprehension renders all coexistence problematical, ambiguous, and insupportable. Evidently this view does not mean that we attribute to the term in the abstract any action whatever in the effective normatization of the subject. Such an attribution is another question.

But if we encounter, at the beginning of certain cures, dreams analogous to the one we have just examined, commonly called "program dreams," in which the entire path the subject will have to traverse is prefigured, is it not that the path is drawn out in advance and that it is incumbent upon theory to explain this?

Before taking another step in this direction, we will indicate our belief that consistent with the common opinion of psychoanalysts, there is no reason to communicate to the patient the interpretation of this kind of dream, because the patient could in no way integrate its meanings at this inaugural stage of analysis.

Among the dreams that patients tell us during the cure, certain ones bear witness to the relationship of the subject to the name of the father, and they will permit us to specify the meaning and the extent of this relationship.

Let us begin with an example.

Mrs. A——— is a patient whose mother tongue is English and who had a long psychoanalytic treatment. After a long interruption, she wanted to take it up again; for if the treatment "changed everything" in her, she remained the same in one respect: she still could not be "the respectable wife of a respectable man." Her analyst sent her to me.

At one point in her analysis she spoke for several sessions of the beautiful and expensive coats that were bought for her when she was a child, during the worst part of the economic depression of the thirties. Who bought these for her? Her father, of course: her mother would never have agreed to such an expense for a thing that, after all, she could have lived without.

Here we open a parenthesis to underscore that this theme did not come out of the blue but arose in the following way: at a previous session, the patient recalled how her mother used to say, each time that the telephone rang, "Go answer it, dear, someone wants to give you something." She said it ironically, because "obviously when someone calls you on the phone, it is to ask you for something, never to give you something." A brief silence followed, then the patient continued: "It's funny, I never know if I am pregnant or not. Each time I have suspicions, it is in vain that I palpate myself again and again, I never know if the child is there or not. Of course it is for you doctors to know. Isn't that true?" For an answer I tell her what I hold to be the explication of this leap from cabbages to kings: the patient's mother, when she manifested her "disillusion," as in the example above, presented herself as someone of whom one was always asking for things but who never received. Now, my hypothesis is that the mother had received something: the patient, to be precise. This would be why the patient never knows whether the child is there or not. Clearly my statement that this was a "hypothesis" was only an expedient in my discourse. It meant: this derives from the fact that a certain number of signifiers introduce an order of meanings into the world, even before the patient's birth, and it is through these very meanings that her being took on body. My words to her recalled this.

Thus, following this intervention, the patient began to speak of coats that her father bought for her at great sacrifice to himself. Then there came a session at which the patient, having just arrived, declared that she did not want to lie down on the couch; she had just come from the hairdresser. But once she sat down she panicked: she was afraid of being fired from her job, afraid that something would happen to her while driving her car, afraid of everything and nothing; her life had been a long bout with fear. All the while she was not able to retain her tears, nor even to think of retaining them. In this context I restricted myself to making the following interrogative remark: it was immediately upon telling me that she wanted to remain seated to keep her hairdo intact that this "panic" invaded her. She responded immediately: "My father always made scenes about my hairdo; my hair was never arranged as he wanted it to be."

In the next session she brought the following dream:

I was in the office, carelessly seated in my easy chair. An officer enters and says to me: "You behave as if you were in a back room and not in a front office." (Reported in English.) Then he adds that when the colonel, another superior, comes back, he will not permit me to have any contact with him, for I am capable of making him change his mind.

Here are the patient's associations:

The way she was seated in the chair. "When I was little, I had the habit of sitting that way." Then she changed her mind energetically: "No, it was not me, it was my sister; I had another way of sitting carelessly."

The officer's reproach. "It is a reproach I did not deserve, since I never sit like that when I am at the office. After all, such a reproach would be indifferent to me, since it is not addressed to me."

What the officer then adds. "This is a reproach that I would like to hear, since it would mean that I can seduce another man (*sic*), and this is something I think I am incapable of."

Back room. "Nothing. A room in which one can be isolated from the rest of society to talk calmly. There is also a song in which there are these two lines: 'Go see what the boys in the back room will have; / And tell them I'm having the same.'"

Front office. "Nothing, a fairly large office."

The form of the phrase "you behave as if you were. . . ." "It is correct. You should not say 'like'!"[11]

In what follows, I will try to reconstitute as much as possible the work being done in my mind as I listened to the patient's associations.

The seriousness with which she asserts: "No, it was not me, it was my sister" is not astonishing when we know the bantering style that is hers. It is as if a distinction became necessary; something commanded the intervention of these two signifiers, *me* and *my sister*, in order to make a distinction that otherwise would have remained in an imaginary confusion.

A *reproach.* How can we not think here of the "scenes" that her father made concerning her hair? Did she or did she not deserve these reproaches? But first, to whom were they addressed? The patient's words to me about her father do not leave me with much time to hesitate: everything led me to think that this man actualized in his relations with his daughter something very primal that had to do with his relation with his own mother. More explicitly, he was the kind of father

---

11. It is a common error in English to use "like" instead of "as" [Original in English.]

who regarded his daughter as equivalent to the phallus. This attitude certainly encountered the daughter's complicity, which in no way prevented her from posing the question, does he address these reproaches to me because he waits for me to be *a* woman (in which case I deserve them) or because he takes me for *his* woman [his wife] (as I would like to imagine; but in this case, paradoxically, the reproaches should be mine against him)? There I brought into play a central notion: can one not say that all psychoanalysis began at the moment that Freud took the position, unheard of in his time, that he had the right to wait for the hysteric to become capable of giving him a coherent narrative of her illness?

A *reproach she would have liked to hear.* How many times have I heard a patient express the wish to be seductive! This wish is always accompanied with a smile that is half shrewd and half ironic. Shrewd? She knew that she was seductive. Ironic? This smile means: as much as I wish to be contradicted for this idea of my seductiveness when I am seated comfortably but carelessly, I also wish to be *really* seductive! Now what she wants to hear is that she can seduce *another man.* Decidedly, the time for the ego to be finally "dislodged" has come.

I invite her to give her associations around the form of the phrase "you behave. . . ." What is astonishing in a dream's proceeding by formal allusion? Did not the unforgettable dream of the *non vixit* deliver up its secret to Freud when a phrase led him, *by its mode of construction,* to suspect the echo of another, the same that he was to use about ten years later to initiate the Rat Man into the mysteries of the human drama, the famous lines of Brutus in *Julius Caesar:* "As Caesar loved me, I weep for him; as he was fortunate, I rejoice at it; as he was valiant, I honor him; but—as he was ambitious, I slew him"?

In inviting the patient to tell me her associations with this phrase, I was in no way expecting that they would be attached to the *correct manipulation of signifers.* The fact is even more significant in that this woman ordinarily took pleasure in speaking colloquially. Who is she addressing when she says, *You should not say "like"?* Who is this you? Is it the thou about which we can say that it is the locus of the conventions that language imposes? Is what is in question a thou that is impossible to tame, which is reflected in the boys in the song?

Let us return to the session. Once the associations are made, she keeps silent for a certain time and then takes up the thread again: "It's funny; ordinarily I am silent because I have nothing to say to you; but now I am silent because I have so many ideas in my head that I do not know which one to choose." I answer in these terms: "Quite so. Besides, your dream appears to be commanded by a question of choice. It permitted us to presume that your father's reproaches about your hairdo embarrassed you: was he addressing you because he was waiting for you to become a woman, or because he took you for his woman?" We can say that this interpretation is more true than "reality." But is it not because it lacked truth that it was not a "reality"?

Having listened to my interpretation, Mrs. A—— keeps silent for a few minutes, doubtless seized by a disquietude that becomes evident in the nervous and willfully babyish tone with which she takes things up again: "It's strange how I forget the time. I tell myself in vain that I must wake up at such and such a time, and the alarm rings, but I do not hear it, and I continue to sleep. And the dreams! There also I often tell myself when I wake up in the morning, I must remember such and such a dream to report it during the session; a little later I have already forgotten it. . . ."

At the next session she tells this dream:

> The telephone rings. I am going to answer it. The call is for Dr. Saddler. I look: Dr. Saddler is jumping out the window. I say to him, "Dr. Saddler, there is a call for you." He answers, continuing his fall, "Tell them that I will call back later." Next I am at home, trying on some dresses. Ordinarily the dresses are hung so that I see them from the sides. But in the dream they were one in back of the other in such a way that I could only see the shoulder and the bodice. This is the way I saw them arranged in a department store yesterday. The dresses were yellow and pink; a very pretty yellow and a very pretty pink with a metallic reflection. But they were all too small for me. At this time the doorbell rang. I am in my underwear and cannot open it. But I intend to open the door slightly to see who it is. It is Dr. Saddler and his wife. I tell them to wait a minute, but they push the door open as though they heard nothing. Both are old and have gray hair. Irene (the patient's friend) is there. I introduce them to her saying, "Irene is delicious." Then Irene smiles and says "Van . . ." (the first syllable of the name of this friend).

That Dr. Saddler jumps out the window and answers while continuing his fall appears to the patient to be completely absurd. Now absurdity signifies, according to Freud, that in the latent content of the dream, the dreamer repudiates or refutes a certain idea. What does the patient want to refute? "Saddler" does not give her any associations except perhaps "deadler," she adds jokingly; this word evidently makes no sense. Nevertheless we cannot fail to notice that the word "deadler" contains the word "dead" in the same way that "Saddler" contains the word "sad." In addition "Saddler," which the dream takes as a proper name, is also a word referring to the making of saddles.

Here are the patient's associations concerning the other elements of the dream: the *yellow color* makes her think of my ashtray, which is made of a yellow metal. The pink, on the contrary, makes her think of nothing. Mrs. Saddler recalls no one, except perhaps her paternal grandmother who, without resembling anyone in the dream, also had gray hair. Dr. Saddler makes her think of an artist of great renown about whom she knows absolutely nothing, she says; this, however, does not prevent her from thinking, without knowing why, that he is an ass. That the two enter as if they had heard nothing, "that means that they do not respect my desire, which is my everyday tragedy." The way she introduces her friend attracts this commentary, which she makes in smiling: " 'Delicious' is an adjective referring to things that are eaten, but obviously I do not want to eat Irene."

We limit ourselves to accentuating the essential in this dream. In conformity with Freud's remarks about the expression of the conditional in the dream, what is in question in the first part is a repudiation of the idea of castration. The consequences appear in the second part: Dr. Saddler, having put off his response until later [primum dormire], reappears in what follows, forming a couple with the dreamer's grandmother. The dreamer can then continue the "everyday tragedy" of her life, a tragedy that consists in always arranging things so that her desires are not taken seriously; she fails to cross the line that must be crossed for her to realize them.

The dream is the extension of thoughts that she had told me at the end of the preceding session, in answer to my interpretation: nothing is pressing; I can put off presenting myself as an oral phallus (Irene—whom she would not dream of eating—is delicious). We note that this negation of castration is accompanied by a feeling of beauty—as in the beautiful color of the ashtray (compare also the "luminous face" in the dream of Mrs. Z——). The concomitance of these themes invites us to reflect on Lacan's idea of beauty. Beauty is something that unveils and hides (by dazzling the viewer) the relation of man to "the second death."[12] Beauty sets up the second and the most powerful wall, where the first is that of the good, encountered on the path through which man accedes to this relationship (to the second death).[13]

Whatever the intensity of the fears and the regression that results from it, we consider as progress the fact that Mrs. A—— has been led to express something about this theme of the relation to castration, even in a negative mode. For we would misconstrue the notion of resistance if we did not understand its function of revealing.

It is the progressive part of this movement that comes to the forefront in the

12. Moustapha Safouan, Etudes sur l'Oedipe, p. 70 n. 1.
13. See Jacques Lacan, "The Ethic of Psychoanalysis," unpublished seminar, 1959–60.

following dream, to the extent that the idea of a certain renunciation is stated there.[14]

> I was in the basement of a department store. There were other people—four or five, I can't remember. There were beige dresses, very, very pretty. I try them on and find one that fits me perfectly. Someone says that this dress belongs to W—— (a woman who because of her age recalls the patient's mother and whose name is assonant with the English verb "to wean"). But W—— says that the patient can keep the dress, which fits her very well, while it no longer fits W——. Then Mrs. A—— adds: I know why the dresses were beige: . . . the color of your walls!

We must specify here that the patient always wore suits; even the idea of wearing a dress caused her an insurmountable discomfort. In the dream she wears a dress given by W——, who contents herself with finding the patient's looks improved. In reality, her style of dress has remained the same. But many things do change following this dream: Mrs. A—— finds a job that is steadier and pays better, rents an apartment with a garden (this time in a good neighborhood), takes charge of the education of her son, education that until then she had left in the hands of her mother-in-law ("in order not to hurt her," she says). Preoccupied by the purchase of new furniture for her apartment, she is astonished at the sureness and rapidity with which she chooses what pleases her and what does not. Another "surprise": she thinks of herself as Mrs. B—— A——, where before it was her nickname (which, as though by accident, meant "small" or "cute") that came to mind, followed by her maiden name.

The four sessions that we have just reported permit us to note, in the unfolding of a psychoanalysis, a sequence of four months, each one of which marks a new position for the subject.

An initial period is often accompanied by symptoms of fatigue and exhaustion, where the subject is found *at the extreme limit of what he can sustain of his questioning of the Other's desire*. The art of the psychoanalyst consists in knowing how to suspend and, on occasion, to reverse all the subject's certainties until he is led to this limit. The dreams that come during this stage of analytic work can be very useful to us, especially in instructing us about the way the

---

14. It is not so much a question of a renunciation as of a sacrifice that the Other makes for her. In other words, in this dream the patient fills in the narcissistic fissure induced by the interpretation by having recourse to a radical fantasy. Some time later the patient provoked a situation that obliged her to leave Paris and thus to interrupt her analysis. The threshold beyond which the patient will not allow his or her narcissism to be questioned is the unknown and unpredictable point of any analysis.

subject places himself in relation to the Other's desire; and we do not hesitate, for our part, to ask for the associations that appear to us to be necessary to penetrate the sense. This obviously does not mean that we give the patient the interpretation.

A second stage occurs when the subject disguises things and lets us hear in the Other's discourse a reference to *a third term*. Here the subject comes out of his solipsism: when a third term is posed, what had been a "dyad" is transformed into "two." At this point more than at any other we can say that the Other is *transcendence, not in relation to an intention but in relation to a dyad*. It is in this way that the subject gains the little bit of consistency and truth that is his. We can say that this third term is the name of the father or that it is the "odd" number par excellence—a third person who is nowhere, even though he is the judge in all relations that are not reduced to being imaginary and even though he is the foundation of all triangulation.

To illustrate this point we cite the example of a sixteen-year-old boy who lives alone with his mother, his father having abandoned him when he was very young: he makes a drawing in which disparate objects are piled up any which way, in a kind of primal chaos but always in opposing pairs (hot and cold, animate and inanimate, and so forth). We find through this drawing three letters, n, y, and p, and three numbers, 7, 9, and 11. Of the letters he says that n and t together make him think of "nature"; p makes him think of "papa." Of the numbers, nothing except that they are all odd. This dream marks the advent of this (third) stage, and it appears to us important to confirm this sense—which, again, does not mean that this dream must be interpreted.

The third stage is that of the *symbolization of castration*, when the subject "signifies" this in the only way he can, which is to say, by repudiating it. This stage derives from the preceding, and here the dream itself sometimes tells us that because of the resistances there is no place for an interpretation—and this is the case for Mrs. A——.

Finally, during a fourth stage, the subject *realizes a certain number of his desires*. At this stage it is not rare to see a modification—when there is a place for it—in the subject's relationship with his name. This fact is particularly significant for Mrs. A——, in view of the symbolism implied in her nickname. But in the final analysis, if a disalienation takes place, is this not because the alienation of being in a signifier is in question: Very often the subject speaks here of an "awakening"; the variety of beings and persons appears to him as though for the first time. *Multiplicity*, for whose symbolization the numbers 4 and 5 often seem to be chosen, does not fail to be underscored. Here the only possible attitude is "laissez-faire."

To examine in more detail the reasons why things unfold in this way would lead us astray. We will only specify that we do not mean that a psychoanalysis always unfolds according to four great divisions. We have only wanted to disengage a certain thematic linkage that can be repeated at very different levels of analytic work and responds to an order according to which *no rehandling of the first relationship of being subjected to the mother's desire is possible without an integration of paternal meaning:* this integration is indissolubly linked to the subject's assumption of castration, to the overcoming of a certain blindness that always covers the identification with the phallus.

Here we touch on a point that J. Lacan vigorously established in his seminar "The Ethic of Psychoanalysis," and this is in my opinion one of the definitive acquisitions that he assured to psychoanalysis: Oedipus's horrible gesture has nothing to do with a punishment; the proof is that this moment is the beginning of his becoming truly seeing, divine; the gesture signifies Oedipus's renunciation of everything that captivated him until then.

To conclude, it is best to recapitulate the path that we have followed.

Our point of departure, which we have not yet made explicit, was this: *there is no other subject than the subject who speaks.*

We have not adopted this principle because it is self-evident, but rather because it has effectively helped us to resolve a certain number of difficulties, such as the following: if we envisage man as an organism (and there does not seem to be any alternative; man remains a speaking animal, and these two terms exhaust the domain of choice), we are certainly able to speak of an "explanation" standing between his organism and his world; but it will be impossible for us to respond to the question of identifying the thread of such an explanation except by a choice in which our ideals intervene, and these ideals, finally, are our discourse.

Do we not have a certain interest in knowing what governs our choice of discourse? Even more so, in that it is only too clear that the "explanation through his world" is only said of the organism metaphorically, thus imposing the task of knowing what this metaphor means in its original domain.

And here we can notice not only that there would be no explanation without words but that there would not be, for man, an explanation through his world if this world had not already been proposed to him in and by words. If the world is at the same time one and many, if things are reflected in themselves and at the same time related to each other, it is because they appear only when they are already involved in the net of language.

The nature of the signifier is to introduce *order* with differentiation; and to tell the truth, this very notion of order is inconceivable apart from the notion of the signifier. If, wanting to situate the subject, we have confined ourselves to the usage he makes of signifiers in his discourse, this is because a discourse, however diachronic it may be, supposes a synchrony that gives us its timing.

Now, psychoanalytic experience has shown us that the name of the father gives the timing. We should have expected as much. It is through a nomenclature defining the "kinship structure" that the symbolic order (or what C. Lévi-Strauss calls the "universe of rules") manifests itself first and universally. Next it is the father-son opposition that, at least in certain cultures like our own, is at the center of this structure, as the axis around which the entire system is equilibrated, and as the law according to which the movements of alliance and the succession of generation are regulated. It is only in relation to the signifier of paternity that the subject can and must situate himself in a lineage.

This task, we have seen, is accomplished in analysis as an integration of the sense of paternity in the discourse. For if the word "father" designates a person, *no previous meaning responds to the signifier "father."* As signifier and not merely as sign, "father" produces all the meanings that are interposed in the relation of the subject to his father. These meanings give rise to the imaginary confusions concerning the father's place and create the subject's difficulty with understanding. But these confusions presuppose the existence of a universe of rules in the same way that there is no "confusion of tongues" without language. In this universe of rules, the subject can only take his place and become the subject of speech in relation to another place, which by its symbolic opposition always signifies the ruin and the transmutation of his imaginary positions.

If Mrs. A—— asks unconsciously, "Am I a woman or am I his woman?" this is because her destiny was such that something was confused for her. From the very fact that she could situate herself in this way, however, even under the hesitating form of an alternative, one can conclude that she is not psychotic. Whatever the confusion of the universal discourse that surrounded her since her birth and made of her what she has become, the imposture was not pushed to the point of obliterating in her all sense of paternity.

The importance of the dream as the manifestation of such a questioning, as the "royal road to the unconscious," is more appreciable where the father is fated in waking life (this is why we compared him to a dream) to be imagined as the Ideal Father.

10   The Apprenticeship of Tilmann Moser

BY MOUSTAPHA SAFOUAN

Tilmann Moser, author of *Years of Apprenticeship on the Couch*, is a Frankfurt sociologist. He is particularly interested in the problems of juvenile delinquency and has published several works on the subject. These works have been well received in his country.

In the early 1960s Moser undertook three successive analyses. His last analyst was a woman. All three of these analyses failed.

In 1967 he applied as a candidate for a didactic analysis in the Frankfurt Psychoanalytic Society. First this candidature was refused, but later it was accepted after one year of face-to-face interviews taking place once a week. The man with whom he had these interviews later became his didactic analyst.

This analysis lasted four years, from 1968 to 1972. It ended on a note of exaggerated optimism, and one year after the end of the analysis, Moser had to come to terms with the fact that nothing had been resolved for him. This obliged him to add an afterword to all of the later editions of his book.

In this afterword he described what he calls the collapse of his illusion of having been "healed" by his analysis. He says that during his analysis he was unconsciously attached to the model of psychic devotion and had substituted psychoanalysis for religious truth. He notes—and this remark is accurate, as are all his others—that his book sounds like a missionary tract, the kind that his ancestors distributed among the Africans and Indians.

Thus it is not surprising that a little after his analysis, he was submerged by what he calls the "buried God image" of his childhood. He had to take up his analysis again, and he had great difficulty engaging himself in the analytic work. He came to ask himself if his precocious separation from his mother had not definitively undermined his fundamental capacity for trust.

His book nonetheless had some success: it was published in paperback and was translated into several languages. At the same time it became evident for him

First published as "Autour d'un ouvrage de Tilmann Moser," in *Lettres de l'Ecole Freudienne* 25: 1 (April 1979), pp. 41–49.

that the *Apprenticeship* represented "only a little more than half the 'truth of the matter.'" This is the sentence with which he closes his afterword.

We do not know who his analyst was, but we do know that this analyst was a student of Heinz Kohut. In fact, the teaching of Kohut is utterly transparent in the style of the analysis, and therefore I am obliged to discuss as briefly as possible the outline of this teaching.

At present Heinz Kohut is one of the most important psychoanalysts in the United States and elsewhere. He was president of the American Psychoanalytic Association, and he is the vice-president of the International Psychoanalytic Association. His theoretical work has concerned itself with what he calls "narcissistic neurosis," and he has published several works on this theme. The title of the most important of these is *The Analysis of the Self* [New York: International Universities Press, 1971]. According to Kohut, the problem is not the Oedipus complex, which is no longer mysterious, either for us or for our analysands who suffer from Oedipal neurosis. These latter are people capable of object relations, except for the fact that the incestuous quality of the objects on which they are fixated leads to unpleasant consequences, of which castration anxiety is not the least.

It is important that the problem is no longer Oedipal, Kohut believes, not only from the point of view of theory but also from the point of view of practice, because the majority of cases at present concern the narcissistic neurosis. How is Kohut going to construct the metapsychology, as he calls it, of this narcissistic neurosis? What is the instrument with which he will work?

Kohut calls his instrument "empathy," which we can translate as a sympathetic understanding, a kind of identification that permits a person to understand things from the inside.

Evidently this procedure invites a question. If empathy is the instrument or the method, and if it is a kind of gift, then what is the purpose of didactic analysis? Ultimately we might be able to determine the purpose of supervision: someone can have a gift and at the same time learn to use it. But what good is didactic analysis, when it suffices to be gifted to practice analysis? I make this remark simply to indicate that the question of "transmission" is closely tied to one's theory of the unconscious and of the method used to support this theory.

Let us see how an analyst works when he does not in the least suspect that he is using his ears. First he remarks that this empathy or sympathy is something that has its limit; it is not infinite, and this makes for the fact that the affective or effective experience of the child, especially during the earliest infancy, escapes us entirely; this is one limit. Happily, we can understand the adult with whom we are working, the patient, and from there we can reconstruct the experiences of his childhood. Later, direct observation of children can confirm our hypotheses. What is important is that this observation does not invalidate or "disconfirm" them.

Here the author forgets precisely that for him an adult is ill only insofar as he is a child, as he remains a child. But with the assurance given by this kind of forgetfulness, he will teach us that everything begins with an original or primary narcissism, for which contact with reality represents a threat or an injury. Faced with this threat the child can respond in one of two ways: he can either idealize the object excessively—this resembles the projective identifications talked about by the school of Melanie Klein—or else he can have recourse to an exaggerated sense of self, which Kohut calls the "grandiose self."

Here is where fantasies enter into play, notably fantasies of exhibition and of omnipotence. According to Kohut the function of fantasy is in some way to supplement or counterbalance the threat to narcissism.

The self is a thing. Kohut does not say exactly which thing it is, but we understand that an imaginary structure is in question, since he speaks very often of self-image. The ego is another thing, which he calls ego reality. The ego is the agency of the real in the subject, or what we used to call the function of the real.

We see that the idealization of the object and the creation of a grandiose self both endanger the ego.

According to Kohut the function of parents is to give appropriate responses to satisfy the narcissistic needs of the child and at the same time limit these responses so that they are compatible with the ego and create self-esteem. In short, this is a function that subsumes disparate functions.

A failure by parents leads to an aggravation of narcissism, and this is a necessary condition for the cohesion of the self. When Kohut speaks of this exaggerated narcissism as necessary for the cohesion of the self, this indicates well enough his concern with the imaginary, with something threatened by nothing less than fragmentation.

Thus the parents' failure at this task produces an aggravation of narcissism, which puts the ego—as a function of reality—in danger. From there the task of the analyst is clear. First, it will consist of favoring the therapeutic activation of the dissociated self and, in this sense, of the unconscious—in other words, for Kohut the unconscious is dissociation. This therapeutic actualization happens in the transference, which will take one of the following two forms: either the analyst will become the idealized object in an idealizing transference, or else he will become the mirror of the grandiose self in a mirror transference.

The problem is that the demands of the narcissistic self are never entirely satisfied; sooner or later the analysand will feel frustrated or deceived. If these frustrations and deceptions are interpreted with a correct sympathetic understanding of the analysand's feelings, significant memories will gradually emerge around the dynamic prototype of the present experience. The remembering of appropriate infantile memories and the deeper understanding of the analogous transferential experiences will converge to give assistance to the patient's ego. The automatic reactions of the past will gradually become more inhibited as far as their goal is concerned and will submit to the ego's control.

At the end of the analysis, patients and analysts can share the recognition of the fact that the analysis itself has necessarily remained incomplete. The correct attitude will join sobriety with wisdom, to the exclusion of both sarcasm and pessimism. At the moment of separation, analysts and patients will admit that everything has not been resolved, that certain symptoms and inhibitions as well as certain archaic tendencies toward the aggrandizing of self and toward infantile idealization still persist. The advantage is that past weaknesses have now become familiar and that the patient is in a position where he can contemplate them with tolerance and detachment. This is the way Kohut's book ends, and this is exactly the way the analysis of Moser ended.

Now, however, we can see that what Moser called his "illusion of being healed" was in fact an illusion shared, if not induced, by the analyst. A British commentator did not fail to underscore the point that not only the patient's narcissism is in question here, but also the analyst's narcissism. Yet this commentator did not see or did not point out the tie between the analyst's narcissism and the theory of ego reality. This latter is founded on the idea of an alliance with the sane or strong part of the ego. After all, it was the idea of this alliance that led analysts astray into a conception of their task as that of an educator who was supposed to produce an emotional education. This conception was common in the 1950s, and we see that today it has been surpassed by a concept of the sympathetic or empathic analyst who is led astray toward an ideal of devotion and samaritan helping, an ideal about which I will say that its sadistic underpinnings are more than evident.

We can easily imagine the technique and the style of interpretation and intervention that are inspired by such a theory, but the interest of Moser's work is elsewhere.

Moser published his book despite the risk or even the certainty of being accused in analytic circles of exhibitionism and acting out. He did so because it seemed to him difficult to bury such an experience, even more so because the medium of many long passages of this experience was language. He underlines this term: the experience took place *in language.*

Moser himself seems to be fairly well informed regarding what seems to have been a misdeal in the analyst's pretended gift of self. He was constantly fleeing the look of this self, except once near the end of the analysis, when he thought that he had never looked at a human face that contained so much affection. On the other hand, he was on the lookout for the least sound that emanated from this wall of silence, and he devoted several pages of his book, written with vivacity, to the description of what he calls the ur-sounds, the ur-noises, as we say ur-speech, these "psychoanalytic ur-noises," which are the ahems, the sneezings, and so forth.

When the analyst expressed himself in words, they were words that were used, as he says, under the pretext of interpreting the transference, to interfere with everything, including the masturbatory fantasy. And the author of *Apprenticeship* labels the analyst's references to childhood as reductive, since they deprive the experience of its specificity. He describes how these interventions and interpretations finished by rendering his progression into analytic trust as something close to torture. On top of that he sees very well how this technique is based on a theoretical aberration. It was Moser who found the nice metaphor for the grandiose self, the metaphor of the dragon, and it was Moser who labeled Kohut a "dragonologist." When he wrote about this in a letter to Kohut, the latter replied by referring to some page of his book.

As for the notion of empathy, Moser puts it in its place with a phrase that is very telling. He heard his analyst tell him that he never became angry with his patients and that if he did, he saw the anger as the sign of something that he did not understand for lack of sympathy. Moser calls this a megalomania and comments, "Through his statement, I heard the muteness of Laius and Jocasta formulated as theory."

This sentence has something almost painful about it, but it is no less significant for that. We come to ask ourselves, what obliged such a man to remain in this hole? What obliges him constantly to make amends honorably and to disown his intelligence with interpretations that arise from principles whose inanity is transparent to him?

What is happening resembles the drama of intelligence: we have never seen a discipline or a system that pretends to spring from thought serve so clearly to enslave that same thought.

Here, evidently, we cannot neglect the weight of the analyst's desire, a desire that happened in this case to be the desire of the go-between or intermediary and was expressed in the most blatant fashion during the analysis. Having had a consultation with a pretty woman patient, the analyst addressed himself to Moser, who was doing group therapy at the time, in the following glowing terms: "That one has to learn how to feel, she needs high-grade analytical nourishment. Do you want to take her on?"

The same desire took another form that was slightly less blatant but no less transparent. The analyst wanted his analysand to marry, and we understand that Moser as analysand had no desire to obey this desire, even if it was really his own. Moser says that his analyst helped him in many areas but failed in the principal task, which was that of rendering him apt to have a durable, trusting relationship with a woman.

Nevertheless, the analysis was terminated because of the certainty that it had lasted long enough. This certainty resisted the examination of the question of whether the date of departure was not determined by the realization that an entire region of the patient's unconscious had remained unexplored and ought to remain so forever.

Even if the analyst's desire explains a transmission of analysis that is something like smuggling, however, we do not have the answer to the question we posed. I find the response to this question in Tilmann Moser's conviction in the afterword, which is in evidence throughout his book, that is to say, his faith in psychoanalysis, in Freud, and in the unconscious.

Curiously enough, this faith in the unconscious, even when presented naively—and no one ever escapes from this naivete—as faith in the science of unconscious contents, is equivalent to the most radical and subtle negation of said unconscious.

A technique can be constructed based on this science of the unconscious—in the objective sense of the genitive. This technique will necessarily be concentrated on know-how, but I will spare you Kohut's description of the three stages in which he thinks analysis takes place. At the same time psychoanalytic transmission becomes a question of form that leaves nothing undecidable. The institute decides at the beginning whether the candidate is apt or not, and when the candidate has been chosen, nothing remains except to prepare him.

Moser's work has the interest of proving by absurdity the fact that no analysis is possible without recognition that the basis of the transference is the analysand's imputing a subject to unconscious or repressed knowledge.

In this perspective a technique that essentially concerns interpretation will become conceivable. This technique will concern itself with the restitution of that which is signified in the analysand's discourse. This technique would subordinate itself to the knowledge that is in the unconscious instead of suggesting that it contained this knowledge. This technique will leave a place for the undecidable. Thus, through Lacan's theory and the technique it founds, we can say that the transmission of analysis is another question, which this theory would not pretend to answer before the question.

It is doubtless worth the trouble to say here how a theory encounters its own limits. This will permit us to specify the sense we give to the word "transmission." I will attempt to do so by referring to one of Freud's dreams, excusing myself before those for whom this analysis will be repetitive.

> The place was a mixture of a private sanatorium and several other institutions. A manservant appeared to summon me to an examination. I knew in the dream that something had been missed and that the examination was due to a suspicion that I had misappropriated the missing article.

(The analysis showed that the examination was to be taken in two senses and included a medical examination.)

> Conscious of my innocence and of the fact that I held the position of a consultant in the establishment, I accompanied the servant quietly. At the door we were met by another servant, who said, pointing to me: "Why have you brought him? He's a respectable person." I then went, unattended, into a large hall, with machines standing in it, which reminded me of an Inferno with its hellish instruments of punishment. Stretched out on one apparatus I saw one of my colleagues, who had every reason to take some notice of me; but he paid no attention. I was then told I could go. But I could not find my hat and could not go after all. [1]

This is a Kafkaesque dream where some unspecified mistake or fault is in question. The dream describes a place that is a hell, a place that one passes through alone, where even the one who has the best reasons for remarking your presence does not do so. This place is precisely the space of analysis.

Others before me have guessed as much, without any preliminary comparing of notes. This interpretation is again confirmed if we look at the verb "can go." With this Freud associated a line from Schiller that he misquoted: "The Moor has done his duty, the Moor can go." To put it another way, at issue in the dream is not the banal metaphor of "going" for "dying" but "going" for "the Moor's death." The Moor's death [la mort du Maure] sounds in French like death's death, and this is the nicest definition that we can give for the end of analysis, for after all, it is a matter of an invitation to live, even if it is paid for

---

1. Freud, *The Interpretation of Dreams* (1900), S.E. 4, p. 336.

with a "de-being." For what has the subject died of, if not that which fixes him in the identical, as Serge Leclaire would say it?

Otherwise stated, the message of the dream, what it signifies, is that Freud opts for a "thou canst know." Signified by the dream, it is a message in which we can have confidence, which can say without being ridiculous, "I choose truth" or "I opt for truth." This is precisely the point that is not decided at the beginning, and we have no way of knowing it at the beginning. I would even say that we have no way of knowing it, not only not at the beginning, but throughout, until the last moment; we cannot foresee what will happen in the next instant. Ultimately, at the end of analysis, the analysand leaves us in a state of ignorance that takes precedence over everything we may have learned about him during the analysis. . . . For myself I find a sufficient explanation in the impossibility of calculating the effects of speech, whether we are thinking of words that have been heard during the course of an existence or, better yet, of words that have been lacking.

Here is where theory finds its limits. Determining or marking this point where effects are incalculable will help us to find the sense of the transmission of analysis.

The term "transmission" is a term of ordinary language, and we cannot transport it into our own field without adapting it. As a term of ordinary language, it bears, we can be sure, an excess of sense that will be nonsense itself.

We can say for sure that there is in analysis the opening of the pathways that lead to the unconscious. The dream is the royal road, Freud said, but it was he who opened this path. Before him no one even suspected the existence of the unconscious. Now, with this opening of a pathway, something is transmitted, but this is absolutely not a transmission taking place between one person and another. It is a transmission to the analysand of whatever knowledge is in his unconscious. Everything else is excess baggage.

PART THREE.   PSYCHOSIS

11   The Onset of Psychosis

BY MARCEL CZERMAK

1

A three-year-old boy, seeing for the first time a man returning from wartime imprisonment, asks: "Who is that?" He hears the response: "He is your father. A father doesn't come out of the blue." Twenty years later, this boy, having just become a father, was doing his military service as a parachutist. Touching down from his first jump, he became delusional. He said, "I am God."

This anecdote will introduce you to the question that this incident poses for me: beginning with a review of a certain number of cases and fragments of cases, I want to clarify what happens at the onset of psychosis. These cases all happen to concern men, for reasons independent of this work itself.

My first subject was in analysis, and it was the analysis that had provoked the onset of his psychosis. The more he progressed in analysis, the more he felt that he was going through an ordeal. The psychoanalyst, as other, appeared to him to be more and more perfect, and when he heard someone on television say that analysts are saints, his intuition was confirmed. In relation to this flawless perfection, he could only think of himself as a failure, a piece of refuse. When, just before Easter vacation, his analyst said, "We'll stop there and we'll take it up again after the vacation," he felt himself literally being "dropped."

A little before this he had had two dreams. In one of them his mother was throwing the garbage over a balcony, and in the other a ram, the head of a flock, was trying to bring stray lambs back into the fold. The ram became mired in quicksand.

When he heard "we'll stop there," this remark exemplified the impossibility of any speech that could make him a subject. Thus he went to see his father. This latter has been defined by the patient in terms of his terrible look and voice. Thus, having left the psychoanalyst, he went to his father and looked at him doing a crossword puzzle. He looked at his father with a look that evidently was

Marcel Czermak is a psychiatrist affiliated with Henri-Rousselle Hospital in Paris. He is also in the private practice of psychoanalysis. This article was first published as "Sur le déclenchement des psychoses," in *Ornicar?* 9 (April 1977), pp. 15–28.

not an appeal; he looked at him and was not able to call to him with articulate speech.

It was not even like the statement "Father, don't you see that I am burning?"[1] He evoked the father, not this father who was there before him, but *The Father*. "Father!" he said to himself.

As he evoked *The Father*, a terrible response came to him: "Son!" This hallucinated response made him feel that he had exploded and that the parts of his body were becoming objects around him.

Finally he got hold of himself, only to engage in a fight to the death. "I will not let myself be manipulated!" he cried out. At this time he could recognize his disappointment that such a fabulous adversary could have borrowed his own father's voice.

In the evening, when the patient was exhausted by his combat, the voice came back and enjoined him, he says, to jump out the window. An attentive examination will show us that the voice said nothing. But the pure, ineffable voice, the pure terrible object through which his body was becoming part of the world of objects, responded, "Out the window." The pure voice catapulted his body out the window. Remember the dream of the trash thrown out the window by his mother. This is what the patient had said about it: "To speak is to bring to life. Speech is fertile, but not for me." At the moment when the pure voice manifested itself, the subject's body translated a radical absence of symbolization, which we can summarize as follows: since there is no act where *to speak is to bring to life*, the only resolution is in a lethal *out the window*.[2]

Having survived the ensuing fall, the patient, become hypomaniacal, screamed. He did not say, "I am God," but rather, "I am the living Christ resurrected." The signifier, never having been at *its* place, emerged as an imperative "Son!" that nailed the subject to *his* legitimate place. He can only experience this as a mortal aggression. It is not an infertile speech but a tyrannical voice, qualified as Divine Father, that brings the patient to coalesce with the first maternal Other, while at the same time making him into dirt or waste to be evacuated in a delusional birth. Then, killed without being dead, our young man begins his struggle with God by proclaiming, "The living Christ resurrected, I will not let myself be manipulated." Lethal conflict where the unsymbolized "to speak is to bring to life" is desymbolized, reduced to an inarticulate command-

---

1. [See Freud, *The Interpretation of Dreams* (1900), S.E. 5, p. 509, for a discussion of this dream.]

2. [In French, *parler fait naître* and *par la fenêtre* are almost homophones.]

ment and then enacted in the fall of a primordial object. The desperate suicide attempt has tried to break apart the coalescence of the pure voice, the pure commandment, with primordial objects.

Lacking a voice to carry speech, the patient, facing his father, had only voiceless speech, a speech he could not articulate. And this speech appeared in the real, in the act, with a defenestration.

All of this is structured like a sentence, even though it could not be spoken. The counterpoint of the symbolic and absent "to speak is bring to life" emerges in a voice without speech whose subordinate clause is a "bring to life" [*fait naître*], a mortal window [*fenêtre*] or pure look that took hold of our patient.

Here you can see that in order for there to be a question, there must in this case be a subject before the question. Because it is absent, when the patient is faced with this father who is merely voice and look, the voice he hears does not question him, he does not feel questioned, and there is not even an internal dialogue. After he evoked his father, the voice (homologous in the real with symbolic speech) manifested itself and sent him the ending of the sentence—"to bring to life"—in a real defenestration. The subject passed through a window that was looking at him. Note how much this voice, qualified as divine father, is discovered to be governed by a discourse in which a mother lays down the law of the signifier.

Beyond that, in the fall, a delusional fertilization by the divine voice occurs. The falling subject risks his life in this fall; he manifests this knowledge—which is language knowledge—that speaking brings life. Speech is fertile and promising. Here, however, the promise of the perfect Other leads to an unleashing of a signifier whose force brings the subject to a suicide attempt whose significance is distorted in the illusion of resurrection. We are faced with a birth that never took place. The subject is left waiting to be fertilized, but fertilization is deferred to the end of time.

An encounter with a pure voice is much more frequent than clinicians think. Our insufficient tests and examinations often miss it. We can find it, however, in the terrible sound of the shofar, horn of the primordial ram, symbol of the ancestor who demands a sacrifice. In the patient's dream this pure voice is that of the ram who calls to the stray lambs to bring them back to the flock— "provided that the ram does not get caught in quicksand," thinks the dreamer.

What he ignores is that since the subject is absent before the question, the voice of the ram will be one that kills [*tue*] because it cannot say "thou" [*tu*].

The automatism, said by de Clérambault to be mental, is to be found in the act through which the body, commanded by voice and look, disarticulates itself and tries to rearticulate a sentence that was never articulated. The attempt to articulate the relation of "Son" to a "Father" who has never occupied his rightful place forces the object *a*, voice and look, to emerge in the hallucination. The object emerges so well in the hallucination that the subject now circulates between voice and look, following the lines of force that are organized around the window. He himself is one of these lines of force.

We say then, that voice and look resemble the inside and outside of a glove. The voice is inside and the look outside. When the glove is turned inside out, the subject becomes detached from the voice and falls out, as waste, only to fall back into the untainted look.

2

Our next patient experienced the onset of his psychosis when his pregnant wife threatened to perform an abortion on herself and had to be hospitalized.

During his wife's hospitalization he cared for his first son by himself. His wife then had an abortion, and for him a child disappeared. Now he had to answer his oldest son's questions. This son was just beginning to speak. He cannot remember the questions that his son asked, but we know the answers that he gave. We find them in his delusions. For example: "People want to make me recognize that I am something other than what I am . . ., others tell me that I am Nothing. . . . A woman wanted to make me say that I am God or Christ. . . ." Then, perplexed but not confused, he tells three versions of a fantasy.

First version: "I was swimming with my brother. . . . We were with others. When we came back, someone had disappeared. . . . My mother arrived, people. . . . Someone is laid out on the grass."

Second version: "I am wading in the stream with my father. A floating bag passes us; my father goes to fetch it and pushes it onto the grass."

Third version: "I am playing with the baker's son." This boy was his closest friend when they were young; he died of a brain tumor at this time. "I make him drink the broth. Father intervenes, but it is too late, he is dead."

Note well that we do not know *who* is dead in this statement. Also, at approximately the same time that the baker's son died, the patient's father had an attack of "mysticism," and his mother said to him, "He has disappeared for us."

Thus we do not know the question that our patient's son asked, but we do know the answer. If it is delusional, this is because, unable to respond, he is not what he is; he cannot follow what precedes him; he is following something other than what he am (follow).[3] Something else, but what? Nothing? God? Christ? From a place where he is nothing or God or Christ, the elder son replaces the fetus that has been killed or taken away. This child is the patient's "analagon"; he does not follow what he follows. Thus, we find, in the fantasy is not only the death of the fetus or the friend but also the patient's ejection. He feeds the broth to his alter ego, to this brother represented by the baker's son, and this person dies, despite the intervention of the father. Reversing the terms, we have a father who is dead but who does not know it, dead not because of the subject's wish but because of what was said by his mother.

The fantasy shows us this in the following two ways: (1) Someone—we do not know who, but it is not a father—has disappeared; his remains are laid out on the grass. (2) The something that has disappeared is floating on the water, an inert bag of signifiers. A father wades into the water to catch it and empty it onto the grass. He wants to give the remains, the empty bag, to his wife.

In the third version of the fantasy, time flows from the source: the intervention of the father (or of what remains of him) will be useless. The son or brother drinks from the cup and will not be saved.

Persons and generations are telescoped: the patient, his father, his friend, his dead child, and his living son converge. Is he God, Christ, or Nothing?

We can understand his perplexity: "What happened to me?"

At the point where delusions emerge, we often find the idea that something has been taken away or has disappeared. Surely, the something that the subject thinks he has lost is not lacking in the real. The fantasy shows us that the subject himself is affected by a deprivation whose bearing is symbolic; and this is why we hear him say, "I was God, Christ, or nothing." Or else, as another patient told me, "I was the global One." And still another said, "The concentric and expanded One whose curving look is reflected back on itself, penetrating into its own cells, which are thus those of the other."

In the second stage of the delusional work, the psychotic subject questions himself about the hole in the real in order to deny this incredible possibility. In so doing he misapprehends his own symbolic catastrophe by evoking a disaster that will eventually take place in the real. His struggle against this danger is manifest when he formulates, for example, a unitary theory of the universe: there is no hole in the universe, for if there were one, the universe itself would fall into it.

Being God, Christ, or Nothing, the psychotic abolishes all enumeration,

---

3. [The play on words between "to be" and "to follow" derives from the fact that in French "I am" and "I follow" are both written *je suis*. In French the dislocation is evident only in the written text.]

annuls all difference, and makes beings and objects interchangeable. The subject's wife may herself disappear or be taken away.

I have said that our subject is perplexed and that his perplexity is not confusional. The person who has disappeared is analogous to the ornamented borders that surround hieroglyphic texts. These borders are the basis for the deciphering of the text. When this border is empty, the symbolic level that it constitutes vanishes, and the translator is stalled.

Before finishing with our patient, I will recall that he had experienced the following phenomena after the death of a friend several years before: an atrocious toothache, the sensation of having his tooth bursting for several weeks, the removal of a good tooth.

The year before, a man had entered his office. He was certain for a moment that the man had come to take him away, to make him disappear. We will return to the role of such phenomena.

3

Now, we have another patient, whose psychosis was set off in a foreign city, to which he had traveled with his fiancée. Just before this trip, she had been pregnant. They decided on an abortion, and several weeks later they began this trip.

The year before, this young man had had the following experience: his mother had remarried, and his stepfather had proposed to adopt him legally for reasons of inheritance. As a precondition for adoption, his father would have had to renounce his paternity; the patient planned to take a new name composed of his own name and that of his stepfather. Now, because of a bureaucratic mistake, the name he received was the name of his mother, attached to the name of his father. The whole family complained sufficiently to convince the authorities that they should reconsider the matter, and a few months later our patient obtained the name he wanted, in which the names of his progenitor and his stepfather were joined.

Now for some of the events in his history. When he was thirteen, there had been a theft in class, and for a few moments everyone was sure that the culprit was his best friend.

A little later, when he was almost seventeen, as he was coming out of the subway, he had seen two men advancing toward him; he was certain that they wanted to take his wallet. Finally he got hold of himself, but from that day forward he always double-locked his door.

When he was twenty, he knocked over and broke a vase at the home of an aunt and uncle while they were out. He went out and bought another, and when they returned he swore on his life that the new vase was the same as the old one. Only after a half-hour did he recognize that the vase was not the same.

The onset of his psychosis occurred during a trip. He was using his step-father's car, which the latter had strongly resisted lending to the young man. Our patient dreaded using this machine. So he left on his trip and was stopped by the police for having crossed a solid dividing line on the road. He had to show his identity papers but was finally let go. He arrived in the foreign city in the evening. Then his girl friend said to him: "Two guys are following us. They want to kidnap me." In normal circumstances she thinks that all men are after her.

In any case, our patient became convinced that someone wanted to kidnap them, both of them. He locked himself into his room that night, and in the morning he tried to flee toward Paris. He went downstairs, but when he reached the place where his car had been, it wasn't there—he couldn't see it anymore. After a moment he saw the car again, right in front of him, and they returned to Paris. They went straight to the hospital.

Having just entered the hospital, the young man jumped out the window—of the ground floor. No harm was done.

Whenever anyone in his presence talks about something lacking or about deprivation—a stolen wallet, a broken vase, a lost car, a kidnapped woman—his delusions begin. They want to kill her, the woman. . . . This is what we call *pousse à la femme*.

In this case the object has so totally disappeared from the real that the patient has negative hallucinations. He has many doubts as to the existence of objects: "But then, this ashtray that I see on your desk, perhaps it is not there." All objects that are receptacles in one form or another are interchangeable when they come to abide in the empty hole of the symbolic—the wallet, the vase, the car, or his future wife, who tells him, "They want to take me away." Here I would summarize his words in the following way: "They want to take me away to the same place where someone else has already been taken, to the place where something of yours has already disappeared. They want to take me away from where I am, from where I situate myself as object. As an object or decoy, I mask what has already been taken from you. If I am taken away, that place will be stripped to reveal a vertiginous gulf. I look at you as the absence of absence; I am the place of the negative hallucination, because Woman does not exist."

He speaks freely of these objects that are *out of place*. In all probability different places designate the successive identifications whose functions he was not able to take on in a signifying sequence. But when I speak his displaced name, he will say to me: "That does nothing to me. . . . No, I really don't have any sense of it. . . . Nonetheless I am a man who is attentive to exceptions, to what is out of place." With psychotics a change in the smallest detail has great importance. This patient, when talking to his aunt and uncle about the vase, said: "It's the same." Only later did he say, "It's not exactly the same."

One day, to my amazement, the delusions vanished overnight, in the following circumstances.

I had been thinking about how to handle this case. The delusions had lasted several weeks and had become more organized. One afternoon, having had enough, I went to him to say: "But didn't this all begin at a moment when someone was really kidnapped?" In fact, I had learned that in this city a friend of his family had been kidnapped. The patient was dumbfounded. The next morning nothing was left of the delusions.

Evidently I did not understand what I had done, except to the extent that I knew that everything turned on the signifier "kidnapped."

May I simply remind you of this note of Freud: "an attempt to explain a hallucination ought to attack not the positive hallucination, but rather the negative."

4

Our next patient introduced us to the unspoken question of the place of the heir, of the successor. The question gives rise to the following problem: he had a mother who was heiress by a female line. She had been, in circumstances that I cannot relate, the true cause of the death of the patient's father, but had imputed this role to her young son, rejecting her own role in the affair. For various reasons, after the death of her husband, she gave her son's rights to his inheritance to the paternal grandfather.

The psychosis broke out when the subject inherited a piano from a maternal aunt, his mother's older sister, who had become head of the family.

He tells me that he is the first man to inherit in a succession of women. "What am I, then, if I am something other than what I am? I'm the first man, perhaps Adam. . . ."

The inheritance of the absence of the subject prior to the question, linked with the absence of the signifier, comes to be materialized in the thing he inherits: a piano.

Just before his arrival at the hospital, he had spent several days during which he could not leave his home and was riveted to his piano, around which he had arranged all the objects of the apartment: "I circulate in this apartment as in a labyrinth, between different territories that do not come together. . . . I must be ready for the alliance." He was screaming, seizing this inherited piano, which made body and world hold together, "So that in and by my body, nations are joined together."

This hypothetical alliance postpones to an indefinite future the promise of a mastery of bodily territory, despite the object that had been abandoned to the jouissance of God—since he was Jewish, this object was the foreskin. "Disorder, in my house?" he declared to his mother, who was outraged by the state of his apartment. "This is my effort to put some order into the objects of the succession."

The reordering of the series of signifiers began with his inheritance, a piano that designated what he had been deprived of.

Remember that for our last patient this mental disorder did not go so far: the objects of the familial succession were also evoked, but only as flickering lights in the holes of the world.

5

I mentioned the foreskin abandoned to the jouissance of God. This is the key for our next patient.

He was the issue of a family that functioned as if men were born of men. He obliged his parents to avow their Judaism, and at the age of twenty, he had himself circumcised. It was at the moment when he had just been deprived of this symbolic part, which marks the Alliance, that the "fertile moment" of the psychosis occurred. His mother said to him: "What we said to you—about our Judaism—we said it to please you." At that moment he became delusional. What he heard meant that the part of himself that he had abandoned to the Name of the Father had not been received, that he was not in a position to abandon this part to the other, and thus that he was not in a position to abandon the other. He entered into psychosis, crying out, "She refuses the law of the return." His mother had reasserted her claim to her child.

The subject is thus seized by a raging megalomania when, trying to put some order into the objects of the family succession, he discovers that he himself has merely been an object succeeding nothing. As such, he is at every moment on the treadmill of a history and spatial organization that can only go around in circles. He is like a stream that in slowing down turns upon itself to see itself in the present wave as the bearer of timeless images.

In time this young man pulled himself together and ran away from the hospital, only to return a few days later. He seemed to be much better, and this was obviously disquieting. There was no way of finding out what he had done while on the outside, until finally, one morning, after he had feigned obtuseness, at the moment when I was about to disappear from view (I was at the door), he seized me to say, with a malicious smile, "I'm going to tell the truth; I went out to steal in order to reconstitute the debt."

There was, alas, no longer a subject to pay off this debt.

Our patient had already had a first psychotic episode when the friend whom he used as a prosthesis (the patient lived an existence of pure facticity by copying the friend's gestures) closed the door on him one day to prepare an exam, thus disappearing from his view. Then he had the impression that he had been kidnapped, that he was tracked, followed, and that someone wanted to kill him. "A friend vanishes" is the image of delusional intrusions, an image that reflects him but in which the subject does not think to recognize himself. That is how he knows he is followed: "I am something other than what I am [suis] when someone is following [suit] me."

Note that this "someone" [in French, on] here functions grammatically as a formula of nullification. Thus the phrase "someone is following me" [on me suit] can be heard as "someone am me" [on me suis], this in place of "I am me." He might have said: "I discovered myself thus exposed, commanded, postulated, when the mental automatism unveiled it, but 'someone' can know nothing of it. . . . 'Someone am me,' since I can only follow this signifier, which can emerge only in opposition to me; it is the signifier that follows me and tyrannizes me. I speak less than I am spoken by my throat, and I can no longer recognize this discourse that it articulates as mine. It is more foreign to me than your speech."

6

Since we mention verbal hallucination here, we will distinguish the various forms into which it evolves, thus measuring its bearing on the subject.

Even before the time when the subject will deny having spoken and in so doing will experience his own saying as hallucination, or else when he will go crazy over the fact that *it* is speaking in his own throat and that his tongue is being agitated against his will, a lesser phenomenon can take place. This is produced when sender and receiver become confused over the message destined for the subject. At this moment of thought confusion, a silent "automatic" articulation says something that makes it impossible to know which part of the message comes from the sender and which part from the receiver. Seglas has already noted this silent articulation, and he deserves credit for showing us that when the verbal hallucination emerges, it is above all else a procedure to which the subject has recourse in trying to maintain himself within humanity. It is not originally a hallucination.

This is the general significance of the phenomena of de Clérambault's mental automatism. I would say the following about it in paraphrasing Lacan's article "L'Etourdit":[4] the fact that mental automatism manifests itself remains forgotten behind what is said in that which is heard.

Looking at what is manifested, we may broach the question of identification in psychotics. These subjects have been living by copying gestures, to the point where they have become—can we still say subjects?—marionettes of pure seeming, fabricated of various random parts, mimicked from people who have crossed their path.

I think of a patient, precipitated into psychosis through having taken LSD just before he had to act a role in a play in his native village, a role that his father had told him he would not be able to act. His voices whispered, "Be a man . . . ," or "Sow confusion. . . ." He confessed this with a controlled and satisfied smile.

It was easy enough in the interview to reach the point where he recognized his taste for sowing the seeds of dissension in order to compensate for his difficulty in witnessing his own discordance with the world's script. This discussion had the effect of bringing about the disappearance of the hallucinations and the emergence of a fragmented discourse, entirely "imaginative," to speak like Dupré, constituted by neologisms and by fragments of talk heard in subways, of popular songs, of politician's speeches, of clichés and stereotyped expressions. It was the pure echo of his master's voice. The fleeting instant was overfilled by the false universal witness with many faces.

I pointed out to what extent his discourse was indebted to others, and the next time I saw him the voices had reappeared.

Briefly, when he was no longer identified by his voices, he became a reflection and pieced together everything that came within hearing distance. Obviously, he was most manly when he hallucinated, and what could I possibly accomplish by interpreting his hallucinations?

The case was exemplary in its apparently atypical quality. It was perfectly intermediate between the pure hallucinatory psychoses and what the classics called "confabulating paraphrenia" or "delusions of the imagination": a

4. [In *Scilicet* 4 (Paris: Editions du Seuil, 1973), pp. 5–52.]

psychosis that sometimes had neither hallucinations nor fertile moment nor articulated delusions without a moment of onset, without anything that suggests a minimum of identificatory crystallization. We would look in vain in such a person for the remarkable way in which some psychotics articulate point by point their delusions about the imaginary of someone who is close to them. In those cases the marking of the imaginary of this other sometimes permits us (relatively) to handle the psychosis.

The elementary phenomenon that constitutes the essential point of the psychosis in question is the subject's way of reflecting one or another characteristic of people who cross his path.

Note well that this trait cannot sustain an otherness or mark a difference or bring about an existential virtuality. Rather, it is a desperately inert way of maintaining oneself inside humanity by occupying any place whatever in the most fluid and effortless fashion, without repetitive scanning, and by escaping as much as possible from any desire coming from others. Pure reflection divided to infinity, outside time and space: these are free men!

We understand, then, the unique aspect in which we appear to them: with the face of the false self, the false doctor, and the false witness, confirming that everything seen was already predicted and that everything said was already seen; we appear to be the emanation of a universal imposture. They are extremely attentive to that which is fleeting and at the same time to the small detail that solicits them without interesting them, which implies no identification with absence, which is wholly within the realm of presence.

For some of them, it takes very little for the gleam of a look to become invading. A fleeting light or a rhythm obsesses them to the point where the entire world begins to bang on their ears or their eyes, or begins to speak. All the world's signifiers, in cacaphonic resonance, become a general language, and the universe, become so fat with its encoding, submerges our subject in such a way that he no longer knows where his brain is, so much so that finally all contours are abolished. All that remains is this famous "thinking of nothing," which one of them nicely called his "lacks" or "silences."

I would like to insist on the frequency of the presence of elementary phenomena well before the psychosis comes to manifest itself overtly. Their meaning is always personal, and they go from fleeting foreignness to a frank xenopathy; they are eruptive and brief, often integrated into the subject's existence without any questions being asked, sometimes as a part of the routine of everyday life. The subject will maintain them in the open or in the frightened silence of his secret garden.

These facts are known but too often forgotten. I would like to accent only what presents itself in our experience very frequently: the subject's certainty that "they" want to take him away, to kidnap him, or better yet, that he is disappearing without being able to talk any more, while beside him or behind him a mute presence emerges, knowing how to think and to talk but obstinately keeping silent. During a dialogue the subject can be seen to abolish himself temporarily, to fly away, and this without his recollecting anything about it afterward and without being terribly affected by it.

When the mute presence emerged for one of my patients, her eyes blinked and then became vacant. She next stood up to move toward the window that looked down on her from a house next door. This woman became psychotic after her husband left her, when she had the feeling one night, after she had put her child to bed, of an ineffable jouissance and of leaving her child while literally seeing candles in the sky.

I began with the story of a man who fell from the sky, and I close with the story of a woman who raises her eyes to the sky. I have come full circle. Thus I will interrupt myself, and in place of a conclusion, I will talk about what the clinician experiences in his relationship with the madman. For me, it is the revelation of the extreme failure of dialogue. Dialogue is always awaited and never attained; its formulas do not bring any conviction, except in marking the logic of this condemnation, this co-damnation, encountering an impossibility that is rather difficult to support but to which we are always brought closer if we keep firm in our resolve, even when we would prefer to maintain our powerlessness by placing ourselves as the phantom guardians of the bottomless barrel of hope.

Valéry refers, as I remember, to the infamy of the most necessary work. Evidently I have kept silent about the necessary infamy in the matters about which I have spoken to you. This position is ethical, and there is no need for me to elaborate on it, since we all know how, wanting to liberate ourselves from infamy, we make it our bedfellow. It is necessary to cultivate that necessary prudence that Gracian speaks about when he says, "It is better not to make of one madness two."

The clinician has no special alliance with the truth, even if he devotes himself to defining how the errors of speech derive from a lie. I drew this lesson from a melancholic as one would draw wine from a keg, and it was perhaps after all to drink to his health in the name of this look that has been in question here and that prevails in the degradation of speech, in its exclusion.

12 Bronzehelmet, or the Itinerary of the Psychotherapy of a Psychotic

BY JEAN-CLAUDE SCHAETZEL

Bronzehelmet—what are we talking about? An object that is heavy to wear, a covering and protective armature hiding beneath its curve a nameless warrior in the fray? Who is under this headpiece? What is the name of one who cannot question his identity when he is suddenly separated from the battlefield, borne away like a body deprived of speech? Bronzehelmet is a student who began his psychotherapy four years ago, without identity or speech, borne by a discourse that is not his.

Dragging through the hallways of the university, seeking one of his professors to explain the disarray that had been triggered by an episode that we will speak about, this young man was intercepted by an assistant professor who referred him to a social worker who sent him to see someone else, so that he finally arrived at the office of a first psychotherapist without knowing what was happening to him. Such is the destiny of an object, to pass from one person to another. Marked and confirmed in his status as an object, the man named Bronzehelmet comes to see a psychotherapist, with whom he will spend two years before leaving him during an acute psychotic episode. He then undertakes another therapy, a second, with me. The results are still uncertain after two years.

The present observation will talk of these two periods of two years and thus will cover four years. It is not exhaustive; the exigencies of discretion proper to any publication of a case necessitate the leaving of gaps in the presentation. While we have tried to keep the essential elements, their foreshortening will give this article a schematic quality that we can only regret.

A brief glance at the biography of Roger Bronzehelmet will permit us to become acquainted with him. He was born in 1943, the second and last child of his family, seven years younger than his sister. His father is a minor bureaucrat, a domestic tyrant a little like a puppet, submissive to his mother-in-law, then to his

Jean-Claude Schaetzel is a psychiatrist practicing psychoanalysis in Strasbourg, France. This article first appeared as "Casque-de-Bronze ou itinéraire psychothérapique avec un psychotique," in *Scilicet* 2/3 (Paris: Editions du Seuil, 1973), pp. 351–61.

wife after the death of his mother-in-law. This death, when Roger was four, seems to have marked the beginning of the father's alcoholism. Since the death of his grandmother, Roger considers himself an orphan, even though his parents, with whom he lived until he began at the university, are still alive. The father lost his father when he was four. Genealogical research, undertaken by a friend of the family, led to an ancestor in the paternal lineage who made armor and bronze helmets during the fifteenth century. Bronzehelmet became the family name in a literal translation of a Slavic language. But for Roger, this genealogical chain has been broken: we will see later for what reason it does not even link him with his father. The matrilineal genealogy leads to the grandmother we talked about above, the mother's mother, whom Roger names "father" and whose name is Butcher.[1]

Roger's family was quickly split into two couples: father-daughter and mother-son. The sister preferred her father, while the mother alone took care of a son whom she later took as confidant. At the age of twelve, Roger underwent a serious operation, during which he almost died from an appendicitis attack that had not been diagnosed. He lost so much weight that he was unrecognizable. Roger had no problems in school, and after high school he enrolled in the university to pursue the same course of study as his sister. Solitary walks and fishing are his favorite leisure activities. We know little about his sex life. He was first seduced by his sister. "They were sexual games," he says, without being specific. At twenty-eight his experience in this domain is limited to masturbation, which he speaks about in relation to his dreams.

The episode that led to the first call for help when Roger was wandering around looking for "his" professor, occurred as follows: a young widow whose blind husband had just been killed in an accident invited him to her home. Even though he desired this promised initiation, when the time of the meeting came, Roger was overcome with anxiety and ran away from the building where the widow lived. He immediately went to look for his professor, his master, to tell him of his state of disarray. Finding the master absent, he was directed by an assistant professor to the social worker who decided for him that he should undergo psychotherapy. Docile, rigid, punctual, Roger continued his treatment for two years and made many discoveries, not the least of which was that the illusion of a relationship is comforting to him, at least as long as he thinks he can control it as he likes. Has not Roger in fact been drawn into a game of object relations by entering into a psychotherapy he did not ask for, after passing through an initially alienating circuit that marked him by sending him from one

1. [As with the patient's name, I have translated this literally.]

agency to another? But being an object is better than nothing, and this is the reason that he remains with a therapist who must henceforth sustain a relationship burdened with the heavy mortgage of a demand that does not come from the patient himself. For Roger this does not pose any problems—as long as his interlocutor plays the game. A symptomatic amelioration comes about and is maintained for almost two years, with sessions taking place twice weekly. Roger speaks of his difficulties, of his childhood, of his family, and when the vein of associations dries up, he finds a new mode of expression through his dreams, which he brings to the therapist in typewritten manuscripts, illustrated and carefully bound. These are truly dream-objects; writing and making them gradually come to occupy Roger for the entire day. He brings them to his therapist, speaks of the text, and often recites it word for word during the session. The symptomatic amelioration is maintained only by making this activity the exclusive mode of therapeutic interchange. Bronzehelmet feels happy. He leaves his parents to live near his therapist, whom he inundates slowly but surely with his literary production.

One day, however, the therapist's intervention modifies the course of things. The content of a dream gives him the opportunity to draw Roger's attention to the impasse in which he finds himself. In this dream Roger is in a golden cage strewn with roses, under the watchful eye of the therapist. Perhaps his dream represents life in a golden cage seen through the "rose-colored" glasses of his admiring physician? Roger grasps immediately that his dreams have a sense that he ignored. This revelation, brought to the fore by the intervention of the therapist at a time when Roger spends all his time writing these dreams and devotes himself to making and presenting these dream-objects, signifies for him that the therapist has just broken the cage. From this moment everything around him takes on a terrifying sense. One day he had noticed a hammer in the therapist's office. This hammer is there, he thinks, to tell him that he is a bit crazy.[2] His name written on an appointment sheet means imprisonment; noises in the hall are there to flout him. A magazine in the waiting room has an article on students and their discontents: "Are students mad?" This question seems directed to him, telling him that he has lost his reason. The question answers itself: we are faced with a psychosis. He receives a letter changing an appointment that bears a stamp canceled with the following phrase: "In case of distress, when you are alone and undone, call SOS." This signifies to him that he has been thrown out. He interrupts his psychotherapy, asking that all his dreams be

---

2. [The French expression for being crazy in this context is *être marteau*. The word *marteau* also means "hammer."]

given back to him immediately. Now, there have been so many of these volumes that the therapist has had to store them in different places; he can not give them back immediately. Bronzehelmet will speak of this for a long time with his second therapist, when he undertakes another psychotherapy, insisting that these texts contained the best part of himself and that the fact that they were not given back immediately injured him very deeply. We leave for a moment these dream objects; we will find them a little later.

We will speak of what he tells us about his quest for identity. "A father like mine," he says, "has no name." He had an "unlicensed" father who went poaching with his son and gave him the role of lookout to prevent them from being surprised by the law. The father himself grew up without a father, deprived of his own in tragic circumstances when he was four. A pastry chef in the army, his father's father was pulverized by a shell destined for the officers at the moment when he was getting ready to bring them some cakes. Roger says, "A father who did not have a father cannot be a father." The patrilineal geneaology was interrupted. Roger imagines it to be like a chain with a place only for someone who can get along with his father: this was hardly possible for him. Thus he turned toward the maternal lineage; this had given him some hope of a possible identification in the person of the grandmother, his mother's mother, who seems to have played an important role in the family as a regent until her death when Roger was four. "She brought me up," he says, "and we were all orphans when she died." "All" includes not only him and his sister but also his parents. The death of Grandmother Butcher is presented as the fact that dislocated the family. The father became alcoholic, the mother took possession of her son, and the sister turned toward the father, but they all remained in the same house, which henceforth was the scene of daily disputes.

Roger moves toward a maternal identification when he speaks like his mother and toward a paternal identification when he considers himself to be an orphan at four, as his father was. But what definite place can he occupy in an Oedipal triangulation when he finds himself thus in a confusion of generations? A long dream illustrates this confusion. He stages a conversation between himself, his mother, and my daughter that ends on this phrase: "All three of us are the same age." One cannot live in a world where one is the same age as one's mother, and Bronzehelmet in fact does not live. One Christmas Eve he makes this appeal to the manger: "God, if you exist, make me exist." But since he no longer believes in the existence of God, the idea of a reverse genealogy seems to him a possible opening toward life. He goes to find his father and says, "Let us forget the past; to live, a father needs a son as a son needs a father." His father's response was immediate: "I'd rather be related to a dog." And Bronzehelmet continues his quest for identity day and night, without relief. At night he dreams of a familial meal. He is sent to find the sausage needed for the *choucroute*. He goes to all the butchers of the town without finding the object, and when he returns to the house, the choucroute is cold, untouched. Butcher is the name of the grandmother whose death orphaned the entire family. During the day he goes through the family photos, in particular those of his birth, to find an image in which he can see in his parents' look a sign of love. He will never find such a photo. He goes to the office of county records and asks to read his parents' marriage certificate and his own birth certificate. He wants to assure himself of his father's name by reading it with his own eyes in the great book where it is forever inscribed. But even after he has sought and found in the real the thing that is foreclosed to him, he cannot, for all that, recognize it. He is not yet sure he is his father's son, despite his visit to the records office.

Robinson Crusoe, who had to fabricate and find all that he needed to survive, said that adversity stimulates the spirit of invention. Bronzehelmet, his surname foreclosed, invented a secret name for himself that finally permitted him to live. This episode occurred during his first psychotherapy and was only revealed to the second therapist.

Let us look at this new adventure of Bronzehelmet. He has the sudden intuition that he can be born from himself and his therapist. To do so he must have a name, which he composes in taking the letters of his first name and the letters from his therapist's surname. As though by accident, this new name is simply an anagram of the therapist's name. He took a sheet of paper to write down what he considered at the time to be his true birth certificate: on such a day, on such a date is born—and then he adds his new name. A cranny in the family home is ready to receive this parchment, which he deposits and covers over so that the spot appears untouched. No adjective is strong enough to qualify the joy he feels this day, and almost three years later he evokes these adjectives, although now they are mixed with bitterness. This "birth" took place at the same time as the long dreams, brought to the therapist at each session until the rupture of the golden cage at the moment of the flowering of his delusions. Then everything fell apart around him in the fragmentation of signifiers.

At the moment when the hammer tells him he is mad, when noises snap at him, when the letter's seal becomes the king's seal, the letters of his new name take their place in the emerging name of a-father. Foreclosure is manifested again, as this cranny in the house that he filled with his "birth certificate." In this breakdown the loss of the name he was born with is mortifying. Only a new name will save him from annihilation, and it is a name that he decides to seek letter by letter. As it happens, this name is that of his therapist's analyst. As a mad adventurer, Roger sets out without map or compass to seek this name, his only signpost being the city to which his therapist had been going for his own analysis. Patients possess from time to time extraordinarily precise information. Bronzehelmet goes to the city where his therapist's analyst lives, but he comes home empty-handed, for even in inspecting the houses and leafing through the phone directories, he cannot win the wager of finding a name that he does not know. Returning to his town he decides to seek another name by addressing himself to the summit of the university hierarchy, to a professor: the professor is a "name." The advice he receives is to pursue a psychotherapy with a therapist of his choice.

Here an event important for the history of Bronzehelmet takes place. He is no longer taken in hand like an object kept by one or referred to another; he is given a choice. Bronzehelmet no longer has the status he had before entering into his first psychotherapy. He is no longer an object that found itself in the office of a physician he did not ask to see, when, two years before, he sought to speak with his professor. Thus the circuit that inaugurates the second psychotherapy: Bronzehelmet is no longer in the position of having to address himself to a therapist designated for him. He chooses a new therapist. We do not know the reasons for his choice. He began his first session by talking about a sister he loved a great deal, the object of his first feelings of love in his memory. This sister lives in Nancy, where her husband is a professor. Are we perhaps too eager, hearing in this first session the surname and the address of the second therapist in a discourse where the patient's sister is often mentioned?[3] In fact, this name has the same signifying resonances as the nickname that he uses to designate his sister. Also, the therapist lives on the boulevard de Nancy! Let us recall that this sister had a privileged relation with the father and was thus a barrier to Roger's access to this latter. At the same time she appeared to be the only possible way of gaining access to this father. Both of the paths that led Roger to a therapist passed through a professor, and the sister's husband is a professor whose name has never been mentioned.

We arrive at the second therapy undertaken in privileged conditions for a case of psychosis. Bronzehelmet takes a personal step forward. Also, the second psychotherapist has just become familiar with the details of the case in a seminar where the first therapist exposed major steps of his treatment, those that led to the delusional episode.

The attention of the second therapist had thus been drawn to the importance of the dream-objects before his first encounter with Bronzehelmet. And since he was also worried by a patient who was so ready to speak of delusions or to

3. [This surname has been withheld for reasons of confidentiality.]

decompensate in grave depressive moments, he decided to refer himself to a third party for supervision. It was during the discussions with the first therapist and the supervisor that the idea of writing up this case came to him.

Here now is Bronzehelmet, with his second therapist. From the beginning the dreams are in question. Roger asks if I accept them. My affirmative response is all ready; to refuse his dreams would be to refuse him. He will say later that his being is entirely in his writings. He says again that in his dreams he finds what is best in himself. Would this be the ego ideal whose recognition he demands? He sees immediately that it is necessary to render that which is given you. These dreams appear to him like a bank deposit whose interest is being represented by the therapist's attention. During the second psychotherapy the dream-objects change cabinets. He brings me the volumes he took back from my colleague as well as his recent writings. The writings abound and are impeccably presented. Bronzehelmet himself is always perfectly dressed and groomed. The pack of writings grows. The author of the dreams spends his nights dreaming and his days transcribing his oneiric activity. During the sessions he tells his dreams and with a monotonous voice evokes memories in such a way that it is often difficult to differentiate, merely by listening, what he wrote down and learned by heart and what he says spontaneously during a session. The dreams seem to be Roger's only reality, to the point where all his discourse takes on the frozen quality of the folders he brings to each session. The dream-objects that he fashions to reveal himself at his best permit him to speak without impediment of all the contradictions of his psychotic universe.

But how can we disengage the message enshrined in the folders and give life to this frozen discourse? It is necessary that Roger not suspect in any way an inclination on the part of the analyst to refuse the growing mass of his dream-objects. Yet to accept these packages at each session—is this not to encourage him to pursue the unflagging work that maintains him, it is true, in a certain equilibrium, but at the price of a sterile displacement that may well boomerang in the future? Faced with this enigmatic material, we decided to emphasize the importance of patient's speech during the session. Thus we marked some digressions about his writings, and some apparently very banal words such as those sometimes spoken at the beginning or the end of sessions. We attempted to show him that speech could be heard and conserved without being written. We restored from time to time the moments of his spoken discourse, accompanying them with a commentary or making him specify one or another point.

Roger's distrust of any word that manifests him or reveals him outside his protecting objects is still very great. He speaks to say this: "Words frighten me. I always wanted to write, but I could not give a name to things. . . . It was as

though the words slid on things. . . . Then I thought that in studying the dictionary from A to Z, noting the words that I did not know, I would possess them all
and would be able to say what I wanted to say." He will abandon this attempt to
retain all the words. If he is not afraid of written words, this is perhaps because he
believes he is their master, as of an object, while all that is spoken, unless it is
read, is only sound or wind—nothing, but also something that can grow and
multiply dangerously. Here we can see the difficulty of undertaking a
psychotherapy with a being who takes words literally, where through the vertiginous sliding of signifiers on signifieds, a word may mean everything and
things can at any moment emerge with a terrifying significance.

After one year Bronzehelmet tells a dream in which I appear with the traits
of one of his friends who bears my name. He seems thus to have recognized me
as a new name-bearer, and he declares in his dream that I am someone with
whom he can talk. Beginning with the next session, for the first time, he does not
bring a dream-object. Now he speaks. Is it because he has recreated himself by
gaining a new name that he can finally lose the first without being annihilated?
Only now does he reveal the name that he had fabricated in secret, unknown to
his therapist. We cannot prevent ourselves from thinking of the combinations of
proper names that Schreber used to construct a delusional genealogy.

After the frequent repetition of the signifier "secret,"[4] evoked in the contexts
of a shared secret, of being put in solitary confinement,[5] and then after a veritable hymn to creation where Roger spares no detail of all he observes in nature
during his solitary wanderings, as though with his own discourse he sought to
create again each object in defining it, the signifying chain is closed with the
expression "to create oneself."[6] Oscillating between mute reticences and prolific
discourses, he finally reveals his secret name, and at the same time the name of
the first therapist and the fantasy of self-creation. Then there is an outbreak of
hate against the therapist, whom he labels a rapist of the unconscious and
accomplice of the medicosocial institution that had decided his psychotherapy.
After this session Roger is calmed and thinks about taking up his studies again.
He stops the production of the dream-objects, which will reappear later sporadi-
cally.

But now we hear in his discourse the gradual development of themes of a
return to a previous state. In his dreams he sees himself following rivers to arrive
at their sources: they are always dried up. In his everyday life he has more
frequent contact with his parents, who had not seen him for months. In the

4. [The French text here reads secré, a neologism that sounds like the word "secret" (secret).]
5. [The French phrase uses the word "secret": être mis au secret dans une prison.]
6. [In French secré and se créer are homophonically related.]

psychotherapy he asks for a return to the reclining position he had with his first therapist,[7] and the dream-objects reappear for a few sessions, with at least two dreams in each folder, a recent one and an older one that he had brought to his first therapist. Will the need for repetition not lead him to return to the delusions?

What echo in me pushed me one day to forget a box of cigars on my desk, contrary to my habits? Am I not in the process of reproducing the scene in which analyst becomes target and arrow for the psychotic gaze, just as my colleague had done two years before, when he had left on his desk the hammer that began to speak and to label the patient "mad"? Roger is manifestly troubled. After a profound silence he sees the box and says: "I am nervous in seeing your cigars. I know that the objects do not have an intention, but I cannot prevent myself from thinking that my first physician smoked the same cigars, and I am afraid that you will also throw me out." The following sessions concern two childhood friends, Paul and Francis, who appear in the dreams. We should specify that these names are those of the two therapists, each time deprived of the first name "John."[8] Roger removes what they have in common. A dream follows that marks the beginning of a depressive period. His father takes him fishing out of season. A policeman surprises Roger and asks for his papers. He is in a bathing suit and does not have them. His father hides. The policeman plunges his hand in Roger's bathing suit and says, "Here are your papers"; yet it was only a bit of fabric.

The depressive period that follows is very disquieting. Roger speaks of death, of withered flowers, of no possible way out except being crushed by a tank or catapulted into the universe. The dream-objects reappear for a few sessions. They are brief, sad, and despairing.

Faced with the aggravation of the clinical picture, I considered the possibility of a hospitalization. But would this not have been to treat him again as a package when he has simply asked to speak? To ask to speak has a very specific sense for Bronzehelmet; he waits for someone to let him speak. But aside from that he has taken my spoken words as his own, and during all the psychotherapy he has never used the phrase "you said" (this phrase so often used by the neurotic to repeat the interlocutor's words, in specifying the place from which it was emitted). Bronzehelmet affirms "I said to you" when he takes up each word pronounced by the therapist during the sessions. If he is now seeking castration, as he dreamt it, are we going to cut off his speech and give him again the status of

7. The depressive symptomatology of the patient had led me to see him face-to-face instead of reclining.

8. [The French names here were hyphenated: Jean-François and Jean-Paul.]

object, since he seems to ask for it, to return him to a previous state through repetition? To play dead, would this not be to propose that he do as much, with the risk that he might take this play too seriously? If the therapist is silent, can Bronzehelmet not understand this as a command to be silent? The dreams speak of a return to the earth that is far from pastoral. To remain in the greatest difference, then, implies being alive. To speak, to invite speech in assuming the anxiety of awaiting the subject's coming into being, seemed to us the correct attitude when faced with one who is still sustained by a discourse that the other proposes.

Bronzehelmet again begins to speak and again renounces bringing his writings. The depressive state stops.

What follows now is one of the latest sequences of this long psychotherapy still in process, whose presentation cannot escape a certain schematism necessitated by the condensation and the cutting of voluminous material.

Bronzehelmet presents the theme of one of his dreams: "The man in 203." He stops speaking after this invocation. Is this not the beginning of a triangulation? Breaking the silence I say, "There are two without three."[9] After another silence, Bronzehelmet speaks again: "It was like with my mother. . . . I was always with her as if I did not have a father. It was thus with my first physician, he was like a mother for me, and then, all of a sudden, I was not a baby anymore. When there were the two of us and I could not do anything for myself, he threw me out on the street. If I came to see you, it was to find out what happened and to leave you one day of my own free will."

The man in 203, is this not a-father who emerged all of a sudden in a third position between Bronzehelmet and his dream-objects, provoking the aggressive drive and the fragmenting anxiety that brought about the end of the first psychotherapy? Recently Roger evoked a moment of his first therapy that illustrated his fear of such an apparition. He had shown my colleague photos of his parents. He wanted to "forget" the portrait of his mother at the therapist's, so that this latter could keep the image. Can we not read in this a wish that he did not dare realize, either consciously or by a forgetting, that the physician keep the mother's image, this in order never to be metamorphized into this father Lacan speaks of at the onset of psychosis, when the Name of the Father, never come to the other's place, is suddenly called in symbolic opposition to the subject?

The project of Bronzehelmet is now to analyze what happened in his childhood and with his first therapist.

Will we always be able to escape the traps of the psychotic investment? We

9. [In French, "203" is a homophone of *deux sans trois*.]

are not certain. Roger shows us the way when he signifies to us that he no longer wants to play at object relations. He has succeeded in breaking out of the bondage in which he had been frozen before his first therapy and he has taken the path to a second therapist to ask him for the gift of speech. This appears to us to be a good omen: through the listening and the speech of his therapist he will perhaps find one day the place that will permit him to leave therapy without having to fall into psychosis again.

This desire can only encounter mine, but the last word belongs to Bronze-helmet.

13 Contribution to the Psychoanalysis of Transsexualism

BY MOUSTAPHA SAFOUAN

We will comment upon some observations reported by Robert J. Stoller in chapters 8 and 9 of his book *Sex and Gender*.[1] They concern the analysis of three boys four or five years of age who at this early age were already avowed transsexuals. We will also discuss the analysis of one of their mothers, undertaken at the same time as that of her son. Since adult transsexuals generally address themselves to surgeons rather than to analysts, these observations offer us almost a unique occasion to see how two desires, transmitted through two generations (that of mother and grandmother) have led to the production of a young transsexual in the third.

How does the author describe these children?[2]

They are anatomically normal. There was no ambiguity at their birth as to their belonging to the masculine sex, and no ulterior examination permits the least doubt on this subject. The sexual chromosomes, in particular, are XY normal. But these children put on feminine clothing each time they have the opportunity, at home, on visits or, later, in nursery school. When they do not have these clothes at hand, they improvise with napkins, blankets, tablecloths or anything else that is useful. They also use hats and feminine shoes, as well as underwear, jewels, and creams; they adopt the gestures, the gait, and the appropriate posture, but only when they are dressed as women or are playing the role. Furthermore, they play almost exclusively with girls and take on the role of mother, sister, governess, or actress. They always sit to urinate.

These are not activities in which they indulge occasionally; rather, this is continuous behavior, lasting at least several hours every day. The mothers all find this "cute," even while sometimes feeling a bit disquieted: "Sweetie, why

Delivered at the Ecole Freudienne de Paris in March 1971 and drawn from a seminar entitled "The Avatars of Reality," given at Strasbourg during the academic year 1970–71. First published in *Scilicet 4* (Paris: Editions du Seuil, 1973), pp. 137–61. Subsequently revised and republished as "Contribution à la psychanalyse du transsexualisme" in *Etudes sur l'Oedipe* (Paris: Editions de Seuil, 1974), pp. 74–97.

1. Robert J. Stoller, *Sex and Gender* (New York: Science House, 1968).
2. Stoller, *Sex and Gender*, pp. 90–107.

don't you let that go for a little while? Please?" But they never discouraged this behavior before the beginning of treatment. They do not have the conscious wish that their boys be girls and do not give them girls' names. But they think that they are beautiful, encourage them in their feminine attitudes, and indulge in daydreams in which they imagine what their sons would look like if they were adult women.

The boys affirm that they are girls and that they will become women when they grow up. They are already thinking of a sex change operation. This is shown in the questions that they ask their mothers: whether they will have breasts and why someone cannot take away their penises.

Parents, friends, and other observers have the impression that this behavior can be due only to a biological disposition, since the children learned it spontaneously enough for it to appear "natural." Each one of the mothers has had many occasions to notice how her child improvises one or another facet of feminine behavior without ever having been able to observe it before. And the children never tire of looking at their mothers getting dressed, putting on their makeup, doing their hair, choosing their dresses and jewels, in short, deploying their femininity.

These children were brought for a psychiatric examination at the age of four or five, although they had shown signs of their condition beginning at the age of two and even before. And in each case the mother asked for a consultation only because of the insistence of someone outside of the family to whom this state of affairs appeared to be abnormal.

In the case of the first child, the taste for feminine clothing began when he had just learned to walk: he had, from this time, put on his mother's shoes and walked around the house as though he had always known how to walk with high heels. In fact this boy showed signs of femininity (whose unusual character his mother recognized) even before he was one year old: seated on her lap he looked at magazines with her, stopped her each time there was a photo of a beautiful woman, and manifested his intense pleasure by modulations of his voice.

With the two others, the evident signs were manifested only at the age of two, but it could well be that a more detailed report from their mothers tells us that the first signs had begun well before.

If we accept, along with the author, as criteria for transsexualism the *fixed belief of belonging to the other sex that leads to the demand that the body be "corrected" in consequence,*[3] we will admit easily that these three boys are transsexuals. And we see as well the clinical and phenomenological differences that distinguish this condition fron simple transvestism.

3. Stoller, *Sex and Gender*, p. 92.

Here we add for our part that transvestism comes from an *exigency of the phallus* such that the subject attributes it to all creatures without exception, since he would not know how to tolerate its absence *in any case*. At issue in this perversion is the universalization of the phallus, founded on the affirmation of the impossibility of its lacking. On the contrary, for our three young boys, everything unfolds, it seems, on the level not of the *universal*, which takes things as they are founded, but of the *general*, which takes things as they are arranged.[4] Now, things are arranged in a way that does not help these children: not only do they refuse the phallus, far from demanding it, but they consider, faced with the unanimous opinion of others, that it is an error to consider them boys, and they include themselves among women. The transvestite *imposes on the real the form of his fantasy and in this sense makes the real imaginary*, and the playful aspect of his tricks derives from his doing so. The transsexual *realizes the imaginary*, as his demand makes evident. The transvestite makes laws according to his desire or according to what this desire comports of castration anxiety, *thus scorning the common classification*. The transsexual apparently accepts this latter and *only contests the place* it assigns to him. Why? Through this digression we rejoin the question that our author asks himself concerning the etiology of this state.

The family constellations in which these children have lived present striking similarities. Let us begin with their mothers.

Whatever specific differences the women have, they resemble each other on two points.

The first is an almost identical way of expressing their *bisexuality*: they are feminine in the same boyish way. Their hair is short, not without style. They wear very little makeup. They show a clear preference for suits—it appears inconceivable for them to wear low-cut dresses with ribbons and lace and so forth. All three have a certain consciousness of being sexually neuter, although they try to erect a feminine facade on this neutrality. This neutrality is colored with a depressive tone, which is a current part of their life.

It does not take very long for the analyst to discover a more severe depression. Heterosexuality does not hold many attractions for them. All were married at about the age of thirty and easily tolerated their virginity until that age. None accepts sexual relations with her husband with joy, although these women do not become unfaithful. None believes herself to have made a happy marriage, and they all agree in saying that no affection, no real communication, exists between themselves and their husbands.

On the contrary, they all affirm that in childhood they had the bearing and

4. See Jacques Lacan, "Kant avec Sade," in *Ecrits*, pp. 765–92.

mannerisms of a boy; they wished to be boys and played only with them, taking part in their sports and fights, repulsing any other girl who wanted to be integrated in the group. This behavior ended with puberty. From this period until the beginning of treatment, one of these mothers had had only one satisfying sexual relation, and this was with another woman. The best friend of the second mother was, during her college years, an openly homosexual woman. For the third, nothing is known on this score.

The second trait that these three women have in common is a profound sense of *emptiness* and incompleteness. But finally, what does this bisexuality signify, if it does not circumscribe some void, and this "anatomically felt" (the author's terms) incompleteness, which is joined with an almost complete absence of desire—what does it signify, if not that we are facing somnambulists, women who live as though hypnotized by the invisible mouth of the virtual image of the vase, to refer to Lacan's optical schema?[5] To express the matter otherwise, these women are attached with every fiber of their being to a phallus without which they feel incomplete but which nevertheless rejects them and absorbs into itself the entire sense of their lives. It is in vain that they exhaust themselves with their social veneer and their way of dressing, to bring back upon themselves the image of this phallus that remains their lord and master, the only one that they really try to tempt. To listen to the description of Mr. Stoller, we have the feeling of finding ourselves in a region that is situated well beyond penis envy, as if a barrier had been crossed: the question for these women is not to save the little bit of desire of which we have only a trace in some more or less episodic, and for the most part homosexual, manifestations that the author has reported to us. This little bit of desire, they have done without it. *None is phallophoric in her own eyes. But with the image of her own body, each one herself tries to occupy this place of the phallus,* of that which her image shows to be lacking: a mirage in which each one nonetheless is reflected. It is not an accident if this term of "mirage" is precisely the one that one of the three mothers uses voluntarily (she is the one who began a psychoanalytic cure) to describe herself. The observation will permit us to grasp the personal experience that pushed her to begin an analysis.

Let us look, then, at the fathers.[6] They also share certain essential traits. All three consider themselves, and are considered by their families, to be husbands

5. See Jacques Lacan, "Remarques sur le rapport de Daniel Lagache," in *Ecrits*, pp. 647–84.
6. Stoller, *Sex and Gender*, pp. 96–97.

and fathers. But all are almost completely absent, physically absent from their families. When their children were infants, these men left the house early in the morning and returned only late at night. The babies were already in bed. Later the children saw their fathers at a dinner that these men ate in silence and in a complete absence of communication by gestures or words. At the end of the meal, one locked himself into his office to work some more, and the two others went out to spend the evening elsewhere, each according to his tastes. During the weekends, the same absences for the same reasons. When their sons began cross-dressing, none was moved very much, nor did any comment that such an effeminization was unusual or ought to be changed. Even more, when someone obliged their wives to consult a psychiatrist, all three balked. Thus the absence of these fathers is not the static absence of dead or divorced fathers but is "dynamic," "living," and "tantalizing" to the highest degree. We have every reason to think not only that these men let their wives "feminize their sons" as they wished but that they (very subtly) pushed these sons along the path of returning to their mother's bodies. None of these men, our author notes, is either psychotic or schizoid. To simplify matters to an extreme, we will say that one is an alcoholic, that another has a personality at the same time passive and aggressive, and that the third is obsessive-compulsive.

It is difficult to imagine so radical an absence of the paternal function. It is on this point that Mr. Stoller's observation—and this is its value—acquires an almost experimental character. In the concrete relations that these three boys have with their parents, there is *strictly nothing that could permit them to integrate in a symbolic order the mute and ghostlike presence of their fathers.* That they have learned to designate these nocturnal visitors as fathers does not permit them to feel the apparition otherwise than as an intrusion into the perceptive field constituted by the dual relation that enclosed them with their mothers. And the fact of noticing that these fathers are "masculine images" cannot incite these children to want to resemble them, when everything happens as though their paternity, the fact that they recognized their children, was held to be of no consequence. Deafness to the signifier that, on the side of the mothers, conditions the kind of cloture or symbiosis that they attempt to realize with their sons. Thus the prop of the signifier is taken away from these children, and it is around this prop that each one should have been able to assume his own sex. While for a neurotic a father exists whose distinction is maintained to the point that he is made into everyone's father, for these three children, the only response in the Other place is a "tantalizing" absence—to use Stoller's expression—that recalls the "leave in the lurch" of President Schreber and is the most moving witness of the radical dependence of the subject on the signifier.

Not recognizing this dependence, Mr. Stoller, who theorizes as though he had never heard of the constituent function of speech,[7] is obliged, in order to explain his observations, to have recourse only to imaginary processes or, as he calls them, "psychodynamic" processes, whose insufficiency he himself admits. This is to his credit, a rare enough fact if we think of the profound affinities of the imaginary with what Jaspers calls "understanding," which seems more and more to constitute the only mental faculty that analysts dispose of.[8]

In fact, how does Mr. Stoller respond to the decisive question that he formulates in these terms: what brings these little males to believe, contrary to anatomical evidence, that they are nevertheless females?

The essential dynamic process seems to be, he says,[9] an excessive identification with their mothers, due to the incapacity of these mothers to permit their sons to be separated from their bodies. These mothers surround their sons with their flesh (which is to say that they do not even tolerate the slight separation that comes about when they wear clothing), with their breath, with their cooling voice and their enveloping movements. Other attentive mothers act in the same way, but not with the same intensity, nor in this quasipermanent fashion.

According to Stoller, the cause of the problem is not that the mother carries her child, but *how* she does it and for *how long*. One of these mothers says that she carried her son all the time against her body because he had a congenital dislocation of the hip; another alleges her determination to make her son avoid what she suffered, an empty mother who took no interest in her. But whatever the reason, the fact is that these children lived an extremely gratifying situation, as close to ultrauterine life as the conditions of extrauterine life permit. Bathing in an atmosphere of love in which everything was permitted them, they saw each of their needs receive immediate satisfaction from extremely attentive mothers. And each time that one of them speaks of her son, we have the feeling that she does not see him as a distinct being, detached from herself. Everything is placed under the sign of "we": "We sat down, and we discussed the thing. Then we decided it would be better to do this or that." These mothers do not feel any need for intimacy or retreat; their children are free to join them in the bathroom or while they are washing.

The author summarizes all these details and others of the same kind under

7. See Jacques Lacan, *Ecrits: A Selection* (New York: W. W. Norton), pp. 218–19.

8. A brief review of Jaspers's examples will show that his "I understand" is equivalent to "it pleases me": "I understand that people kill for jealousy" is equivalent to "It pleases me to get rid of a rival"; "I understand that people commit suicide more frequently in the autumn" is equivalent to "It pleases me that it always be spring." Since the world is not made to please Jaspers, it is not surprising that statistics show more suicides in the spring.

9. Stoller, *Sex and Gender*, pp. 97–98.

the term of "symbiosis." But there is symbiosis and there is symbiosis: the usage of a general term does not render this situation identical, he underscores, with a living relationship. A symbiotic relation with the mother is in play with a schizophrenic child or with a normal child—and this proves, for the author, not that such a relationship is pathogenetic in itself, but only that it communicates certain messages subtly from mother to child. The experience of the child destined to become a transsexual is doubtless limited to a constant sensation of pleasure or an absence of tension, which render superfluous for him the necessity of conceiving the frontier between his body and the maternal body. But in what way does the symbiotic experience of the schizophrenic differ? The author leaves this question unanswered.

A few pages later he takes up the question again from an anthropological point of view: the child's prolonged gratification seems to be the rule in certain primitive societies, without any excessive identification with the mother. Mr. Stoller responds by invoking what constitutes in his eyes the second etiological factor: the fathers of these transsexual boys are absent *"in a very special way."* Without telling us which way, he is content to remark that this absence, besides depriving the child of a man as an object of *identification* (as though that were the essential part of the paternal function!), leaves him defenseless before the effects of excessive contact with the mother. It happens that this contact constitutes, in his opinion, the decisive factor in determining an excessive identification with the mother. Then his question rebounds: no argument, concludes the author, no citing of authorities, can resolve the problem; only the *dependable,* concrete facts will permit this.

Here the empiricist credo of Mr. Stoller serves manifestly as an alibi. The observations concerning the mother-child relation in schizophrenia are so numerous and so detailed that we ask ourselves if an observation which discovered things that no other method had found would still be an observation of a schizophrenic. Or should we await an apparatus that would detect the "subtle communications" that pass from mother to child?

In order to be fair to the author, we must, however, quote the reasons he has for excluding a hypothesis toward which many analysts would lean:

So much has been said, from Freud's earliest papers on, about the crucial effects of fear of castration on the little boy's growing masculinity that the reader may wonder how one can discuss extreme femininity in little boys without relating it to castration anxiety. Most of us, for instance, have seen effeminate boys who have sacrificed some of their masculinity to save their maleness (penis). Are not these transsexual boys the same? The answer suggested is that these little boys are clinically quite different in appearance and have different histories. It is hard to believe that this femininity, which is observable in these children long before the classically described phallic phase—in one case by age one—is the result of the kinds of castration fears that are known to be fully developed only years later. Also it seems very unlikely that the blissful state of closeness that such a mother produces can cause the boy so much fear of his penis being cut off that he pleads to have it cut off, and that he can preserve his sense of maleness by becoming female.

It may be worth noting that castration anxiety, phallic behavior and fantasies, and neurotic (defensive) reactions have in fact appeared in one boy treated successfully so far. However, they were not present when he was permitted to be transsexual; they only occurred after many months of treatment, and only when his femininity had died down and he began to enjoy being a male and being masculine. It was when he came to feel that having a penis was worthwhile that he became concerned about losing it.[10]

Though it would be difficult to disagree with such an analysis, we ought to formulate the difference between the *neurotic* and the *transsexual* in an even more explicit way than the author does. *The one wants to keep his penis, the other to get rid of it*. If the first, to accomplish his end, finds himself led to adopt a feminine position (which is what the author means by "sacrificing masculinity"), this is because the neurotic child is trapped, unbeknown to himself, in a game in which a partner *whose face he does not know* intervenes. The threat of really having his penis cut off with a pair of scissors is no more real than an encounter with a wolf in the city streets—which does not prevent our children from being afraid of wolves. The transsexual does not *play* at being a woman, he is one; and the only other that he recognizes is the one who *knows* it and who is the other to whom he can address a demand that does not have an obscure desire beyond it; thus this other is first the mother, then, as his apprehension of social reality develops, the surgeon, to whom he addresses *the same demand*, to correct his body. The difference between the attitudes of the neurotic and the transsexual toward their own organ leads to another no less essential difference that remains completely unnoticed by our author and concerns the *apprehension of the Other*. And this difference leads us to examine the relationship of these three boys with their mothers from another angle.

If we remember that the relation of the fetus to the maternal body is in truth

10. Stoller, *Sex and Gender*, pp. 100–01.

one not of symbiosis but of parasitism, it would be correct to affirm that each of these mothers was for her son in one sense more than a uterus, in another sense, less.

More than a uterus, since the child considers himself as a part of her and does not want to be separated (to the point where the description of Mr. Stoller makes us think of the reactions of pursuit described by Lorenz),[11] at the same time considering her to be a prolongation of himself. She did for him all "the specific acts," to use Freud's expression from the *Project:* so much so that the three boys were "physically fearless," says Mr. Stoller, adding that this was the case because "each of these children felt that he could do everything that his mother could, being merely her extension." These children, in sum, lived enveloped by providence, even becoming this providence themselves by the assimilating and dissimulating force of an imaginary identification. The note of contemplative fascination, characteristic of the identification, is far from being absent in this picture; in fact the children never let their mothers out of their sight. We are hardly astonished that such a capture has produced in them effects of impregnation or sensibility that are entirely comparable with mimetism—whose principle resides, according to R. Caillois, precisely in a fasciantion, in "a temptation by space."[12] This would not only explain what Mr. Stoller calls their "extreme femininity" but would also include this talent for improvisation that they make use of, which dazzles those around them.

Nevertheless, this identification in itself does not in any way explain the *conviction*—which we would not hesitate, for our part, to describe as "delusional"[13]—of being a woman. Being effeminate is one thing; this conviction is something else. The two phenomena are most often separated in fact. In another chapter of his book, the author tells us of an adult transsexual who was nevertheless not particularly feminine. *The sole recourse to an imaginary mechanism explains nothing.* If the opposite were the case, transsexualism would be much more frequent than it is in fact: all of us breathe more or less in the space of the maternal uterus, if only metaphorically; and the hold of the maternal *imago* is often so dominant that it determines later all the fundamental options of

11. Konrad Lorenz, *Studies in Human and Animal Behavior* (Cambridge, Mass.: Harvard University Press, 1970).

12. R. Caillois, *Le Mythe et l'homme* (Paris: Gallimard, 1972), p. 27.

13. Stoller wants to reserve this term "delusion" for any idea that is formed as a defensive reaction to a traumatic reality, as if Freud—and for the best reasons, those dictated by the most attentive examination of clinical facts—had not been led from the beginning to limit the place of traumatism in the etiology of neuroses by postulating that no event exercises a traumatic action without the intermediary of a reminiscence. We believe that the best way to place oneself in the line of Freudian thought is to affirm that no traumatic effect can be explained without consideration of the subjective relationship with the symbolic order.

existence, without becoming transsexualism and without any resulting "feminization," in Mr. Stoller's sense.

But to stay with the author's observation, if it is true that the feminization of these boys is manifested well before the phallic phase, and we have no reason to doubt this, it remains true that their *transsexualism* probably dates from this phase: it is in fact difficult to imagine that these boys had begun to formulate their preoccupations before the age of two and a half or three.

Whatever blindness brought the fantasy of symbiosis to realization in their sons (the same fantasy that Mr. Stoller wishes to give a theoretic reality), these mothers were not able to prevent the *mediation of speech* in this relation itself.

Now, it is the nature of speech to place the subject in relation not only to the other who is its destination but also—and this is infinitely greater in its consequences—to something situated well *beyond* everything that can be articulated in this speech as a demand. If we have said that for each of these children, the mother was *less than a uterus*, this is because speech is not simply the vehicle of intersubjective communication, and among other things it can also be an object of exchange or communication. The spoken word opens a breach, or if you like, a window that looks onto an object that is not visible and cannot be reduced to something visible. Nor can it be reduced to a demand. This, the *object of desire*, will give the intersubjective relation its particular style.

Everything indicates that the mothers of these boys were women who wanted to lead their lives in conformity with what can be articulated as demand for, or as exigency of, this object. But everything happened as though this object had already flown away at the moment when the women had made this decision. They remained as unsatisfied as before. What object undid all the "lures of power"?

Since it is no longer a question of "contact," as our author writes, but of desire, we have no need here to detect the "subtle communications" of Mr. Stoller in order to talk about it. However inarticulable it be, this desire is nonetheless spoken through every pore (as Freud said); it is perfectly readable: even if only through the first name in which each mother dressed her son, which is not, as one would expect, a first name that can be used for boys and girls but has for the mother mirific resonances of heroism and exoticism. [14] Then, without our speaking of the position, which is that of a parasite and which these mothers have succeeded in allotting to husbands who are more than acquiescent and complaisant, we learn from Mr. Stoller (but here the child knows as much as the most acute observer) that these women who live as though dispossessed of their

14. To give us an idea of the first names, which he must keep secret, Stoller tells us that one of these boys was named something like "Lance." When he chose this camouflage, he was doubtless thinking of the first name that a celebrated American millionaire picked for his son.

essence, which is for them masculine, have nevertheless an extreme aversion for that which represents the other sex, and most especially for its genital organ, which appears to them to be "ugly" and "grotesque": no penis is phallic enough for these mothers.

They have, however, found the phallic luster in an object that is real enough: precisely in the *penis of their sons,* which appears to them to be "beautiful." There they have found their lost essence, and doubtless they do not deprive themselves of the opportunity to manipulate it occasionally (the author does not say this specifically, but his description of the atmosphere of promiscuity in which these women live with their sons leaves no doubt on this question). Now, as good an observer as he is, our child is here incapable of seeing the deviation of the maternal desire from the symbolic order into which he ought to be introduced: he can only submit to the consequences. He cannot be his mother's phallus, that is to say, he cannot please her absolutely, be her sole principle of pleasure, except on the condition that he be excluded from the masculine gender . . . : and this is what he demands.

Better yet, if it is true that the mother has found the object of her desire *in the real,* it is no less true that she has found it outside herself, in her son. Where, then, is he going to find his own? Where is he going to deceive his mother's lack, when there is no lack? *Where the neurotic sacrifices his desire to safeguard his phallus* (this is the only sense we can give to the formula already quoted, by Mr. Stoller), *the transsexual* is obliged *to get rid of his phallus to make room for his desire* or to become desiring. Someone will perhaps ask, but what object will he find when he has learned from his mother to detest men? Yes, but he has also learned to adore himself, and he will not fail to find an object that reflects him: *it is precisely in order to be in the position where he can search for (or find again) such an object that he demands the sacrifice of his penis.*

Doubtless, the fact that this organ has appeared to be his mother's as much as his own has rendered this part of his body excessively anxiogenetic for the boy: through it the image of the mother, like his alter ego, risks being transformed into the image of the double. The ubiquitous phallus threatens to become real. And perhaps in conceding this organ the boy concedes to some sort of solicitation of a gift, since the maternal affirmation "It's mine" (whether she says it or simply signifies it by her behavior), if it is jurisdictional for the child, does not change the face of the world; rather, it signifies the mother's suffering. But we cannot advance these hypotheses with certainty, since Mr. Stoller, alas, tells us nothing of the material obtained during the analyses of the children. Our knowledge does suffice to show that the alienation that constitutes human desire as desire of the Other, or if you prefer, this servitude, is such that where the real seems to be compact, without a breach, a hole is nonetheless introduced, whether we like it or not, a hole that is more costly than that which the child plays at digging in the sand at the beach. The philosopher would like to see in this hole a manifestation of the negativity of the human spirit and its liberty.

This seeming, this delusional plenitude of the real, this successful deception of symbiosis, does not happen without producing a *foreclosure of the name of the father.*

So that no one will take these children for psychotics, Mr. Stoller warns the reader that they were all three charming children, even charmers, who were pleasant to talk with and had lively and inventive minds, to say nothing of their talent for dancing or singing. Is it as if all these talents and others, even more worthy, were not more than reconcilable with intimate, nameless disasters? And yet, what does all this signify, if not that these children were perfectly molded by the socialized and socializing *demands*, of their mothers? It is important that for them *there is no beyond to the demand*, or to say the same thing, *it is they themselves who were occupying this beyond.* In their existence they only encountered one caprice which, being exercised on them without restraint, enslaved them and was directed toward nothing outside of them. These children certainly knew how to distinguish men and women, and they identified with the latter, even if they did so only to object to identification itself; but their lives unfolded as though there were only masculine and feminine images. It is not as models for masculine identification that their fathers were absent: this absence can easily be compensated for. They were *absent as holding a symbolically different position, despite* the imaginary resemblance. With this defect in the symbol whose function as indispensable prop would be, we see, very compatible with the absence of the person or of the image, it is the lack itself, or the "beyond" of the demand, that is lacking for their sons. Beyond their articulated demands, these boys do not ask to be the phallus. On the contrary, *they ask*—this is their madness—*not to be it, while the neurotic for his part is not contented to be a man; he wants to be a real man.*

In short, through a path that we hope we have described correctly, the *foreclosed* castration in these boys, *foreclosed as symbolic castration, appears as a real castration* that the transsexuals demand with a passion not in the least playful, to the point where sometimes they do not hesitate to endanger their lives if the demand is not satisfied. Thus castrated, they are, we will say in risking a misunderstanding, the only true women.[15]

15. For the general diagnosis of transsexualism, we find it difficult to disagree with the conclusions of Jean-Marc Alby in his doctoral dissertation, "Contribution à l'étude du trans-sexualisme" (University of Paris, 1956), which diverge significantly from those to which Mr. Stoller is led.

It would doubtless be interesting to know what destiny created the emptiness in the life of the three mothers that they tried to fill with their sons—the result of which was a foreclosure that the boys suffered at the "springs of life."[16]

Happily, in the idea that such an enterprise could not fail to contribute to the elucidation of transsexualism in a boy, the research team directed by Mr. Stoller arranged for one of these mothers to begin an analysis at the same time as her son[17]—the only one of the three boys whose treatment brought some results.

It was Mr. Stoller himself who took charge of this woman's analysis. He draws this conclusion, insofar as we can summarize it: the woman has an imperative need for her son to cure her of the void that she received from her own mother. This need is also the origin of the bisexuality and penis envy that have dominated her life. The boy is thus the victim of her hatred and of her castrating intentions toward men (the feminization of the child sends back to her the mirror image of what she wants him to be);[18] he is her phallus (more specifically, her feminized phallus); and finally, he is her transitional object, first in the sense that he is a part of her own body, suspended at the moment of the transition towards his becoming a separated object, then, in Winnicott's sense, "in that he bridged

16.
> And thus untaught in youth my heart to tame,
> My springs of life were poisoned.
>
> Byron, "Childe Harold's Pilgrimage"

17. In contrast, almost three years were needed to convince the father that he should see an analyst from this team at least once a week. Another important point is that only the reprimand of a neighbor and the mocking looks and insulting comments of others made the mother decide to bring her son for a consultation.

18. In truth, nothing in the smattering of details that Stoller gives us from this analysis (and we can only regret his decision against describing the process of the analysis in favor of concentrating on the results that explain the son's disorder) permits the conclusion that any particular hatred is operative. In any case, it is striking that such an effect could be attributed to penis envy by an author who, some pages before (*Sex and Gender*, chapter 6), believed himself capable of arbitrating—to the detriment of Freud and through observations that he found crucial—the dispute concerning the phallicism of girls. Having observed women who were genetically, anatomically, and physiologically normal except that they had been born without vaginas, Stoller noted that none wished to become a man, that all wanted a vagina, and that all were happy after their operations to discover the hitherto unexplored pleasures of coitus—even though one of them, admitting that the operation had been a step in the right direction, nevertheless indicated that she had the feeling of not being like other women, since she had not been born with her vagina. Stoller draws this conclusion: "If Freud had worked with a woman without a vagina, I think he would have seen that the only thing a woman wants more than a penis is a vagina. It is only when a woman has normal genitalia that she can afford the luxury of wishing she had a penis" (*Sex and Gender*, p. 51n.).

For our part, we find nothing astonishing in the fact that the sense of the phallic phase escapes an author who utilizes the terms "phallus" and "penis" interchangeably, without asking himself at all why the one always emerges with the verb "to be" (Lance *is* his mother's phallus) and the other with the verb "to have."

the incompleted separation (*sic*) between herself and her own mother."[19] Lance's mother would have curbed her son according to her desire, but she would have done it by being loving, full of worry, overprotective, surrounding him with a warm atmosphere in which her need to ruin her child's masculinity mixed invisibly. Surrounded as he was, the dimensions of his body (his body ego) have unfortunately remained open, to include, as a part of himself, the body of his mother and her bisexually twisted femininity. When the father does not intervene in this process by which two beings of opposite sexes devour each other's feeling of sexual gender identity, a human convinced of being a girl despite anatomical maleness will be created.

We will leave to the side our remark that the transsexual boy is not a boy who feels himself to be a girl but is rather encumbered by his penis as by the feeling of being a boy, to the point where he demands his own castration . . . in order to become woman! We have already sufficiently insisted on this point as well as on the pathogenetic source of this general state. To go straight to the crux of the matter, we ask: *what is the void* behind all this disorder; is it that of the mother or that of the child?

When Mr. Stoller, leaving to the side the "anatomical" sense, or if you like, the objectal sense of this void, speaks with the patient of the emptiness "she received from her own mother," the expression signifies very precisely, according to him, that she has not received enough love from the mother.[20] But then, we do not see why she requires, to cure this sense of emptiness, not another love or an equivalent love, but the phallus. The question at this point is not love but a dialectic of desire, which escapes our author as much as it does the patient.

Now, not only did the patient's mother refuse her love and lack interest in her—even more, she assigned her daughter, if we may say so, an inferior rank on the scale of creation. It was, in fact, a "cultural tradition"[21] in her family: men are superior beings in relation to women. Born between two brothers[22] whose virility—too marked—was their excellence in the eyes of a mother whose look reproached her femininity, she herself was nothing—not a lacuna, but worse: it is preferable to be "nothing" than to be a being destitute of all love. And yet, she has maintained herself in being. How?

19. Another phrase that leads us to ask whether a slip of the pen or a typographical error has occurred: after having affirmed that the feminization of the boy reflects his mother's desire, Stoller adds (*Sex and Gender*, p. 109), "We shall be especially concerned with her problem of separating himself [*sic*] from her son."

20. We note that Stoller himself does not seem to notice at any time the double sense (terrestrial and celestial) of this void.

21. We know that it is most often women who perpetuate this kind of tradition.

22. One was two years older and the other three years younger.

It is not for nothing that Mr. Stoller underlines the patient's "special interest" in cloth and clothing, an interest that should not be connected with fetishism, "since rather it is a sensual pleasure approaching voluptuousness in the feel of cloth."[23] He is of the same opinion as de Clérambault, whose remarkable clinical observations led to this same conclusion.[24] According to Mr. Stoller, cloth and clothes are for her a transitional object, the primary object being "skin." But what does the patient herself say?

First, this interest is closely associated with her desire, nourished throughout her childhood, to be a nun (a nobody, if we write it "none"). She associates it also with the taste that she had from latency to adolescence[25] for theater and plays in which she played the roles of both men and women with equal success.[26] She comments, "When you take off your own clothes and put on different clothes, you can be anyone."[27] She did not need to read Homer to find a way that permitted her, without being anyone in particular, to be a kind of "negative grandeur" symbolized by *nun-none* or by *anyone*. But it was favored, this interest,[28] that of an artist or an artisan,[29] by clothes and fabrics that provided a way of hiding a nudity identical to that of her mother. Her mother must have felt this, even if only for a moment, as a castration: what is she for her mother, if not the ineffaceable memory of this very instant? *She has taken charge of the effacement of her mother's castration.*

We see that her desire is *the desire of her mother.*[30] It is also a *dead desire.* This is signified in a dream: "I had died and was now dead. But my mother kept sending me to the store on errands because she hadn't even paid enough attention to know it."[31] Dead and submissive, we could not put it better.

She is not really dead, however. We must consider the desire of the mother if we want to know what retains the daughter in being, what contains her desire for effacement within the field of language or of the symbol. That this mother had a preference for the brothers of the patient—this we do not doubt. As it

23. Stoller, *Sex and Gender*, p. 110.
24. See Gaetan de Clérambault, "Passion érotique des étoffes chez la femme," in *Oeuvre psychiatrique*, vol. 2 (Paris: Presses Universitaires de France, 1942), p. 683.
25. This latency period occurred, no doubt, between the age of six, when a sister was born, and thirteen, when a third brother was born. We will see the importance of these events for her.
26. Her family was proud of this ability.
27. Stoller, *Sex and Gender*, p. 112.
28. "Her father was noted for his beautiful needlework and weaving. Her maternal grandmother and great-grandmother were prize-winning lace makers" (Stoller, *Sex and Gender*, p. 110).
29. "The patient herself was a very creative dress designer before marriage, and still works daily designing and making all her own clothes" (Stoller, *Sex and Gender*, p. 110).
30. On the double sense of this genitive, see M. Safouan, "De la structure en psychanalyse," in *Qu'est-ce que le structuralisme?* ed. François Wahl (Paris: Editions du Seuil, 1968).
31. Stoller, *Sex and Gender*, p. 113.

happens, however, nothing indicates that she had been as subject to them as the patient is to her boy, Lance: the possession of a penis did not give them a right of sovereignty over her. What did she then want? Or: what *more* did she ask for?

It is in the distance of the "more" that the phallic image is going to "bend" the subject, boy or girl, who is going to be identified with this "more," which from that point on will polarize his *desire*, since he identifies himself with this image not as with the object of a *demand* (even if he thinks that the Other is asking for it) but as with an object that no demand would be able to articulate, and especially not the sexual demand that presents it most clearly. This object, then, cannot circulate as a gift and is refused to him. The child can only resolve this refusal, as Lacan points out,[32] by identifying with a mask.[33]

Now, bringing the phallic *image* on stage constitutes an *effect of the symbolic*, to the extent that this image functions as a metaphor of paternity. What matters for these three boys is that this effect has been defaulted.

This is why we feel certain that at issue, for the mother as well as for the daughter, is not some vague middle ground between "gratification" and "aggressiveness," "contact" and "distance," or what have you, but rather a *stopping of the symbolization of desire* in its reference to a third order, the symbolic, without our even mentioning the *default* of this reference.

If it were otherwise, if the mother were as addicted to one of the patient's brothers or to the patient himself as this latter is to her son, if the want-of-being opened by speech were completely obstructed, the daughter's frustration would be even more intense, since only her having the phallus could render her capable of being it. Liberated from its symbolic attachments, the phallus would have become for her the object of a demand that would accept no substitutes. And it would not only be what she demands, but it would also be what the Other asks from her in order for her to be someone, or better, that she be; it is precisely for this reason that she asks for the phallus in her turn! Only real death or madness would still be a way out, and yet no gift, no love, can placate this demand, the only one that she will confront in the Other place, beyond all demand. This demand for the phallus will have induced in her the most heterogeneous imaginary identifications, whose character, being as unconditional as the demand itself, threatens to throw her into depersonalization or delusions or else to submerge her in an uncontrollable anxiety.

Mr. Stoller's patient is pleased to repeat that she is *nothing*—but the *thing* is still preserved even in the negation; she is a "mirage" that retains her in being,

32. See Lacan, "The Signification of the Phallus," in *Ecrits: A Selection*, pp. 281–91.
33. Stoller, *Sex and Gender*, p. 113.

even if it makes her discontented with the real, a cipher, a message to whoever wants to hear it. Whatever her fortune, what little she has of it, she will not have lacked the signifier that breathes ambiguity into speech, and without which no subject can advance—she has felt a void that is not *nothing*.

All of that—it is true—renders inexplicable her later deviation, in which object relations were slowly but surely dissolved, only to reappear concentrated around a rejected child whom she tries ultimately to reintegrate. By accident, Mr. Stoller reports a fact whose importance will escape no analyst, that if the patient had the feeling that her mother did not love her or did not love her as much as her brothers, she was largely compensated for this by the care of a father for whom she was manifestly the preferred child, despite her changing moods. It was he who comforted her when she was sick and accompanied her to the doctor, he who took her, excluding her brothers, to athletic contests, and he who bought her clothing. Then, when she was six, a sister was born, and overnight she lost this favored position. Her deception and her resentment were such that from that day forward, her father no longer existed for her. An unresolved Oedipal complex became unresolvable. Henceforth the clinical manifestation, which will persist until puberty, is the regret of not being a boy or the desire to be one; this is clear in all the behavior we have seen, be it in masquerade or in the active participation in the sports and games of boys. We would be wrong to see in this participation a rivalry with boys. The rivalry was with *him—Oedipal*, as always.

It would be an even worse error, the one that perpetuates our misapprehension of the order of desire, to think that the patient felt that her menstruation and the development of breasts were traumatic events that put an end to "her hopes for maleness."[34] *It was not a question of being a man but of being the phallus.* This aim might also be expressed by "cultivating the appearance of femininity." Once her femininity had become a fact, she devoted herself to cultivating it . . . , without there being any break in her development.

One event took place during this period of her existence, whose unconscious consequences, perfectly deducible from the material that we have at our disposition, sealed her destiny. It was the birth, when she was thirteen, of a third brother. She claimed this brother as hers and appropriated him as the fruit of her incest. We are not surprised to learn that the patient first blamed her mother for the transvestite practices manifested very early by this brother, only recognizing later that she herself had initiated him.

This brother had been the first object she used to make her lack tolerable or, if we can say so, the first depositary of a penis *as not one*. If he was also her first

34. Stoller, *Sex and Gender*, p. 118.

victim, and if the problems with her son later reached the limit of real castration, it was, we see, without her wanting it: the castrating intentions that Stoller attributed to her did not determine this result; rather, their insufficiency did so. The unconscious brings about results not always in conformity with the likings of the subject.

The man whom she did castrate in the imaginary was her father. From the age of six, her existence was dominated by a resentment toward him that can be formulated as follows: "The phallus, which I lack—I do not seek it in you; I am it." At the same time the father became a counterpart and nothing else, an absolute rival. In fact, when she attained puberty, disputes began that ended only when she was sixteen and left home. After that she hardly ever saw her father until the time of his death. The brusque and irrevocable character of this departure reveals the radical meaning of these disputes: it is him or me.

From the age of sixteen until her marriage, all we know of her is that she worked as a milliner.

Of her marriage we know that her husband got along beautifully with her mother and that the emptiness of this mother was only equaled by that of her husband. Stoller takes note of the fact that this resemblance between the husband and the mother cannot be held as a coincidence, but without explaining this otherwise than by reference to the reasons pushing the patient toward a choice that reproduced the model from which she suffered the most.

A first child was born of this marriage, a daughter. Six years later, doubtless in commemoration of her deception or her revenge, she had a second child, her son Lance. "I had to have a baby," she explains.

Her last brother had been named Lance.

PART FOUR.   PERVERSION

14   The Perverse Couple

BY JEAN CLAVREUL

I cannot fail at the beginning of this communication to underline the fact that there is a paradox in speaking about the perverse couple. The principal themes of my discussion will bear on this paradox, and I will be open to criticism asking by what authority I link the notion of the couple with that of perversion.

Recent works on perversion—I refer essentially to those of the Freudian School of Paris—obviously prohibit us from considering the question of the perverse couple as that of the influence of a perversion on the life of a couple. Such an approach would necessarily imply that we consider the perverse act to be a fantasy enacted by a normal or neurotic subject. Now, all the recent works tend to show that on the contrary, the perverse act is engaged in by subjects whose libidinal investments, whose relations with desire and the Law, are profoundly different from those of the neurotic. That is why, rather than speak of perversion (in the singular or plural), we speak of the perverse structure, since this term permits us to approach the problem of perversion independently of the particular form that any perverse act may take.

Here we encounter the paradox: in isolating a perverse structure, as distinguished from that of the normal or neurotic subject, do we not deny to the pervert a knowledge of and participation in the ultimate goal of libidinal evolution, the greatest achievement of sexual life, the "love" that each of us would say is alone capable of maintaining the solidarity of a couple? Is the perverse structure compatible with love? This is the first question to which we are tempted to respond in the negative. But if there is no love, what is the tie that assures the extraordinary solidarity of certain perverse couples? This could be a second question. Finally—and this is not the least important of the problems that I will raise today—what happens in the psychoanalytic relation when a pervert is introduced into it? Does our conceptual apparatus permit us to speak of the

Jean Clavreul is co-chairman of the Department of Psychoanalysis at the University of Paris VIII. A psychiatrist, he practices psychoanalysis in Paris. This article was first published as "Le Couple pervers," in *Le Désir et la perversion*, ed. Piera Aulagnier-Spairani (Paris: Editions du Seuil, 1967), pp. 91–117.

couple formed by the pervert and his analyst? Notably, is it possible to take up the notion of "transference" as we utilize it in the analysis of a neurotic?

We do not pretend to respond to these questions here; our aim is only to articulate them: we have chosen the theme of the perverse couple not to provide a clinical study, which could only unite some very disparate elements, but to create openings, both in our approach to the perverse structure and in our more or less explicit idea of the love relationship, of the libidinal investments implied in the life of a couple.

We can now mark the opening through which we can legitimately introduce the pervert into the life of a couple. *Love*, which we speak about easily and even nonchalantly when we are talking about couples, is a complex feeling, whatever sense we give to it, and we have difficulty in explaining how a libidinal investment is fixed on a privileged being. We must notice that perverts often are those who speak of it best. Discourses, poems, romanesque descriptions— whatever the form of expression, the uninformed reader cannot be assured that his judgment will permit him to recognize whether or not the author is perverse.

And again, is it not patent that on the whole, erotic literature has been made up of writings by perverts? Again we must add that from the point of view of eroticism, the "normal individual" is presented, next to the pervert, as an inept yokel unable to elevate his love above a routine. The sexual good health that he brags about appears to derive from a lack of imagination. We cannot fail to notice that the ordinary hetrosexual seems very often to be a prisoner of this "vulgar love" denounced by the participants in the *Symposium*, who themselves do not hesitate to dismiss as uninteresting the bestial coupling that is only good for assuring the necessary and uninteresting mission of the perpetuation of the species.

Let us say, then, that we could not dismiss perverts from the field of love without getting off the track. In large part it is they who have sustained its discourse the best. Everyone is more or less conscious of, and easily lets himself be fascinated by, the relationship between the pervert and erotic love. But if someone normal eagerly looks to the pervert for lessons, he is not inclined for as much to take him as a model, and he rejects, often with intolerance, the practice of perversion. This characterizes the ambiguity of our position, which accommodates itself in order to gather a discourse while at the same time it denounces a practice.

Doubtless it would be possible to justify such a position by saying that knowing how to speak of love does not mean that one knows how to love. This would be to avoid the difficulty and, in any case, not to take account of the problem that a perverse patient poses for an analyst when he speaks of the love he bears for his partner. If such "material," when it is given to us, is not readily interpretable, we are no less constrained to have an opinion on this tie, which is often very lasting and which the patient will talk about throughout his analysis. Perhaps in such cases we should denounce the inadequacy of the notion of love, saying that this term is only employed by gross analogy, and speak rather of "passionate bond," which evokes more the absoluteness of psychosis than the diverse attachments of love. I will not, however, raise the question of passion envisaged as an entity distinct from love. Not that this question is not pertinent, but introducing a distinct category could only obscure one of the points that I want to talk about today and that I have just indicated. What the pervert talks about and pretends to talk about is surely a *discourse on love* and on nothing else, whether he is writing a literary work or doing a psychoanalysis.

To be more precise, and to interpret at the same time the aim of his discourse, let us then say that when a pervert talks of his love, we cannot be satisfied in thinking that he is giving a simple description of the passionate state that he experiences. If he speaks of love, what he says about it must be situated in relation to what he can know about people's willingness to forgive amorous states and to justify all of the abuses of these states in the name of a cult of Eros. It is certain that this is not proper to the pervert and that any analysand who invokes love is going to obscure the issue. We know well that at such a moment a fault is being hidden from us; but in the case of the pervert we must mention a note of challenge that seems to provoke us to tell him that if he wants to be cured, he must triumph over his love as well as over his perversion—his homosexuality, for example. More than of passion I will speak of "alleged love" to designate the sentiment that the pervert uses when he comes to us. To justify his perverse practice, he invokes a feeling about which we would be tempted to say that it constitutes one of the most solid criteria for a harmonious affective development, according to either the most currently admitted prejudices or to a psychoanalytic theory that is obliged to speak of investments, of object relations, but has certainly not said its last word about the role played here by the presence or the absence of the real penis. We can thus introduce a question: in alleging love, is not the pervert the one who first captures us in our own trap, using it for his own purposes and thus assuring the inanity of our eventual interventions? The love we often talk about is one of the central elements of the challenge that he throws at us. We now see the limits of his position, for when the pervert maintains it in the name of values that we are supposed to respect, he is revealing the importance of his reference to a universal discourse.

Rather than denounce this challenge, we speak of alleged love to designate the feeling through which certain subjects succeed in misapprehending themselves completely in their perversion. These subjects pretend to do nothing other than submit to the perverse practices of their partners, and this because of something that they call duty, pity or, more often, "love." Such a feeling is supposed to justify all weaknesses and all liberality. Thus we should not, even while invoking the pretext of love, spare ourselves from questioning the role of the wife of the fetishist, of the husband of the kleptomaniac or nymphomaniac, and even of the older woman who takes some very pretty pederasts under her wing. It is too easy to discard this difficulty by referring to signs of morbid complacency in one who submits to the other's perversion because of love. We would say, on the contrary, that the fetishist's partner is even more in question than the fetishist, for it is clear that the relationship between the fetishist and his fetish is sustained only when this fetish has the power to fascinate the other. This is one of the most important elements of the perverse structure, and since it is through the pervert that we understand the role of the other in this structure, we will return to him.

Thus love may be invoked by one of the partners to justify his perversion as being compatible with the most respected values. It can also permit the partner to live his perversion without thinking himself a pervert. The alleged love constitutes the ambiguous link, the common theme in which the two partners find each other. The ambiguity of this link is such that it would seem to merit very little interest; the link would be very close to a simple misunderstanding if its persistence through time, its resistance to mishaps, were not there to show once again that a good misunderstanding has all the chances of lasting for a long time—and not only in analysis! Now this remark—and even this comparison with analysis—permits us to indicate that this pretended linking through love functions like a contract in the sense that a contract united Sacher Masoch and his partners (a very precise contract, resembling a notarized document, defining the authorized limits of abuse) and also in the sense in which a contract linked Gide to his wife, who was condemned by the artifice of a ridiculous marriage to be a witness and accomplice to practices that she could only suffer and condemn. Here there is no need to recall the innumerable facts that are easily recognized as related to these examples.

The eventual breaking of such contracts has a completely different sense and a wholly different bearing from that of the failure of love between normal or neurotic subjects. The fact that these contracts are secret, that their terms and their practice are only known to those involved, does not in the least signify that the third party is absent. On the contrary: it is this absence of the third party, his being left out, that constitutes the *major element* of this strange contract. This third party, who is necessarily present to sign, or better, to countersign, the authenticity of a normal love relation, must here be excluded, or to be more precise, he is present but only insofar as he is blind or an accomplice or impotent. For this reason the eventual breaking of a perverse relationship is very different from the breaking of a love relationship. In the normal relationship one speaks of suffering, the infidelity of the partner, and the waste of time; the third party has no other role than to register the failure. But for the pervert, to the extent that only the "secret" kept from the third party constitutes the foundation of the contract, it will not be the infidelity, the suffering, the indifference of one of the partners, or the waste of time that will lead to the breakup. It will be the failure to keep the secret, the telling of a third party, and the ensuing *scandal* that will bring about the breakup. Thus the perverse couple will support without difficulty any suffering, meanness, or infidelity. It is sufficient that the secret be preserved. But on the contrary, we see the couple torn apart when one or the other makes a public allusion to their practices; for example, a professor or a priest will be sincerely revolted if his protégé reveals the acts to which he (the protégé) lends himself. Finally, the third party himself will be scandalized by such revelations: thus Krafft-Ebing was revolted that the wife of Sacher Masoch revealed to him the secret contract. In any revelation of an intimate secret, it is difficult not to have scorn for the one who gives it away. We cannot overestimate the importance of such a secret contract, without which we could not begin to understand how the most extreme perverse practices can be perpetuated for such a long time, leaving the occasional spectator fascinated and finally an accomplice because he cannot give away the secret.

Perverse bonding, passion, alleged love, secret contract—these notions permit us, then, to approach the solder joining the two partners in this couple. It is necessary to note a point that is currently observed but is dissimulated by the fact that perversion lends itself particularly well to the role reversals that characterize other couples. We remark that homosexuality unites the same with the same, that the homosexual relation can be triangulated indifferently with a third party who is of the one or the other sex, that sadism can turn into masochism, exhibitionism into voyeurism, and so forth. This is certain. But a possible role reversal does not signify a symmetry. We should note how different each partner in a perverse couple is, precisely in the most lasting couples. The couple's *disparity* is always remarkable. And I cannot fail to recall here that Lacan in his seminar on "subjective disparity" referred continually to the homosexual couples of the *Symposium*.

Thus we find the athlete linked with a puny little kid, the refined intellectual with the hillbilly, the massive woman with an angel of femininity, the immoral alcoholic with a saint, the vicious dirty old man with the prepubescent adolescent, the sociably respectable person with the hobo. We would not finish if we tried to enumerate the infinite variety of strange couples who seem to defy the third party who observes or would observe them, so much are the disproportion and ridiculousness shocking. Yet the meaning of such unions goes well beyond this exhibitionism, scandalous for the bourgeoisie. The alibi of love will not prevent us from seeing an essential characteristic of the perverse structure in these dissymmetries. Only the most radical ambiguity permits the pervert to pursue a tightrope act, we can only guess how close he may be to a bad fall.

Such disparities do not allow themselves to be reduced to the waverings of our categories. The masochist would not be so interested in seeing his torturer in action if this latter did not incarnate some model of force or virility. And even the characters of the divine Marquis [de Sade] are not interested in Theresa because she is a masochist. For Theresa is first "Justine," which is to say "the misfortunes of virtue." What would she be, this designated victim, if she did not incarnate a value, one of those values that the entire century venerated? It is through her, through this victim, that the perverse act finds not only its sense but also its place in a contemporary discourse—this in the same sense in which we said above that love, more than being an alibi, is a *moral reference.*

The recent trial of a couple of sadistic Scottish murderers awakened the fantasies of a number of our perverts in analysis. Their commentaries are precious, even though they chose very diverse facts to focus on. They all told us that the erotic excitation that comes from the contemplation of the other's suffering sustains itself in only one certitude: that the *other is innocent.* Also, even more important to the sadist than the victim's cries of suffering are his protestations of innocence and his pleading for mercy. All the stories of Sade insist on facts of this order, and we can only underline their importance. The pervert is not indifferent to his choice of partner.

Of importance about the other are his activity, his commitments, the insignia that he bears, the virtues that he possesses. The crossing of two paths, let us say, of two ways that are profoundly different, the fascination in an uncommon encounter where the aim of the one is in no way similar to that of the other, the misunderstanding, the quid pro quo that is inseparable from the act itself—this the pervert seems not only to submit to but to *seek.* Perverse eroticism is most certain to be sustained if one of the partners defends himself in the name of certain values and thus precipitates himself even more quickly into the other's game, first as a participant, then as an accomplice. Not only the eroticism, which is to say the desire, but also the anxiety; each of the partners takes care to misapprehend the field of the other's desire sufficiently for the erotic game to be played in an affected ignorance of the partner's aim. This makes the emerging anxiety and jouissance closer to the everyday outcome of an unknown desire.

We thus recognize one of the singularities of the perverse couple in this deliberate misapprehension of the other's aim. It will suffice for the functioning of the couple if one partner knows definitely which signifiers imprison the other; it will suffice for him to know what the other cannot extricate himself from, for then he will use this knowledge to make the other attain the summits of anxiety and jouissance. With these givens there are enough elements to activate the delicate and fascinating mechanism that makes the two partners into consenting playthings, impotent to be anything other than consenting. Jouissance will come especially from everything's unfolding according to the law of an implacable mechanism to which the disparity of the partners is reduced. This permits us to understand why it is not only possible but rather indispensable for the other to conserve his autonomy, his role of unknown. Perverse partners do not fail to flatter themselves for being, years later, as attentive toward each other as if they had just met for the first time. We must also note that they take the necessary steps to renew this illusion every day. And as proof of the love that they bear each other, they give the respect that they have for the intimacy, the secret, and the liberty of the other. The transfixed observer will never fail to be astonished in remarking how perverts reconcile their extreme delicateness with the total disrespect for the other that their practice implies.

Such are the clinical facts that need to be pointed out before we go any further with the question of the "perverse couple." Obviously it is out of the question to pretend to make a complete study of this topic, as much because of the extreme diversity of the facts we should have to consider as because of the complexity of their interpretation. The only goal of my remarks is to attract attention to a certain number of particularities that, without neglecting the privileged importance that should be given to the *fact* of the perverse act, will permit us to discern a certain style, a certain mode of relationship with the other, that overflows the traditional and relatively narrow frame of perversion. To tell the truth, it is through the relation with the other, or thanks to the lever it gives us, that we may attempt to discern in the perverse structure the elements that will permit us to move away from that which in practice always remains marked with the seal of contingency. Perverse practice, the perverse act, in soldering the elements of the couple and in constituting the major element of their contract, is always something that appears to be a "find," in the sense in which one would say "a clever find or a poetic find." If the gestures of the perverse ceremony are so clearly dependent on cultural background, even on fashion, the actors are no less conscious of their participation in a kind of "black mass," which doubtless could not have its value if it were not also a mass but whose wit is contained especially in the fact that the challenge it brings has no name and no face except for the few initiates who have been able to find the place and the mode of its ceremony. Thus the perverse ceremonial is always profoundly marked with this seal of secrecy, of a secret whose fragility (we will come back to this point) is the illusory guarantee in this ceremony that the "unknown" is to be found.

Since we are proposing to go beyond the clinical facts into the psychoanalytic interpretation of the perverse couple and the perverse structure, we cannot avoid referring to the question of disavowal, exactly as Freud discusses it in his article on fetishism. I do not have to recall the questions raised about this matter, notably those that led Freud to utilize notions such as "splitting of the ego" and "coexistence of contradictory beliefs," notions that are finally obscure but whose sense appears clearer, thanks to the elaboration given them in Lacanian theory through the notions of "subjective splitting" and of noncoincidence between "knowledge" and "truth". . . .

What I want to talk about today, the emphasis that I want to give, does not concern the *object* of the young boy's discovery, that being the absence of the penis in the mother, but rather the child's *subjective* position. If it is true that the discovery of this absence of the penis in the mother counters the presence of a penis in the child, and if it is true that such a discovery brings with it the theme of castration in showing that what *is* can also *not be*, we must also recall that Freud always designated the true knot of the castration complex as the acquiring of *knowledge* about this absence. And he has said that this acquisition is made at the cost of great internal struggles. Then, aside from the threat (of being castrated) that this discovery brings virtually (it is possible to be dispossessed of it), there is something else that bears on the discovery, which concerns knowledge itself. And this is that knowledge can be deceiving. The child discovers that his previous subjective position has been based on an erroneous knowledge (all beings—including his mother—have a penis). To be more precise, the child must recognize at this moment that he had been living in a universe of certainties where there was no place for the problematic nature of the existence of the penis. Thus, beyond his discovery, the child has to learn that he must leave a place for a "not-knowing" whose importance is primary, however, since it touches the field of his libidinal investments.

Now the question can also be posed in other terms (at the moment of the discovery?). Is the child spectator or voyeur? explorer or jouisseur? This question recurs constantly in any consideration of perversion, and the exhibitionist asks the same question about anyone who sees him exhibit himself. This questioning concerns a *look* (here, the Other's look). We can pose the question in the most precise way, "precise" as regards psychoanalytic theory, in the very terms Freud used in his article "Drives and Their Vicissitudes," where he speaks to us of the separation that we should make between the external, exogenous excitations, which one can be rid of through an appropriate act, and the endogenous drives. It is worthwhile to modify this distinction, since the drive, or better, the drive circuit, necessarily includes its object, which is generally on the outside. We will interpret the discovery made by the young boy differently if we consider either that it is in some way accidental, something given by the external world, from a "reality," as we say, that imposes itself on the child despite himself, or that this reality is discovered by the child because he was moved by a desire to see, by a scopophilic drive. Evidently our interpretation of this moment of discovery is suspended according to what we will say of this drive. This recalls the fact that we cannot have a correct psychoanalytic concept of reality without referring to the reality of drives, which is to say, finally, to the libidinal economy which is dependent on the pleasure principle.

Freud does not really take a position on the question of the drive in his article on fetishism. We can even say that in isolating the moment of the discovery, Freud's text lets it be understood that the discovery is in some sense accidental. But no text of Freud really states that the libidinal development is perverted because the child was taken unawares by a traumatizing discovery. Freud's interpreters have never moved in this direction, and in any case, we do not see where such an explication could lead us. It appears impossible to understand the event if not as a function of a scopophilic drive that was inciting the young boy at this moment.

In isolating this moment of discovery—we can consider it to be mythic— Freud separates a "before" from an "after." And if it is vain to decide arbitrarily whether the child wanted to see and to know or whether he only interpreted the discovery retrospectively as the endpoint of such a desire to see, it is important to note this other fact whose bearing I indicated above: the child must also discover that he was ignorant of the reality of sexual difference. What we learn here concerns the fragility of a subjective position: it is a question not merely of having to accept a singular but contingent anatomical fact but also of having to integrate the other fact, that only the *lack* can be the *cause* of desire. It is precisely on this point that the pervert brings his disavowal to bear: it is not the *lack* that causes desire, but a *presence* (the fetish).

The discovery of the difference between the sexes is for the young boy the occasion for a reinterpretation of the cause of desire, and it is this reinterpretation that the pervert misses. We must add that this reinterpretation has a retroactive effect: how could the child have made his discovery, by what scopophilic drive could he have been moved, if a *lack of knowledge* had not provoked him? Thus the discovery of the absence of the penis will normally lead the child to recognize not only this lack as the cause of his sexual desire, but also his *lack of knowledge* as the cause of the scopophilic drive that led him to the discovery. Thus the desire to see and to know is not structurally different from sexual desire.

The pervert's disavowal bears first on the lack of a penis as cause of desire and then on the lack of knowledge as cause of the scopophilic drive. Here we find the incidence of the retroactive interpretation that follows the discovery of the absence of the penis in the mother: the child has to discover that concerning *the object of his love, his mother,* he ignored an essential aspect that concerns him as a sexed being, as a desiring being. Better yet, the child must still learn that as concerns the object of his desire, his mother, someone else—*sharing the same* desire—knew more than he did, knew what he had ignored of his own desire. The father's role, the role of his priority or his anteriority in knowledge, gives the sense of the avowal, as indicated after the report of Rosolato: this is the avowal of the priority of the father (the avowal that someone knew his [the son's] desire at a time when he [the son] himself did not). It is here, around this knowledge of sex and desire, that the subject discovers his place in the signifying chain, the place where he finds himself marked by a desire to which the Other, the Father, has the key. At the same time the child has his place identified for him, and since he is alienated from his desire, its object is unconscious.

On what does the pervert's *disavowal* bear? In terms of the relation to *knowledge,* it signifies that the child did not recognize himself as the one who did not know and who *wanted to know.* In terms of the relation to the father, it signifies that the child does not submit himself to the sovereignty that is his father's by virtue of his preceding the child in knowing. This leads the pervert to place himself in the position of never again being deprived with regard to knowledge, and most particularly knowledge concerning love and eroticism. Here we find one of the themes that I evoked at the beginning of this report, concerning the pervert's wager, where it is easy for us to recognize the challenge that he presents to our position with respect to the "supposed subject of knowing," to use Lacan's term. The pervert's knowledge is equally a knowledge that refuses to recognize its insertion in a "not-knowing" that precedes it: it is a knowledge that is given as the truth, it is the "gnosis" to which Rosolato has attracted our attention. Finally, this knowledge is rigid and implacable; it cannot be revised in the face of facts that belie it. This knowledge about eroticism feels assured of obtaining the other's jouissance under any circumstances.

I will not return to these facts, which are not essential for pursuing my argument. I will ask only one essential question: what is the quality of a knowledge that does not leave any place for the field of illusion? We know that this field of illusion is necessary to the constitution of the symbolic order in which Lacan has designated the object *a* as the first term of the only algebra where the subject can be recognized. It is there that the subject discovers the only subjective position in which he can get his bearings and identify himself, that of the desiring subject. Where is this object *a* to be found, which in revealing itself to be deceptive, evanescent, illusory, and substitutive confirms the subject as a being of desire? We know that that child looks for the *object* in his mother. The lack he encounters there cannot lead him to anything but this desire evoked by the lack, which makes plain the fact that this object is missing at the same time that its value for access to truth becomes apparent. The object of desire will forever remain marked by this sign of the illusory, and thus when we speak of love in the normal subject and in the neurotic, we never fail to remark that the love relation is founded on a first experience of illusion, which is to say that any chosen object will always be a substitute. Only through an investment will a chosen object occupy the place left by the lack, a place that draws its signifying function for desire only by having been left empty, by being seen as illusory.

We see that the theory of the disavowal does not permit us to consider the pervert as choosing, as investing, a privileged object whose function would be to occupy this eminent and fragile place whose contour is given by the object *a*. If the pervert in his disavowal maintains that he has discovered nothing concerning sexuality and his mother, this contention signifies above all else that there is for him no difference between a before and an after, that there was no illusion or disillusion. Nothing permits him to think that he loved what he did not know, that he could have wanted to know what he loved, which is to say, that he could have wanted to know and to lose in the same movement what was most dear to him.

The danger that the pervert is always bordering on—I must repeat it here—is psychosis, and we see then that it is on the level of the absence of the subjective root of the "not knowing," of the desire to know, that the difficulty emerges, since then an absolute knowledge, outside of time, outside of the dimension of the illusion, may come to prevail. But such a knowledge would be psychotic, and the pervert does not let it take root. The specificity of his own position and its originality lies in his success in parrying this danger by reconstituting the field of illusion elsewhere. This elsewhere is the fetish. It is also the masquerades that perverts are so fond of, the travesties, the transvestitisms that are so close to psychosis. Finally, these are the games, the arts in which one is supposed to create an illusion and, if I dare say so, to fetishize it. The pervert seeks not only to create this field of illusion but also to limit its range so that it does not attain to the function that it acquires in the normal subject, that of being the means of access to the Truth that the Other necessarily discovers on his path. This fetishization is marked by the fact that the activity, the knowledge, and the interests of the pervert must above all be *rigorously of no use,* to lead nowhere. Anything validated by the pervert is marked with the seal of uselessness.

The decision to establish a field of illusion is obviously not sufficient for its emergence. The illusion, in such a scheme of things, must be self-sustaining, and this does not happen without difficulty. In confronting this difficulty the pervert demonstrates his own genius. The necessity that constrains him to move into the useless obliges him to glow with a particularly lively light in the eyes of those who observe him and who are supposed to be dazzled by him. There is another difficulty that we must now consider again. We return to the interpretation of the scene where the young child discovers the absence of the penis in his mother, since we must elucidate the very important question that P. Aulagnier has rightly posed: *with what eye does the mother see her child, who looks at her?* It is here that we find the question, left to the side for a moment, of the scopophilic drive, of the look. Can the mother believe that her child is looking at her innocently? . . . We can continue with another remark, bearing on the mother's look. Each one of us has often learned, from the confidences of our patients, with what evident complicity mothers are attentive to the effect produced on their children by these discrete exhibitions.

But here there is no response, there is only a question. The look and the eye retain their mystery. And it is thus that for the pervert the eye will have a problematic place that neurotic and normal subjects reserve for the phallus and the loved object. This eye, which did not consent to recognize itself as deceived or tricked, discovers itself and lets itself be discovered as deceiving. Is the eye there to see, to look, to jouir, or better yet, to seduce? It is always there that the pervert will have to employ his charms [spells]. From the side of this "seeing" that proposes itself as true, he will have to reconstitute the illusory.

Coming back to our argument more directly, we ask ourselves what becomes of the Other in this affair, of the Other as partner in the perverse game. It is clear that insofar as he brings a look, the Other will be the partner and above all the accomplice of the perverse act. We touch here on the distinction between a perverse practice, in which the Other's look is indispensable because it is necessary to the complicity without which the field of illusion would not exist, and a perverse fantasy, which accommodates itself very well to the absence of the Other's look and asks one to be satisfied in the solitude of the masturbatory act. If the perverse act is distinguished without equivocation from the enacted fantasy, it is at the place where the Other's look is inscribed that we discern a frontier. This look, whose complicity is necessary for the pervert, denounces both the normal and the neurotic subject.

We understand thus the importance that the mother's look may have. Assuredly she is the young pervert's spectator at the decisive historical moment of the discovery. It is thus that this look participates in the creation of the field of the illusion. But it will be necessary in what follows that this look continue to let itself be seduced by the charm of the fetishes, by the child's gifts. You will easily recall these mothers, fascinated by the talents of their boys, who let them settle into a homosexuality in which the mothers play the role of accomplice. These mothers pretend not to see the direction taken by their sons' sexuality and remain in a curious position where they can guess everything, without really knowing, in a reverse reproduction of the scene Freud talks of. We know that if the mother fails to play such a role, the pervert will not fail to find some other, somewhat elderly lady who will offer him the same complicity and sustenance. How many women love the company of these men who are so gracious toward femininity without making the women sense that as men they possess a penis, which the women are deprived of! Here the complicity is patent and is designated for what it is, the refusal of a desiring look, the refusal to enact a disparity that would be rooted in an anatomical reality.

But if the mother's look has such an importance for the pervert, it is because this look is equally the one that knows how to see something other than the illusion that her son proposes, and it is also because it is the one that refers to the father (who is thus not entirely lost), the one through which a relationship to the law is found, the one that it is interesting to seduce because it is sufficiently moored to a family and social foundation for the challenge of detaching it or perverting it to retain its value. This challenge also determines the interest that the pervert always has for people well placed in the social order, for the people who sustain social order, which is manifested, for example, in the project about which homosexuals speak so willingly among themselves as a joke: to succeed in seducing... the policeman or the priest.

Without going to such extremes, let us rather say that most important for the pervert is the fact that the Other be sufficiently engaged, inscribed in the social structure, notably as someone respectable, for each new experience to have the sense of a debauchery where the Other is extracted from his system in acceding to a jouissance that the pervert has mastered. There is always, in any perverse act, an aspect related to rape, in the sense that the Other must find himself drawn into the experience despite himself and that this experience must be a falsification of his social position.

To avoid confusion we must specify here that the desubjectification whose essential role we have signaled in perverse practice signifies not the absence of subjectivity, the anonymity of a partner who would be indifferently replaceable by an other, but rather a loss or abandonment of subjectivity. This implies that it existed at the beginning and had only to be erased; subjectivity must constitute the canvas on which the pervert's mastery of the fetish will have to affirm itself, be it with a whip or with an erotic technique.

We must add that it is of little import, finally, whether the pervert's partner is or is not an important person whose dignity, purity, and power are debauched. If it can happen that a respectable person lets himself be drawn into perverse practices, it may also be that the perverse partner plays at being a respectable person. The essential point in the illusion is to maintain enough verisimilitude to cause anguish and enough of a lack of verisimilitude and of fantasy for all this to be interpreted at the desired moment as a simple play at which it is not possible to take offense without appearing ridiculous.

We see that the perverse couple will be led to reestablish the place where the Law is represented. And if the presence of the Law is necessary to assure the quality of the challenge, we must also remark that even here this step has the function of restoring an illusion that, in the problematic proper to disavowal, has been eliminated to prevent the deceptive character of the mother's desire from appearing. This desire lays a foundation because it is deceptive.

This tightrope act that the pervert must maintain does not continue without difficulty and may even lead him to the analyst's office. What does he come to do there, and what couple does he count on forming with the analyst? I attempted in 1964 to give a first answer to this question, and at that time I placed emphasis on the fact that the transference is falsified and eluded by the pervert because his demand cannot be superimposed on that of the neurotic: it is not a demand to know, a demand for a knowledge that can cure and to which the neurotic aspires. I think that it is useless to return to this point after what we have just said, that it is impossible for the pervert to take the position of the one "who does not know" before a "supposed subject of knowing," a position of "avowal" [aveu], where one can recognize oneself as the "solicitor" [avoué] of the one who knows something about the object of one's own desire that one cannot know oneself.

If this position, which is the foundation of the transference, is in default, what can our role be? What is the pervert asking for when he asks for an analysis? The analyst's role can best be approached through an example that was brought to me as a fragment of an observation and presents the advantage of having close affinities with theory.

It concerns a young man with homosexual and fetishistic practices. This young man also has a particular liking for striptease. Now, after such a spectacle, but never after the other practices, he has the unbearably intense feeling that a look has been fixed on him and that he is being followed or trailed. The painful impression persists and only disappears when he goes to confession. This curious phenomenon continues until the day when a priest is disturbed by the role he is being made to play.

It is not necessary to underline the interest that the story of this look can have for us. This look weighs on the pervert as soon as he puts himself in the position of the voyeur. We see how anxiety is evoked by this look, and the subject may at any instant become prey to a delusion of surveillance or to some other psychotic process. It is striking to find vividly presented here a devolution of the priest's function of granting absolution. It makes little difference who is giving the benediction, as long as it is given in the same way, with the soutane in play. This action makes the priest the accomplice of the act that is being erased. Through a ritual gesture surely denuded of sense for the penitent, there is the assurance that someone who has an affirmative relationship with the Law looked at his voyeurism with a blind look because he was secretly fascinated and thus an accomplice.

Merchant of illusions—here is the role to which they confine me, this priest said with a melancholy tone, but happily he was sufficiently reserved to see that there was no urgency and doubtless some danger in denouncing the role that he had been asked to play.

Merchant of illusions, or better, charlatan [marchand d'orviétan], a patient said of me, finding this nice word "quack medicine" [orviétan] as a substitute for our more modern "placebo." But she told me this (experienced analysand that she was), only because she knew me to be a bad merchant, not generous enough. Being able to recognize her true demand constituted progress, nonetheless, for this masochist who, after having failed to get herself strangled on several occasions, was preyed upon by oneiric anxieties in which a hallucination with the theme of persecution appeared. The view of herself as the buyer of quack medicine [acheteuse d'orviétan], was new to this alcoholic, and yet she could have known that she sought some quack medicine [orviétan] in alcohol. I could have been maladroit, and I might have been offended by what she was saying, had I seen there an expression of lassitude concerning the length of her analysis. She did not hesitate to explain to me that this quack medicine [orviétan] brought all kinds of golds [ors], but also slowworms [orvets], and that this had been going on for some time now [de tout le vieil or]. In short, this word brought with it a mine of signifiers that was, without doubt, of primary importance for this woman, who made the art of writing a privileged activity and excelled in it.

I am not the first analyst to observe that the demand for analysis from a pervert is particularly strange and ambiguous. Its challenge cannot be avoided. The courteous appearances that perverts affect generally do not deceive for very long. The analyst questions himself about the nature of a challenge borne in this way. Does the pervert seek from us protection against eventual medicolegal troubles, thus reducing us to the role of accomplice or protector? Or does he seek to prove his good will in the eyes of a third party? Does he come into analysis to seek scabrous images that will aid him in ameliorating his perverse practices? Or better yet, does he want to get rid of some minor problem while remaining firmly decided to modify nothing of the essential?

All the questions that one may ask oneself, that one *does* ask before or at the beginning of the analysis of a pervert, constitute the principal reason for the extreme reserve with which we greet such a patient. This explains—without justifying it—the preliminary precautions that are often taken, for example, a close questioning of the sincerity of a homosexual's desire to be cured, as though we wanted to verify that the analysis is based on a "firm purpose." Or we may place the rule of abstinence in the forefront. Sometimes this may represent the technical alibi behind which the refusal to analyze is hidden, but it can also be a way of misapprehending the patient's perversion by focusing the relationship between analyst and analysand on a particular element (acting) and thus pushing the relationship toward a sadomasochistic mode.

In fact, whether it is a question of the technical rules of analysis or of any other consideration, one can only ask whether the analyst does not respond to the challenge posed by the pervert in taking refuge in such familiar terrain as alliance with the sane part of the ego, refusal of acting out, and so forth. Such actions finish by "moralizing" the analysis, in the sense in which it is always possible to say that within the correct psychoanalytic norms matters should present themselves in such and such a way, well codified.

Doubtless we are provoked by this questioning of the ethics of psychoanalysis or by this questioning of the analyst's desire, which is the same thing. Who will sustain the desire to be cured when it can easily become identified here with a suppression of perverse practices? Or else, if we agree—at least tacitly—to attach only a secondary importance to the symptoms and to make the analysis an end in itself, what demand on the part of the analysand will come to sustain the undertaking? We understand the impasse that we would confront if we tried to reduce the analytic act to purely gratuitous research that proposes no preliminary goal. Such an undertaking would be tacitly accepted by the pervert without difficulty. *It would reduce the analyst to the role of pure voyeur.*

It appears that the analyst finds himself reduced to a position that is either moralizing or perverse, capable of passing from the one to the other very easily. This is not surprising when we know the structural analogies between the two positions. We understand that analysts often refuse to take on this impossible role, since it touches them at a point where the questioning of their practice and theory is impossible to elude. To tell the truth, we expect no less from the pervert. He aims at precisely the place that constitutes our Law and is sustained by our desire. Here we find, in the context of the practice of the psychoanalytic cure and of the couple analyst-analysand, exactly the same question that we posed concerning love and the perverse couple. Are we going to say that the pervert is incapable of love and of life in a couple? and that he is even incapable of the transference and the analytic relation? Why not? But we should expect that the challenge will be picked up: we will see perverts rejected from the psychoanalytic paradise, but they will be those (if this has not already happened) whose discourse on love, transference, law, and desire most people listen to. We note in passing that the pervert shows his true adroitness when he is sustaining a discourse that does not appear to be his own but is argued in response to a challenge declaring that only the demonstration of a virtuosity without object is important.

Reduced to the role of pure spectator, of pure auditor of a pervert whose discourse has no other end than to affirm the total gratuitousness of its content, the analyst—no matter what he says about the fact that the aim to be pursued should properly come from the analysand—finds himself reduced to impotence. Whether he is called upon to witness the delusional phantasmagoria of an orgy or to try to make sense of a tortuous narrative in which the patient leads him on between clarifying metaphors and deceiving images, between honest avowals and the corrupting exhibitions, the analyst finds himself trapped in his own discipline. The pervert will thus have succeeded in creating a situation with a tacit contract founded on the impotence of the analyst and the sterility of the analysand's discourse. To escape from this trap, we must remark first that it could not have been set except by our own hands, that the challenge can only exist to the extent that we feel ourselves challenged.

Another approach is possible if we begin by observing that the illusion we are asked to accept and to share it not entirely unknown to us and that its place is not negligible in our theory. This permits us to be neither fascinated nor ignorant in relation to the quack medicine, which we can finally accept for its exchange value as the medium in a relationship where the merchant and the buyer find themselves in a disparity without which there would not be a subjective position. After all, why would we not haggle over the price of this quack medicine? We analysts are particularly well placed to know the price. We know that if our function is to make a hidden truth emerge, this truth will not appear definitively until it has been revealed as elusive, until it has shed all the masks of false imitations, mirages, or illusions.

The analytic relation is thus dependent on the analyst's ability to sustain the discourse of a patient for whom the field of illusion remains the privileged register, where the perverse structure permits him to glow in such a way that the person who listens to him feels himself always more or less threatened. And in fact it is there that the analyst's knowledge is definitively put to the test. The challenge that the pervert throws at him, this challenge from which he tries too hard to preserve himself—the analyst only feels it as such to the extent that he *in his relationship with his knowledge* feels himself threatened by the ambiguity of the perverse position. We can see this threat emerging in relation to the place that we must accord to this disavowal [*Verleugnung*], which we are always tempted to misread as the denegation [*Verneinung*] or the rejection [*Verwerfung*]. In either case we end by denying the particularity of the perverse structure. The term "disavowal" that we use to designate the position of the pervert faced with the discovery of the absence of his mother's penis cannot take on its veritable sense unless we give it a place among the other markings of the perverse structure. Behind the question of the real presence of the penis, we find another concerning the significance of a discovery that introduces the place of a phallus whose existence is only specified as not being lacking. Beyond the problem of reality is the definitive issue of the Other who guarantees it. As such, the Other is disavowed, and the entire analytic relation finds itself transformed from the beginning, when the pervert refuses to the analyst this place in which the neurotic would see the "supposed subject of knowing." The analyst is defied to the extent that he wants to find refuge in this place, and this defiance can be interpreted as a refusal to be treated like a neurotic, which thus signifies the pervert's attempt [in the analysis] to stage the fundamental elements of his structure.

I will close by leaving suspended the question of the perverse couple, first, to create a place for discussion, but also because it does not appear to be possible to do much more here than to disengage ourselves from the more or less implicit and vague notion according to which the pervert seeks with his partner a complementarity in which his predilections can be satisfied. Often clinically inexact, this "complementarity" is in any case insufficient to account for the complexity of the relationship. For whatever the form taken by the couple's relationship (and the forms are many and varied), the decisive influence on the solidarity of such a couple will be the presence of an eye susceptible of judging the perverse game— this eye, impotent accomplice, whose blindness must be renewed day after day, even if this entails making it a partner, occasionally or permanently. The true partner of the pervert will always be this eye, which because it lets itself be seduced and fascinated, proves at every moment the existence of the register of the illusion, even if it could not have had for the pervert the historical function of founding the accession to an object relation that it does for the neurotic or normal subject.

In sustaining such a wager, in spying on the place where he will succeed in imposing himself on the Other's look, the pervert displays his expertise. His abilities are astonishing without being convincing. But we cannot ignore them, and perhaps the current interest in the perversions derives precisely from the fact that his challenge questions us on the most delicate and uncertain point of analytic theory. For that reason this report will leave many questions barely opened, even though they are essential because they touch us at the quick. They do not touch us in the same way as the love and hate that the neurotic uses to catch and to imprison us. At this point we are most profoundly bound to a theory that, like all knowledge, has its blind spots and is silent about the essential; here the lack of knowledge finds itself filled, not by a delusional discourse, but by the dazzling know-how of the pervert.

15 Essay in Clinical Psychoanalysis: The Alcoholic

BY CHARLES MELMAN

1

From the multitude of drinkers—so diverse in their condition, passions, and habits—the profile of the alcoholic emerges, its weakness organized, with a perfectly geometric rigor, by at least three traits:

1. The apparently unique affinity of this mental affection with a social class, the proletariat. The problem with jouissance leads us to ask about a sociogenesis.

2. The subjective drama is stereotypical and unalterable: the family tyrant with his fortunes and misfortunes. A scene is constantly played out in which paternity is impossible, and this leads us to ask what signifier is thus denied [*Verleugnung*].

3. The libidinal disaffection toward the medical corpus can be marked as a third trait, significant for the evaluation of the alcoholic's psychical economy and also for the deployment of a therapeutic tactic.

The Impossible Avowal

Despite the evidence of the facies, the stigmata, and the alcoholic's biography, he denies; clinical tradition sees this as an example of bad faith. We suggest that this is an error; the subject's recognition of his addiction is inefficacious—it even may aggravate his condition: now he drinks to forget his addiction.

We must note here that the construct of the drive (as Lacan inscribes it on his graph) implies the eclipse of any subject.

Something in him, "it," craves a drink; as subject, he can only slave at working to satisfy the demand.

This article was originally published in three parts. The first, "Essai pour une clinique psychanalytique: L'Alcoolique," appeared in *Scilicet* 4 (Paris: Editions du Seuil, 1973), pp. 161–66. The second was entitled "Alcoolisme II" and appeared in *Scilicet* 5 (Paris: Editions du Seuil, 1975), pp. 105–10. The third, "L'Alcoolisme: Troisième et dernier tour," appeared in *Scilicet* 6/7 (Paris: Editions du Seuil, 1977), pp. 179–86.

This primal splitting accounts for the representation the alcoholic alone has of himself: a good boy, generous, devoted, a worker who would never leave his friends in need. He seeks with the best faith to have this representation recognized and validated, especially because people want to see him as strange and dishonest.

This split between a true private representation and the degraded image for which he is reproached by society is at the origin of a fundamental misunderstanding that may well embarrass the therapist who would try to establish a transferential relationship.

The Transference Is Cursed

The sterotypical quality of the subjective drama validates the unpleasant necessity of having to consider the alcoholic as a class without concern for the individuals who would give this class its particularity. The reason for this consideration will be found in alcoholics' generally sharing a fantasy that can perhaps be isolated.

The difficulty of inciting the transference in an alcoholic is secondary to the fact that there already is one in him before any therapy begins. This transference is aimed at his wife, in an erotomaniacal mode.

Studying the discourse and the attachment that links these two people will not lead us astray. For her part his wife understands full well what is going on; she enjoys the omnipotence attributed to her. Any relationship, even one exalted into homosexual fraternity, will fall apart when confronted with the alcoholic's inexorable fixation on his wife.

Still, it is important to note the subjective disparity that marks his relationship with this strange, avid, insatiable, and omnipotent figure. Much as he would like to defend himself or beat her, he is held in the relationship without being able to attain her or to let her drop.

The wife's place is that of Medusa. The complaints that he addresses to her are exactly those of the drive that controls him.

Thus the emergence of a transference in a therapeutic situation will count as the beginning of a cure.

The Humiliated Father

In the group of addicts, the alcoholic is isolated by his choice of the family as the stage for his subjective drama.

So defeated, flouted, and impotent is this man as father that no sign of the other's subjection can correct his feeling of insufficiency. The excess he puts into his tyranny only separates him further from assuming the place that he claims as his.

What would recognition accorded by feeble-minded and weak beings be worth anyway, when it comes from people whom he nevertheless cannot prevent himself from interpellating, since this impossible game is played out on their field? His claim is for justice: is he not master of his own house?

This legitimate aspiration for recognition is sustained and exacerbated by the well-founded conviction that there is, living in and dominating his own house, an Other whose imaginary characteristics he denounces. And these denounced traits show that he can tolerate himself only as the one who can take up the cause of the [symbolic] paternal metaphor. He must be the guardian of the Law and true progenitor.

This is the best place to see the split between the Name of the Father and the incarnated father when the failure of the latter leads to the emergence of the pure omnipotent presence of the former.

We suggest that such an emergence, the ceaselessly renewed possibility of provoking the Other into a confrontation where a father's failure is attributed to wife and children, is behind the selection of the family stage as privileged place.

Jealousy and Truth

The alcoholic's natural conviction of the omnipresence of an Other in his own territory founds his jealousy. To label it "delusional" does not touch its cause, which is logical.

It is more remarkable that everything is a *sign* of this presence: an ash, the fold of a sheet, a sudden paleness, and so forth are irrefutable stigmas.

Thus there is the possibility that an interpretative state is produced within a geographically circumscribed space: the space is heterogeneous. The interpretation designates the alcoholic himself as ridiculous and superfluous, threatened in this place: his attack is only a crafty defense.

The family territory also acquires the characteristics of this presence, a tirelessly fleeting shadow, which marks and challenges the alcoholic's mastery.

The avowal that he demands unremittingly from his wife can be conceptualized as the thirst to drain to the dregs a truth that is dissimulated, fleeting, and resisting. We know to what lengths of extreme violence, to what disregard for all modesty and intimacy, his need to extract it from her body can go.

This perturbation of the relation to truth accounts for the ease with which the alcoholic tolerates the interchangeability of the objects of his accusation. He accuses one person and at the same time points at someone else. And the limit that this someone else, unattainable for being elsewhere, imposes on his jouissance also defines the masochistic fixation on the family scene.

Inside and Outside

Once the doorway of the family space is crossed, a fraternal and homosexual space opens. Egalitarian exchange orders the relations with others (even when they are of the other sex), creating a process by which the world is peopled through an infinite reduplication of mirror images.

Solidarity is exalted to the hypomania of "puffing oneself up" so that one will have nothing to fear in being measured against the Other. This induces a nostalgia requiring that the grouping be only provisional (which classically was provided by military service).

The relation to the other as double accounts for the fact that without any worry and seeking only help, this jealous individual can introduce this other man as a rescuer into his conjugal bed.

But the homosexual act that would not be surprising in a climate of virile excitation marks the limit beyond which the alcoholic will do a sudden turnabout to denounce and strike at the image of the double in a movement of paranoiac misapprehension.

Sociogenesis?

The fact that this type of pure alcoholism (as opposed to ethylism, which is polymorphous and general) is basically limited to a social class, the proletariat, suggests that a sociogenesis may be involved.

How can we evaluate the effect of the infantile neurosis (since we can date only from that the formulation of the fantasy to which the problem with jouissance will bear witness later) of the relationship with a fallen and castrated Father whose social position publically deprives him of any link with Mastery?

Since infantile neurosis may remain perfectly silent, our only thread is still the psychoanalytic cure of those cases where the family structure, whether a social reality or the realism of the fantasmatic interpretation, was revealed to be operative.

This thread defines a hysterical structure articulated around the fantasy of paternal impotence, of belonging to some fallen race; in this structure the prevalence of an oral fixation, sustained by the ideal of a therapeutic object, is common to all addictions.

For this man in exile, the social consensus that designates a national liquor dictates the choice of the fluid object that may make him commune in a permanent feast. Can we propose a better medication?

Yet we are more interested here in the political factor: the way that capitalist exploitation deprives a class of supposed citizens of its rights.

Is there a better means to the authentication of the cursed drive that he struggles to satisfy than to attribute it to the lawless imperative of this exploiting Other, omnipotent and insatiable, pumping up the jouissance of bodies, without any concern other than this limit that the maintenance of life imposes: fantasy of the unlimited jouissance of the Other?

The only jouissance that remains for the alcoholic is to bite down on the very life of this body, on the object that bears witness to this life in procreation.

Treatment

The perverse tendency of the jouissance defines the misunderstanding that links the alcoholic to his physician. The physician remains without recourse where there is foreclosure of the principle that founds his power, which principle is the exigency imposed on the subject to renounce the plus-de-jouir of his own body.

This defect gives the alcoholic the curious courage in which he tricks death: we could say this better in noting that death as Knowledge [*connaissance*] is stolen from him at the same time as his phallic appendage. The only thing that remains for him is the implacable demand of this Other: to satisfy, to nourish, to make it enjoy [*jouir*] ceaselessly, to the last glass. The last? We know the quasifetishistic taste of the alcoholic for bottling, his numerical estimation of the quantities he has absorbed. But this numbering gives him access to what? Infinity? Precisely not, for this attempt to attain it by the naive path of the innumerable is quickly closed by the physiological barrier of the body.

Cures by disgust or conditioning, inspired by Pavlov, tend in a very logical way to an artifical correction of this vector by establishing an approximate limit.

The drawback of this procedure is that it frequently has the effect of provoking and accelerating the dipsomania, or else it leads to the constitution of a neopersonality sensitive to all pressures, characterized by a resigned and obsequious foolishness hardly less unpleasant and noxious to the family than its antecedent. And then? Isn't the impasse faced by the therapist related to this truth: it is not (happily) medicine that can cure a political problem? Yet where the pathological structure is manifest in a second generation with the formation of an active, psychic reality by fantasy, we gain an opportunity and a responsibility when the patient demands his rights and, in so doing, recognizes his debt.

2

The discussion above sought to sketch a clinical picture that is coherent and thus does not owe its unity to that of the observer's subjectivity but rather to the unity that we suppose to be at work in the formation of the picture itself. After all, there is a clinical picture; and it is not a representation or a model (of what?) but the effect of a structure.

In any case, we can only make a supposition here (even if alcoholism suggests it, in particular) that the individual drama is organized in a limited series of short plays, and that the intersubjective relation is organized in only a few roles. Erotic behavior is reduced to a few gestures that in making subjects act otherwise than in their singularity, appear to be sufficiently stereotyped to provoke the anxiety of the interlocutor: he feels himself confronted with a mechanical man, a fantasy produced in the real.

We will then suppose a structure and try to give it value and pertinence through a reconsideration of the clinical facts that it makes necessary. We describe it in the following way: it is a structure in which the lack is inscribed as that of an object designated and said to be plus-de-jouir.

Assuredly the structure we disengage is *perverse*, and we will attempt to see how it regulates both the alcoholic's acute intelligence (he knows what he wants) and his consummate stupidity (what he wants is not very much).

Plus-de-Jouir

As we said before, the theatricality, the modalities of the demand, and the orality of the drinker evoke more clearly *the hysterical structure*. One characteristic, however, distinguishes the drinker radically from the hysteric: the total absence of disgust. This affect is neither hidden from view nor sanctified; it is nonexistent. Disgust does not function as a barrier; from vomit to excrement, from incest to perjury, from perverse manipulation to investigative sniffing, there is even an appetite for waste; and frank intimacy extends to the alcoholic's spontaneous exhibition of himself as such an object.

Here the alcoholic consummates his break with medical ethics. Medicine sees somatic degradation as a sign and as pathology, where the alcoholic lives it as normal and natural. Stated differently, for medicine, the problem remains invisible. Medicine denounces intemperance as a moral fault (this well before our religions), and this denunciation comes to be a heroic gesture, the fulfillment of a duty. The object *a* whose quest motivates this dynamic does remain linked for a time to the physiology of the body and its ability to accustom itself. But the object is an ideal aspired to as a beyond: another effort, the "one more drink" that calls to the alcoholic.

In fact, the particularity of the object *a* when it derives from the oral field makes for its being reached only in the transitory clouding of consciousness: the confusion or the sleep of drunkenness is parallel to a phenomenon elsewhere pertinently called "little death." It is not a matter of enjoying death, unless in the sense of taming it, even for a short period of time. Here we notice again how much death and its fear are absent from the perceptive field of the drinker.

In any case, the clouding of consciousness makes for the fact that this object fades away at the very moment when it is reached or that it is reached only after a long time. The object's defect prohibits it from being seized quickly or permanently and seems to place the object relation under the sign of complaint and dissatisfaction which leads to a fundamental and paranoiac demand for the end.

The alcoholic wants the whole truth; he speaks frankly, without mincing his words, comes right to the point, and does not fail to ask for a willing reciprocity that will be betrayed by the underhanded style of the interlocutor. It is easy to show that if he does not tell the truth, even when he lies with the most natural good faith, he is aiming precisely at the truth. The reference to this truth is hardly sustained by his approximating [the act of] saying [something]. The problem is that in this approximation his goal of attaining the truth escapes him. Thus the family is for him his wife's territory: everything signals her presence, which is dissimulated and refused only from him. . . . This is her treason and her crime; and he wants to wring her neck until she vomits, to bring forth what she conceals, to get her to spew out her guts. . . . No less remarkable is the value the drinker gives to the truth when he thinks he has it and exhibits it generously for everybody's jouissance: he shows it as the cause of evil. In his thirst for truth, he can paradoxically not speak or swear; nothing can subsist, faced with this desire to gulp down the truth. He destroys it with the same movement that he uses to make it emerge, and thus the cycle of demand and appetite begins again.

And if he "lies" sometimes in disavowing his ethylism, he does not do so because he has anything at all to dissimulate: launch an inquest and sniff about. But at the same time he must validate the excellence of the object that constitutes the good of the family and, in exhibiting the truth of its overripe face, he must annul it with the best faith.

The Disavowal of Castration in the Other

The alcoholic appears to be a good example of the active intervention of the Other in the determination of the subject when consanguinity is established by an imperious and dreaded pact to a disavowal (here mutual) of castration. The maternal, feminine Other whose omnipresence is manifest in clinical work with the drinker alienates all possible future relationships into dual relations where reciprocity is exacted. The limitless oblation of the one is inseparable from the permanent suction of the other. Reverse vampirism.

In its considerations of the choice and transmission of neurosis, theory seems to neglect the way in which a seemingly banal fact, the castration of a progenitor who has been elected to dominance by his offspring, may act on him in inscribing its debt as a duty to offer reparations. It happens that this debt, in being made explicit and in being extended to a collectivity, may motivate the demand for a national pride. Being thus a legal debt, it can give rise no less inevitably to a default of payment that can extend to what is called treason.

But the weight of this debt becomes heavier and its figure limitless when the creditor makes himself known not by the force not of the law (which is the same for everyone) but by his weakness (private)—not by what is said but by its saying.

In this case it is essential that the Other's saying be deployed or bring interpretation to the field of the hazards of jouissance. The massive predominance of ethylism in the male puts us on the trail of a type of default, or injury interpreted to be the Other's, which comes to support an imaginary castration and ends by valorizing the penis as supreme, signifying it as object a.

Thus we find a paradox in which a paranoiac attachment to the feminine imago (invested by the object that it is supposed to conceal) coexists with an exaltation of the male organ that brings the homosexual passage into action, preferably in fellatio. We also find the ambiguity of the coat of arms, exhibited in ridiculous combat, through which the Other would signal her presence: the phallic breast emerges against the background of the sea. The drinker's fixation on an older man who can raise and nourish him is not exceptional.

The private geography of the drinker is demarcated by the places where he can drink: the chance of being in want leads to the panic of anxiety and the threat of dislocation; we know of the quarts accumulated under the bed for Saturday night. We see well enough the place the object occupies in the fantasy, the object whose lack threatens to reveal the Other.

Is it necessary to evoke the *delirium* of the alcoholic being weaned from this object?

Continuation

The father is continually being distanced in the most natural way from this constellation, which has been ordered around the maternal star. There is neither conflict nor rivalry, but rather the silence of a castrated creature whose value for the mother is second to that of his objects, his male productions. The father's reaction will be to use bragging and tall tales to make himself recognized as an imaginary superman. This can account for the paradoxes of the drinker's behavior in the home that he will make for himself later on, around another woman. But when he becomes a father this time, he will be claiming an impossible place. There he will have the feeling of being persecuted, excluded, cheated, of having his own children as rivals. But he will also invest activities of nourishing, of education, and of everyday care, which are ordinarily the activities of a wife. And he wants to show (not even hesitating before incest), that his love is superior to hers. This superiority marks the annulment of his love. It is noteworthy that the drinker ignores this affect; certainly he is rich in feelings, often effusive, seeking a body-to-body or soul-to-soul relationship.

Nothing, however, can assure the stability of a relationship that is inevitably a misfit, except perhaps the paranoiac attachment to a partner who is supposed to hold the object: and his own prodigality never fails to wager this object in the appeal to a reciprocity that is always deceived. And they will have the nerve to accuse him of failing in his duties?

In Practice

How can we not fail with him?

If the physician is not the object of an investment for the drinker, the psychoanalyst can interest him more, because of his taste for the truth. The truth to which a psychoanalyst can conduct him has another consistency and inevitably passes through defiles where "depersonalization," or to put it another way, the "putting into cause of the fantasy," is more than elsewhere an inscribed stage, whatever its dramatic quality. The possibility of following this road depends especially on the psychoanalyst's renouncing all certainty, which is precisely what he wants to drive out of his patient. On this will also depend the completion of this work.

3

In this last section we will confront systematically the questions that we have until now either left hanging or prudently avoided, and we will then conclude.

1. The first difficulty is introduced by the alcoholic's *particular mode of relation to the phallus* in the general clinical form that we treat.

We have already remarked that alcoholism is the only addiction with a clinical picture organized—in prevalent, demonstrative, provocative fashion— around the phallus: the claiming and affirming of virility and the denouncing and scorning of feminine castration coexist with homosexual passages into action that are passive as well as active.

That we have to work with the only addiction whose clinical picture presents this particularity (the others seem precisely to ignore or crush all phallicism) permits us to declare that alcoholism is at the origin a *neuropathic condition* and not only the effect of overuse: we will see later whether it is neurosis or psychosis. But this etiological assurance leads us to consider it in terms other than those of the pharmacodynamic effect of the relation to alcohol.

2. Let us pursue our questioning of this mode of *relation* to the phallus. This mode is distinguished first in that its *coming back* implies no limit, prohibition, or duty; on the contrary, its *going out* claims a generosity and an inexhaustible abundance that, joined to the liquid character and the absorption *per os* of the delivered product, evoke unfailingly, at the place designated, the presence of the breast. Thus for the drinker a contradiction is established such that a breast is made to respond "phallically." Obviously it is impossible to resolve this contradiction.

We understand the mode of anxiety proper to the drinker: since nothing in the structure can attest to the permanence of this breast, this latter becomes attached to its sign: the bottle, the bar, elevated here to the dignity of the fetish.

3. One more step: oral jouissance and its particular consequence, here drunkenness, become themselves the necessary guarantees, constantly to be furnished, of this permanence. Drinking becomes a duty as well as a homage, and we can understand that any prohibition is counternatural, or better, counterlogical.

4. But why wine or alcohol and not a neutral liquid? To tell the truth, we know the delectation with which the drinker, being weaned, approaches any liquid, even the inoffensive, provided it be bottled. But, aside from the fact that wine is a part of an ancient Mediterranean cultural tradition, alcohol has a pharmacodynamic effect that we can now mention. Alcohol provokes the fading of the subject.

The exalted triumph of the drunken man is nothing but an evacuation of the subject in favor of a speech immediately become that of the Other.

The fluent speech, the megalomania, the omnipotence and omniscience of this moment, the boundless generosity, as well as the violent response to any constraint, are notable as attributes of the Other: a time in brackets, where words and acts cannot create memories, since they are broken off from any history that could be assumed by a subject; this history comes back with a painful and gray awakening.

5. A remarkable and essential characteristic of this moment, which has no equivalent in any other addiction, is the necessity to introduce speech as logorrhea in the ardent addressing of an other.

The paradox is that this moment of supposedly egoistic jouissance is social and does not happen without speech and an appeal for the recognition of others; an impossible recognition by the other, since the other is denied by the omnipotence of this speech.

6. Thus the alcoholic's life has a binary rhythm; it alternates between a brief time of feasting and a time of exile, when he is fallen, depressed, fearful, and obsequious. When the transvestite puts on his costume, he can know these highs, which vanish with the morning light, going from triumphant inex-sistence to painful inex-sistence.

7. The care and conservation of his body are not a source of concern for the drinker, even when drunkenness does not anesthetize him. He does not read on his body the stigmas of its being attacked: ecchymoses, hemorrhages, trembling, polyneuritus. . . . He knows nothing of death and respects nothing of life; and yet we cannot talk about repression or foreclosure. The alcoholic seems to be from another world, ignorant of birth, aging, or death.

With his scholastic prejudices about the necessity to preserve life, the physician has a language that the alcoholic cannot comprehend. The drinker has been educated in another medicine, the powerful healer of all ills; his prescription of wine to his neighbors is a pure oblation.

8. His image is slovenly, but its disorder and disgrace are invisible to him. And these two symptoms of body and image can be understood as the default of recognizing any debt to the Other.

9. And yet, he sniffs out any fault that is revealed in the other, this in order to reject him and to disavow castration: he scorns the wife he can only appreciate as a mother, and this on the condition that he can supplant her offspring to become her only child; he has an ambivalent scorn for the foreigner, the alien who renders his double present in a threatening way.

10. Thus his relation with the male other oscillates between a depressive, fearful, self-depreciating submission and the exaltation of a perfectly transitive relation with his mirror image (his brother in poverty with whom he shares everything). This latter leads in its turn to a paranoiac turnabout ("he took

everything from me," "he betrayed me"). The common appeal to intimacy and fraternity finds its origin here.

11. The alcoholic's commission of a homosexual act shows a sexual ambiguity. The virile protest can banally punctuate the femininizing effect of an ideal pushed to its limit. But it is also from a feminine position that the drinker claims an assumption of virility, making it his duty to dislodge the castrated creature who occupies this place.

This effort encounters not the opposition but the complicity of women, as though he could do nothing other than to pursue an archaic feminine fantasy: that of a God whose infinite bounty would leave no prayer unanswered and who would thus be the true therapist of castration. As Other, a mother always seeks to embody this God.

12. Our analysis of the facts is exclusively founded on the application of the Lacanian matheme of sexual identification and on the postulate that the male alcoholic places himself unconsciously on the feminine side ($\overline{\exists x \overline{\Phi x}}$ and $\overline{\forall x} \Phi x$).[1] It seems to us that this evaluation can account with economy and originality for the paradoxes of the alcoholic's behavior, preserving him from moral judgment (temperance) and medical prejudice (conservation of life as a duty toward the Other).

Thus there is no bad faith or dishonesty in the drinker; he is simply following different rules, where to enjoy *one more time* is based on the impossible duty to affirm an ex-sistence ($\exists x \overline{\Phi x}$)[2] that would found these rules by authorizing the evasion of the castration that would permit it: from this there is the exigency of a breast in place of the phallus, the echo and validation of the feminine fantasy of feeding. The drinker's claim of a virile position involves even more conflicts because it originates from a feminine position, but it does not fail to resonate for a woman—here we see the well-known masochistic collusion of the spouse, amused and interested that a man far from the superb assurance of virility takes up her drama on his own account, suffering on the same side that she does.

It is clear that a therapeutic intervention is only possible if the drinker admits the otherwise normative point of view of the other side—male ($\exists x \overline{\Phi x}$)— for which his excess is a symptom.

1. [These two formulas determine a feminine sexual identification. They should be read as follows. 1. $\overline{\exists x} \Phi x$ means that there is no x, or there is no one to say no to the phallic function. 2. $\overline{\forall x} \Phi x$ means that for not all x, the phallic function is valid.]

2. [This is one of the two formulas determining masculine sexual identification. $\exists x \Phi x$ means that there is an x, or there is someone to say no to the phallic function. The other formula here is $\forall x \Phi x$, which means that for all x, the phallic function is valid.]

We know that if a constraint is imposed, it can only be pathogenetic, aggravating the anxiety and dipsomania.

But a transferential relation cannot fail to revive the presence of an Other whose unfoundedness provokes anxiety and thus depersonalization. His silence will be registered as impotence (to flee) or provocation (to conquer), while his benevolent intervention will justify the alienation of the appeal for "one more." The analyst will be captured in the alternation between a dual relationship pathetically invoked but justifying the constituting alienation and a properly analytic relation, generating pathogenetic anxiety: this he must play out, if he can.

The question of knowing whether alcoholism is a neurosis, a perversion, or a psychosis—is it thus resolved? We see, in any case, the direction in which we have been moving.

16   Fetishization of a Phobic Object

BY RENÉ TOSTAIN

*Splitting of the subject? This point is a knot.
We remember where Freud defines it: around
the mother's lack of a penis in which the nature
of the phallus is revealed. The subject is split
here, Freud tells us, at the place of reality, on
the one hand seeing a gulf open before him
against which he will build the barricade of a
phobia, and on the other covering it over with a
surface on which he will place a fetish—that is
to say, something that maintains, displaced,
the existence of the penis.*

    For the one we extract the "no..." [pas
de] *of the (no penis), in parentheses to transfer
it to the no-knowledge that is the no-hesitation
of neurosis.*

    *With the other, let us recognize the effec-
tiveness for the subject of this gnomon that he
erects to designate at any time the point of
truth.* —Jacques Lacan, "La Science et la vér-
ité," in *Ecrits*

I could have entitled this article "On Taste and Disgust." In fact, the terms
"phobia" and "fetish" seem to be so codified in psychiatric semiology and now in
psychoanalytic usage that I am afraid of facing the criticism that will come from
those who still hold to the labels.

    Psychoanalysis teaches us that there is only a nuance distinguishing between
"I don't like crowds" and little Hans's inability to leave his house for fear of
encountering horses in the street.

    It is this same nuance that separates "Bring me a scarf that covered her
breast, a ribbon of my beloved," of Goethe's Faust, from the shoe collector in the
Journal d'une femme de chambre of O. Mirbeau.

    René Tostain is a physician practicing psychoanalysis in Paris. This article first appeared as
"Fétichisation d'un objet phobique," in *Scilicet* 1 (Paris: Editions du Seuil, 1968), pp. 153–67.

Taste and disgust are considered to be normal reactions. "All tastes are in nature," someone has said, speaking of the same nature that Leonardo da Vinci recognized as "full of infinite reasonings that are not in experience."

At what moment do these reactions of attraction and repulsion become abnormal? I will not decide the question here. I will limit myself to noting their existence and their opposition. For there is a manifest antinomy between the behavior of a fetishist and that of a phobic.

The one employs the same perseverance in fleeing that the other employs in seeing a particular situation. The extreme disgust of the one is opposed to the elected taste of the other, repulsion is opposed to attraction, suffering and anguish, to pleasure and perhaps jouissance. Finally, stupefaction or retreat is opposed to the movement toward, the perpetual seeking. The only thing that unites them is the irrational character of their reactions, which are, for the one as well as for the other, inexplicable, or as another age would have said, fated.

The fetishist's mixture of affection and hostility for his object has often been remarked. Freud noted the fetishist's aversion to the female genital organs, and he saw in it the indelible stigma of a repression. In the case of little Hans, he wrote a footnote saying, "Theory demands that what is today the object of a phobia was in the past the object of a sharp pleasure." But we had to wait for his last unfinished article on the *Ichspaltung*, written in 1938, for him to describe the similarity between a fetish and a phobia.

Freud does not tell us what fetish has been chosen by the little boy he is speaking about. As for the phobia, it is a fear of being devoured by his father, and this contains an oral element that we always find at the origin of a phobia when the analysis has been pursued far enough. But it also happens that it is intolerable to this boy for someone to touch his toes.

That one object may at the same time be the object of attraction and horror, simultaneously sought and avoided,—that, it seems to me, has not been described. This eventuality will be the focus of our interest in retracing the analysis of a patient.

One beautiful summer evening John was playing in his room when he heard his mother call, "John, darling, come help me."

He ran to the bathroom, where his pretty mother was getting dressed. She often went out in the evening. He liked watching her get ready. He found her as beautiful as a fairy. She liked hearing him say so, and he often did.

This evening she asked him to fasten a dress with buttons on the back. She could not do it alone. Happy and attentive, John did as he was asked. But a strange trouble seized him. He felt himself blush, his legs trembled, and in his haste his gesture became more and more uncertain. Then, from the depths of his being, just as the enchantment of the moment was broken, there surged forth a brusque and painful pleasure. John had just come. He was six years old.

Twenty years later he comes to his analysis and speaks to me about his object.

This object is grammatically in the category of "things." Inanimate thing, dead thing. It happens to be the most insignificant of objects. And yet we are going to see how intensely he lives it, what unbearable weight it will take on.

It will be at the same time the object of horror and of fright, the object of repulsion and of insurmountable disgust, an object bringing evil and an object of death. But it will also be a love object, irresistibly attractive, the object of all seeking, the apparently elected object of desire.

This terrible and fascinating object, this object of prudishness, analytic *par excellence*, is a button.

Yes, a button. Not a pink button, not the button that rings the doorbell, not even one of these blemishes [*boutons*] that we doctors are happy to class among the pimples and blackheads[1]—no, it is a button on an article of clothing, nothing more.

It is really an idiotic object. Such concern about a button cannot be taken seriously.

That is exactly what John thought. In the end he decided to do a psychoanalysis. The point is that this button really disturbed him. It is not funny, he said, to have to dress oneself every morning as though buttoning one's shirt or fly were not disturbing. when accidentally seeing any of these buttons on a table forces one to look away. When one of these buttons fell off, he panicked in terror, and he could not even pick it up because he would have had to touch it. The simple idea of a woman holding a button between her lips prior to sewing it on a garment filled him with an immense disgust that nauseated him.

Even pronouncing the word was such a torture that he avoided it by using words like "watchamacallit." Seeing, touching, or naming this object was for him odious and repellent.

But at the same time, along with this invincible repulsion, he felt with equal force an irresistible attraction to this same object, providing that there was a slight modification in its presentation.

The condition that made it pass from one extreme to the other was this: it had to be multiplied.

I will explain. Clothes with an important number of buttons attracted him. On the street he looked at women who wore coats, dresses, or shoes with numer-

---

1. [In French, *bouton* can mean "pimple" or "blemish."]

ous buttons, and with an expert glance he could count the number. Thus a dress that had eight was better for him than one that had seven. The only requirement for erotic stimulation was that the buttons be rigorously identical, set out in a row, and especially that there be none missing. If one was different from the others by its placement or by its form, color, or absence, what had been the object of attraction an instant before became irremediably the object of an extreme repulsion.

Thus he observed on the shelves of clothing stores those articles that responded to the exigencies of the curious canon of his vestimentary esthetic. When he encountered a woman dressed according to his taste, he felt a strong sexual excitement. Charmed by the buttons, he completely ignored the face of this woman; fascinated by the sole object of his interest, he stared at it for a long period of time.

I skip over the other details to insist on the facts that for John all the buttons had to be correctly buttoned and that only buttons made of bone or pearl mattered for him. Those covered with fabric had practically no value in his eyes, neither in one sense nor in the other.

Finally, a woman had to be the wearer of the article of clothing before the full erotic effect could occur. A man wearing similar clothes did not affect John. Strangely enough, he pretended that men wearing clothes of the sort that would have interested him were homosexuals.

All these details were of course supplied with reticence, requiring long elaboration, for the facts, which seem to be so precise, were mixed up in a sort of chaos in which he had a lot of trouble finding his way.

We summarize: if the same object, the button, was alone, singular, it was the object of an anxiety, which I have tried to express in my title by calling it "phobic." On the other hand, multiplied, put into the plural, the button became an object of attraction, which I have called a "fetish."

These facts at least are indisputable; they are the symptom. John had never spoken to anyone about his strange perversion. I say "perversion" because, despite everything, he recognizes, not without hesitating, that he is being delivered over into excesses that he regrets. Imagine the scenes that take place in games where he or his partner (he does not know very well which, and we will see how important this is) is dressed in the kind of clothing that is adequate to his pleasure.

But how did he come to this point. How did he reach this aberration, which I, following Freud, would willingly call a delusion? We are obliged to recognize that the mobilization of such an energy in pursuit of an object that is so far from the goal of normal sexuality implies a loss of a sense of the real, providing that this word has meaning.

BEING

To understand John's symptom, we will have to go back in time into a past that the present repeats in an eternal return.

About the conditions in which John came into the world I will say only this: his maternal grandfather thought that his daughter (John's mother) should not have children. For that reason she married the only man acceptable to her father, one they suspected of being unable to engender any.

Such is the fairy tale that sealed the crib of John's destiny. Born of a father defined as absent and of a mother cursed by her own father to be childless, his place was narrow and painful.

He was often sick. Colds and bronchitis with thousands of infectious complications necessitated daily medical care that was often painful.

Of this period his mother said she would not have wished such torture on her worst enemy.

But her son was not her worst enemy; rather, he was a little bit of herself that took on a very strange function in her relation with her father and her husband. Only one as faithless as a psychoanalyst will see the indecency involved.

In the evening, when John had a slight fever and was softly blowing his nose, his mother entered his room. Her child was then the object of attentive maternal care. She inserted the rectal thermometer and held it with her finger long enough for the mercury to rise. Other things rose with the little column of mercury. Before the reading of 99 or 99.4 degrees—we should not hesitate to call this fever desire—John's mother intervened. A very hot fumigation, a burning cataplasm and, to fight a supposed constipation, an abundant enema, to be held in as long as possible.

John listened to the verdict with a secret joy. When I say "secret," I mean that he did not exteriorize it. He did not jump for joy, and he did not speak; this was his way of saying that it was not worth the trouble. But in fact this unavowed secret was shared with his dear mother. They knew, the one and the other, that these innocent treatments had a sense, a very specific one.

Suffocating under his blanket, asphyxiated by the vapors, burned by the mustard plaster and bloated with water—who was he? Who was he to have an erection given to him by this unavowable pleasure? Then, perhaps in the paroxysm of suffering and congestion, he comes, in a disenchanting succession of spasms. Who is he? Here we evaluate the evidence to see that reddened, bloated, stiff, and irritated, he is . . . a penis in erection.

Yes, it is not agreeable to notice this, but it is certain. And John knows it, although not in these terms. His mother knows it also, although also not exactly in these terms.

But this boy learned what he had to be for his mother: her lack, a toy to inflate, a serious toy for a reasonable adult, a living dildo for her exclusive use.

This euphoric period where the child is the decoy of his mother's desire, the metonymy of her lack, does not occur without some moments of anxiety. This object of desire is the living object of all excesses, most especially here those of destruction.

Thus we have reciprocal destruction and fear of this destruction. These moments of troubled pleasure where the identity is almost perfect—what can they lead to, if not to the vertigo of a being hanging on the disappearance of the one in the other, of the one by the other? This is always at the horizon of such mortal play.

In addition, there comes a day when this game of being everything for her no longer amuses her, this decidedly difficult mother, and a question arises concerning the "being for nothing." The sense vanishes. He had in vain been sick, sick almost unto death, it was almost but not entirely that; and yet there is still a beyond to her desire.

What should he now do to continue to be what she desires? Should he renounce being it to have it, since he also has it, the penis? John thus turns to his father. Is it he who holds the key to the mystery?

Not in the least, and this has been known for quite a while already; the father does not have it to transmit, the famous phallus. It was through this clause of the contract that John was born. Not only does he not have it, but for his wife the son is understood to be it, replacing his.

At this dramatic moment John finds the solution he knows well, and he gets sick.

In the middle of the night, he is running a fever of 102 degrees, he vomits, and he has a pain in his stomach. The doctor, called in for the emergency, makes the diagnosis of an acute attack of appendicitis. His mother says, "He is having an appendicitis attack for me." For once she is wrong, and we will see why.

Operated upon that very night, he sees upon awakening, while still under the effect of the anesthesia, his father at his bedside, with a radiant smile, holding in his hands a jar in which, as a formless shadow, the appendix of desire is floating.

John, who for six years was nothing but a prey offered to the pietà, will never again be sick.

This intervention, which is no more nor less than what is represented in a circumcision, permits John, according to the Law of the Father, no longer to be his mother's penis in sufferance and to accede to the question of having it.

To Have It, the Phobia

It was in the months that followed, when John was about six, that the scene I described at the beginning took place. When his mother asked him to help her to get dressed, he was requested to have it for her. Until that time his entire body consummated an imaginary incest. Now his real penis is required. But this penis is fundamentally inadequate. It is too small. She even tells him that it is. She calls it "your little bit" [*ton petit bout*].

Also, when she wants to thank him for having helped her to button her dress, she says, "What would become of me without my little man." John, who knows what it means to speak, having experienced its brutal consequences for six years, will never again want to help her.

When she calls to him, he cries out from his room, "I don't have the time, ask papa to do it." His mother is astonished and scolds him, but to no avail.

On that day John, as if in a dramatic *peripetia*, forged himself a phobia.

What does that mean? First, one does not choose an object of repulsion like that, no matter how significant the moment. There must have been other elements that predestined it to this function.

Doubtless John has a few other memories that antedate this scene.

—The first is very vague: when he was very little, he received medical attention that necessitated unbuttoning his coveralls between his legs.

—Another: sick and alone in the house, he played at lining up the buttons on the dining room table as he waited for his mother to return.

—About the age of four, playing with some friends older than he, he was given the role of the baby. The others dressed him in a pillowcase from his parents' bed that had been closed with snaps [*boutons pression*]. He remembers having had a sensation that he calls "voluptuous" when he felt himself enclosed by this pillowcase.

—About the age of five, a memory relating to wearing pants that had a buttoned fly and were not, as they had been when he was younger, kept in place by suspenders that he had to lower when he wanted to urinate.

For a little boy the passage from baby clothes to boy's clothes represents a consecration. For John it appeared to raise a problem. For whom? For his mother? For his father? He does not know. Finally, some other memories, which appear to me to be fundamental.

—He heard his father one day describe what he understood to be his mother's sexual organ as a "button."

—His father always intervened to remark that perhaps his wife could get dressed by herself. Such are the memories that he brings to me, apparently insignificant, as memories of childhood often are; but their evocation in context explains the overdetermination of the symptom.

During the course of his analysis, John's searching for an objectification of his choice will make him move toward studying a past that is comprised of etymology and history. In etymology, this incestuous adventure of knowledge whose erotic character is known to some people, he found that "button" comes from "butt," which first meant "to strike," then "to repulse," then "push," then "out of," in the sense of a growth, of something that germinates or pushes out.

As for history, he read that in the twelfth century the button was introduced into France with its contemporary usage of closing. Originating with the Nordic countries, it was employed for practical reasons.

During this time, elegance demanded that the cuffs and collars of the dresses of the women of the court be strictly aligned. For this the Roman broach was of no use, and the dress then had to be sewn on the person who was to wear it. Before the dress could be removed, the stiches had to be taken out. Buttons remedied this inconvenience and have maintained, since their introduction into fashion, a usage that everyone will recognize easily.

We are progressing very slowly indeed. In our defense we will invoke the contradictory and completely enigmatic character of John's symptom. How can we conceive of one object as simultaneously attractive and repulsive? Apparently this phenomenon is totally illogical. And yet we know that the great scandal of the unconscious is that it is strictly logical.

Let us return to John. What remains to be told is absolutely inseparable from the progress of his analysis. I found myself in the position of guaranteeing its limits, which Georges Bataille would have called the ineluctability of its profound impossibility. John often told me how much he found me narrow-minded.

THE ONE

As we have seen, the phobia is intolerable, untenable. It spreads itself limitlessly; it overflows the borders of reality; fallen from an elsewhere, it occupies the entire scene. It is completely full, dense, opaque, and yet totally ungraspable. For it to take up so much place here, something must be terribly lacking somewhere else.

In the case of little Hans, Freud has told us that because the horse pulls the wagon, the phobia derives from the horse, through the constitution of the signifiers *Wagen* ("wagons" in the plural) and *wegen* ("because of"). We find this phonematic, here homophonic, aspect of the signifier again in the uncertain quality of the statement in which we recognize our certainty, the one that comes from the imprecision of certain elements of a dream. What does it say?

"Yes, Button, your bit, little button, your little bit."[2]

There it is: the phonemes are displaced. It is anagrammatical, but the unconscious is not very demanding, and a sense appears, the one that will specify the scene of the memory.

The button is your little bit, your little penis, whose being solicited—we have no doubt but that his mother provokes it in this scene—shows to what extent its real presence has always been problematic. It is not just yesterday that this little bit of flesh was destined to become a major signifier.

But this signifier is equally metonymical, manifesting the function that Freud recognized in the dream through the form of the combination of one term with an other.

The distance is not very great between the buttons of the fly and the penis. Yet the distance is immense in consciousness, practically impassable in the consciousness that guarantees the metonymic displacement.

In this context John brings us, in the course of his analysis, a story that he had heard.

It takes place in America. Coin machines are at the disposition of the clients. On the machines there is the inscription, "Enter, you will feel at home." On the front of the machine there is an orifice. A man, supposed to be in erection, introduces his penis in the orifice and senses at the top of his organ—a button.

"Yes, yes," he tells me. "This story is idiotic: your pants are your home."

It is certain that this story, which John did not make up, objectifies, happily enough, not only what sexuality can become in America, evoked here in a humorous mode, but (more interestingly for us) the passage from the penis to the button.

Another time it is in *L'Age d'homme* by Michel Leiris that John, always ready to pounce on what he finds strange, finds a passage where the author, speaking of his relations with his brother, says:

> Aside from having threatened me with an appendectomy with a corkscrew (an operation that he had had under conditions more normal than John's), he had spoken once of "making me eat button soup." At this time one of the

2. [In French the connection is closer between *bouton* ("button") and *ton bout* ("Your bit"). I have chosen to translate with the word "bit" because it approximates the first syllable of "button."]

soups we ate the most often at our house was a broth to which noodles had been added, sometimes in the form of stars, sometimes in the form of letters of the alphabet. I imagined pearl buttons floating in the broth in place of the noodles, and my disgust was so great that even today I cannot look at a button on a shirt or on shorts without imagining it in my mouth and beginning to feel nauseous.

Reading that, John remembers his own despair when, at the age of seven, obliged to wear a buttonless shirt on the beach to protect him from a sunburn, he put on a tie to hide the fact that there were no buttons. His friends took great joy in this and nicknamed him Johnny the Tie.

We leave off these digressions, however instructive they may be, and we return to the object that is horrible when singular. We will say that it is necessary to recognize the close relation that the object has with the metonymic signifier, the phallus.

The function of the signifier is not to represent the meaning but to fill in the gaps. It is when the meaning is lost that we again find the cobblestones of the signifier.

The signifier designates the lack, the absence, but it primarily engenders this lack. It as around the hole of what he says that the subject is structured. And from this hole has fallen the waste product that has taken on for John so much importance in defining one of the boundaries of his being. The signifier makes reference to a spoken word, to the one that speaks the truth in unveiling the well. But for John, at least, this speech is unsayable, even though he cannot avoid it.

We would be a bit shortsighted if we thought that the anxiety that apparently throws John to the ground before this object and prevents him from touching it, from seeing it, and from naming it could be linked to a fear that the object would be defending him against—for example, a fear connected with masturbation or the representation of a castration threat, real and dreaded.

No threat has ever been made to him, and he has never renounced mastur-bation. We know well enough that anxiety is not the fear of an object but the confrontation of a subject with the lack of an object.

Thus for John the button is the emblem of a lack beyond measure.

It evokes at the same time the gap of a situation, an absence that he renders present, a "no . . . " that is situated at the level of the Other, and the radical inability of John's being to come to terms with it.

He says, or better, he cries out, that his mother does not have a penis. John knows it, he saw it (the "not-seeing" of the phobia), this bottomless hole that calls to him. He has been delivered over, a defenseless prey, to the excesses of this void, which attracts and terrifies him. Certainly his mother desires him to fill it and lose himself in it. This has been her desire from the time when she began to feed him. There is a truly incestuous dimension in this retrograde movement that would deny the first cutting and would thus deny the subject.

This object is also the support of the anxiety around which something at the level of the name of the father would be foreclosed. Who would deny that a phobia is like a psychosis in being limited to very little reality? John has no father; at least, his father does not have the phallus that guarantees the lack and would prohibit incest and permit John to accede to a desire. And the button of bone or of pearl—these dead remains recall the all too possible wish for his death. Is he not already killed in his name, which he has been able to assume? Not touching it, for if he did he would turn to dust, like the tree downed by lightning but retaining the appearance of having its old force.

Finally, this unnamable object is also John.

It is John-with-a-penis that doesn't make sense, to which no one can give any sense, but especially the button is John as subject, the "no" place for John, the "never having been born" that presided over his birth, in conformity with the Law of his maternal grandfather.

And he knows it, equal in that to Midas when he found the sage Silenus and asked him what a man could find best and most profitable in life. Midas heard this response: "Miserable race of men, children of chance and pain! Why do you want to hear something that will be of no benefit to you? The supreme good, know that you cannot attain it: it is never to have been born, being nothing. But the good that comes after is not out of your reach, it is to die very soon."

John does not exist, at least as a subject. Who would recognize him? Not his father, who is missing, not his mother, for whom his existence represents her transgressing a paternal prohibition and is thus a cross to bear. She could only recognize him as sick, ready to die, as he was during childhood. But for John, and perhaps for all of us, death is only deferred. In the course of his analysis, John came to remember a distant time in his childhood when he had decreed that he was dead, that no one knew it, and that surely enough he continued to live as before, with only he knowing that he was dead. He reserved for himself the right to live again, to be reborn at the opportune moment.

Thus John, caught in the dialectic of being and having, searching pathetically since his childhood for a lack designated as such and not exaggerated, creates in the urgency of a privileged moment a derisory object (himself).

This button, suddenly untouchable, is like the notice of a registered letter that awaits you and that you know contains a bill to pay. It tells us that the father's debt is unpaid and unpayable, that the mother's desire is a desire for death and that her lack cannot be designated. All of which means that John in his parents' discourse would have been better off never having been born.

But He SAYS It

And even though John makes every effort to know nothing of all that—of all this knowledge and of what it implicates (which is the dimension of the zero)—only the One and himself separate him from it. For the simple but radical reason that one day, during his incestuous play with his mother, his father named it. His father, as we have seen, one day used "button" to designate his mother's sexual organ. With his desire he thus designated, however slightly, a lack from which afterward everything can originate.

Thus John holds onto this word and to the object that fell away in being named, above and beyond everything. His anxiety is that it might disappear and thus unveil—the buttonhole that would swallow him up.

The One, not countable but unitary, structures the edge of his knowing being. But it is insufficient, untenable, inadequate to all division. There must be two edges before there can be a Moebius strip.

The Fetish, the Subject

For those who have followed me to this point concerning the repulsion linked to this object, I will propose now to envisage its attractive force, through which John finds himself in a perversion.

How did the button pass from a horrifying singularity to an erotic plurality?

It is tempting to want to find here a simple return of the repressed: John finds in his perversion the delicious sensation that was his when he helped his mother to button her dress. If this is the case, making the object something horrible represses the object.

But it has appeared to us that the phobia is not repression but rather the failure of repression, an immanence, possible and recognized, of what one would want to know nothing about.

This moves in the sense of the fundamental equation of fetishism formulated by J. Lacan: what is loved in an object is precisely what it lacks. John himself has oriented me in this direction.

Here is how things present themselves approximately. A button is horrible, insupportable.

A lot of the same button is veritably exciting. This can be seen as a double arithmetic operation:

One is made of:

—nine-tenths anxiety, whose sense we have seen in the "no . . .".
—one-tenth that, without knowing why, John calls his father's part, which we can specify in linking it to naming.

The number n (the object as plural):

—The nine-tenths of anxiety are divided by n; thus the greater n is, the better things are.
—The one-tenth is multiplied by n and tends toward one.

In fact, the One was speech opening into the truth of a hole but not delimiting it sufficiently.

On the contrary, the number n, which is not at all a measuring apparatus, must be conceived as indicating the function of the lack and as structuring the cut.

From there we can oppose the phobic One, a metonymy of the exaggeration of a radical "no . . . " that it preserves badly, to the fetish number, the metaphor of a structuring lack.

In the first case, his mother has a penis, maintained by an absence that is displaced.

In the second, father's phallus is truly the guarantor of the lack, reconstituted in this number that represents the signifying chain that has no missing link—all are identical, permutable, and these conditions, we note, are those of the organization of his fetish—and in lacking no link saves the truth.

Finally, John himself is safe. Around the cut that prohibits incest, he can finally structure himself as divided. The fetish constitutes the second edge of his being for truth.

Evidently, since it has always been so, the question that John has thus resolved is that of the Other. It will then be necessary in his fantasy for travesty to play its role, where clothing traditionally hides that which is there as well as that which is not.

"It can't be known"; it is that which the fetish preserves better than the phobia. Is it necessary to complete this statement: "It can't be known that that cannot be fixed up"? Yes, if we are interested in articulating clearly the truth that the "nice fetishist" sustains in disavowing it.

It sustains him, and he sustains it with his baroque and sadly laughable props.

Also, this fetish, which constitutes the being of the subject in its edge of truth, as the phobia was constituting his edge of knowledge, makes for the fact that we should not be too quick to contest the structuring value of this inaugural *Spaltung* of the subject confronted with the impossible reality of the difference of the sexes.

This is what John reminded me of when he said to me, like Thomas the Obscure: "I hear a monstrous voice through which I said what I said without knowing a single word of it."

That was the voice of the Other.

Index of Psychoanalytic Terms

Index of Proper Names